100 IDEAS THAT CHANGED DESIGN

Charlotte & Peter Fiell

100 IDEAS THAT CHANGED DESIGN

Charlotte & Peter Fiell

Laurence King Publishing

Introduction

Every design starts out as an idea and is also an expression of an idea. So it makes sense to be publishing a book on design that is all about ideas. And not just any old ideas, but those that have changed the course of design practice significantly. These are the big ideas in design that have improved our lives immeasurably through often brilliant **innovation**, helped us experience the world, and ultimately shaped our material culture.

Design is foremost a problem-solving process that seeks solutions to all sorts of different needs, concerns and desires. While the vast majority of designs are the result of this particular approach, however, there are other designs that are simply manifestations of sheer creativity, conceived for the delight of producing something new or beautiful for its own sake. There are also certain types of design where the primary function is to act as a vehicle for conveying concepts, opinions or propaganda. Yet whatever the underlying intention or motivation is behind a design, it always begins its life as an idea.

So how should one define 'design'? Probably the best and most concise definition is that it is the conception and planning (forethought) of an artefact, environment or system as well as the physical outcome of that process – the idea realized in physical or digital form. The word 'design' is actually quite slippery because it is a verb and also a noun: an action and its result. The meaning of 'design' is also very wide-ranging, covering everything that is man-made, from pottery and textiles, to consumer appliances, transportation, medicines and gaming environments. The practice of design straddles the worlds of art and engineering, so exactly where a specific design falls within that crucial intersecting area between aesthetics and science largely depends on what is being designed. This means that the ideas that have shaped design are surprisingly expansive, running from those that relate to the more artistic (**creative expression** and **decoration**) to those that are more technologically based (**interface design** and **robotics**). Yet despite this broad scope, the word 'design' fully lives up to its root origin: the Latin verb *designare*, meaning to select, order, plan or scheme – all of which involve some form of thought process, wherever on the design spectrum a designer chooses to operate.

Designed artefacts are also a physical testament to their creators' ideas – their thoughts, opinions and aspirations – and are often the only material proof we have of someone's life lived. Despite this, however, all too often when considering a design we assess its here-and-now physicality and how well it fulfils its intended purpose; we do not really think too much about the people or the processes that brought it into being, or the ideas that lie behind it. One goal of this book, therefore, is to delve beneath the surface of designed objects and explore the multiplicity of ideas that have compelled designers throughout the centuries to come up with alternative and, in some cases better, design solutions.

Designs also embody the spirit of the time in which they are created, for no designer has ever worked in a cultural vacuum, and nothing shapes the creative essence of an era more than the collective ideas shared by a society at that specific moment in history. This explains why over the decades different design ideas have come bubbling to the surface in response to the ever-changing economic, political and technological landscape. It is no surprise, for instance, that the ideas of **rationalism** and **functionalism** in design found such fertile ground after World War I, when there was a consensus that society needed to be rebuilt – socially, politically and economically – by harnessing the machine. Likewise, during the 1930s Depression the idea of **planned obsolescence** in industrially manufactured goods was formulated as way of boosting the economy, while in the 1970s, in response to growing eco-awareness, the idea of **sustainability** in design came to the fore. As a result, when we look at an object from the past or even the present, we can read it as a veritable sign of the times, an encapsulation of the ideas and ideals of the society that created it.

So what makes some design ideas 'big' and others not? At a minimum, a big idea must not only have had a substantial impact when it first emerged but also a certain 'stickiness', which means that its influence has left an enduring legacy on the practice of design. One also finds that history has a habit of repeating itself in design, with certain big ideas cropping up repeatedly at different times, according to how the **style** pendulum is swinging.

Another goal of this book is to sort the 'ideas' from the 'isms' – so while you will find entries on **historicism**, **vernacularism** and **essentialism** (which are all ideas), you will not find any entries relating to design styles per se, such Neo-Classicism, Futurism or Post-Modernism, although within the various entries you will find them mentioned repeatedly. The reason for this approach is that this book is not intended to function as a compendium of styles, but rather as a useful and thought-provoking work on design thinking.

Within the 100 selected entries, all the well-established ideas are included, but there are also a few that are of a slightly more esoteric nature. Among these you will find, for example, **There is always a better way of doing things** and **The world of tomorrow**, which might not be as doctrinally laden as **Form follows function** or **Less is more**, but have nonetheless inspired designers to do what they do and have in their own way changed the course of design. It is remarkable how many of the selected ideas overlap and link to one another, as our system of bold type cross-referencing makes clear.

Over the last few decades, most people's understanding of design has both broadened and deepened. Thanks to this, we are now seeing the transformative power of design being better recognized among businesses and governments. The upshot of this is that design thinking is being increasingly deployed not only for commercial gain, but also as a tactical response to some of mankind's biggest challenges. Today design has completely transcended the physical world of making stuff, and is being used more and more to develop better systems and practices.

Quite simply, anything and everything can be designed, whether in the physical realm (such as a building, a chair, a car or an airplane), or in the digital realm (such as an immersive gaming environment, a social media profile or a fitness app). Relentlessly, bits and bytes are replacing nuts and bolts as the **digitalization** of design takes hold, which in turn has transformed the physicality of design, with apps on a smartphone often replacing whole product typologies. Indeed, the practice of design is itself becoming digitalized, with **parametricism** being just the first step towards more advanced types of autonomous **CAD/CAM** software programs.

Yet whatever direction design may take in the future, it will be – as it always has been – based on key ideas. If history is anything to go by, a proper understanding of what the important ideas of the past have been should help inspire the next big concepts in design. As ever, these will generally follow either an evolutionary or revolutionary tack. In other words, they will be premised on existing ideas and try to build on them, or they will reject the status quo and seek radically new approaches. It is crucial, therefore, to know what the really big ideas in design are in order to move design thinking forward, because ultimately, we need more intelligent design thinking to enable us to solve the biggest problems we face, from global warming to clean energy generation and overpopulation. We also need innovative design ideas to ensure that design remains the vital civilizing force it always has been, richly enhancing all aspects of our daily lives. ■

Intelligent design thinking
for step-change progress

INNOVATION

Every design starts with an idea, but some of those are so groundbreaking that they actually constitute a major innovation. The concept of innovation has long motivated designers to believe that **there is always a better way of doing things**, which has driven them on to develop better solutions than those that previously existed.

The world's greatest design innovator – Thomas Edison holding his revolutionary incandescent light bulb (patented 1880) in Building One of his West Orange Laboratory in New Jersey, c.1910.

Innovation in design is also often driven by entrepreneurship – the belief that monetary gain can be achieved by coming up with a new invention, which is what many designs marked by innovation actually are.

Human beings are naturally inventive, and the idea of design innovation has, over the millennia, shaped human civilization – not only our material world, but us as people, too. It has given us countless world-changing inventions: bricks and ploughs, coinage and printing presses, ships and trains, cars and planes, telephones and computers, to name but a few. Most innovative break-throughs in design are fundamentally born of frustrations with what already exists, and the realization that something does not necessarily have to be the way it is, but can be improved upon through the application of intelligent design thinking. Innovation in design is also often the direct result of necessity. Indeed, when people are faced with seemingly insurmountable problems, it is inbuilt human instinct to try to overcome them, because ultimately that is what has enabled mankind to survive and thrive from its earliest beginnings.

Innovation in design starts with understanding the exact nature of what already exists and then casting around for a better solution. Sometimes this can come as an Archimedes 'Eureka!' moment, a flash of design-thinking inspiration, but this is quite rare. In fact, one of the surest ways of designing something that is technologically innovative is to take an iterative approach to its research, design and development. The great American inventor Thomas Edison was the most famous pioneer of this scientific approach to problem-solving, which is based on systemized trial-and-error testing. While this process can be painfully slow and costly, it is the most surefire way of developing step-change innovation. As Edison famously noted of this tried-and-tested method, 'Genius is 1 per cent inspiration and 99 per cent perspiration', and yet, this is what enabled him to create so many life-changing inventions, including the world's first commercially successful incandescent light bulb – the iconic form of which is now itself a visual metaphor for an innovative idea.

As the British design-engineer entrepreneur James Dyson – a complete devotee of the Edisonian iterative approach to innovation – explains, during the design, research and development phase of a product, 'You must only make one change at a time, otherwise you won't know which one made the difference'.[1] And it is this meticulous process of testing and

retesting that brings each prototype one incremental step closer to technically innovative design perfection.

Today, strategic design thinking is used by many leading manufacturing companies, such as Apple, IBM, Nike and Tesla, as a way of boosting product innovation and consequently their bottom lines. These types of organization understand well that in today's highly competitive, globalized market-place, innovation in design is what gives their product offerings the all-important differentiating 'wow' factor, and engenders an owning lust among potential buyers, and brand loyalty among existing customers. The business writer Gary Hamel has put it in rather stark terms: 'Out there in some garage is an entrepreneur who's forging a bullet with your company's name on it. You've got one option now—to shoot first. You've got to out-innovate the innovators.'[2] As history has shown time and time again, companies can only do this by using the transformative power of design thinking so that they can innovate the proverbial 'better mousetrap', as Ralph Waldo Emerson once called it. ∎

AM01 Air Multiplier (2009) by Dyson – this bladeless table fan is another step-change product by James Dyson and his team of ultra-talented design-engineers.

Design on the move, from handily compact to knock-down and flat-pack

PORTABILITY

When thinking about the creation of products, the term 'portability' simply means devising objects that can be easily carried from one place to another.

One of the very first pieces of furniture to feature designed-in portability was a type of X-form folding stool that was used as a sort of mobile throne by the Ancient Egyptians. The Ancient Greeks likewise developed their own type of folding stool, known as a *diphros okladias* – a more practical design that appears to have been used widely, according to archaeological evidence. The Romans, however, took the idea of portability a step further by designing furniture to be used specifically by its travelling armies, including another type of lightweight X-form folding stool. Such pieces fall under the category of 'campaign furniture' because they were specifically devised to be easily transported from one military campaign to the next.

Later, a demountable (rather than folding) seat design, known as the Glastonbury chair, was used mainly by travelling clergy and nobility during the Early Middle Ages, and then enjoyed a resurgence of popularity in Renaissance Italy during the fifteenth century. The real heyday of portable furniture, however, was during the nineteenth and early twentieth centuries with the expansion of the British Empire. This type of campaign and expedition furniture – including a butterfly-form sling chair known as the Paragon (1870s) – was rationally conceived and often

incorporated highly innovative constructions. Designs like these tended to be quite plain in appearance, relatively light in weight, and either folded or broke down so they could be easily transported to far-flung destinations.

Other early instances of portability in design include typewriters – such as the compact Blickensderfer typewriter patented in 1891 by George Canfield Blickensderfer – and various portable sewing machines, including some made by Singer. Yet these early portable designs were really exceptions to the rule, for certainly in the early twentieth century, goods tended to be large, heavy and pretty immovable – most notably, furniture and later electronic items such as cabinet-encased radios and televisions. This was because, historically, most larger-scale manufactured goods had associations with status and permanence, and often the technology they employed in their manufacture was not advanced enough for much else.

But as technology progressed – be it with the introduction of latex foam for upholstery, or the advent of transistors for 'wireless' radios, which ultimately ushered in a new age of **miniaturization** – so designers were able to design objects that were far more compact and lightweight, and therefore had a greater degree of portability. Indeed,

the first pocket-sized radio, TR-63, introduced by Sony in 1957, was an important milestone in design portability, as was the company's subsequent launch of the world's first portable transistor television, the TV8-301, in 1960. Sony's later first-generation Walkman® personal stereo of 1979, officially known as the TPS-L2, likewise heralded a new level of portability in consumer electronics design.

Another landmark in portability was the introduction of IKEA's first self-assembly piece of furniture – the Lövet table (1956), which came about when its designer, Gillis Lundgren, removed its legs to get it into his car for a photo shoot, thereby inadvertently sparking the ensuing flat-pack furniture revolution. Products such as these were cheaper to

Valentine typewriter (1969) by Ettore Sottsass for Olivetti – this colourful machine, with its own bucket-like carrying case, was designed with portability in mind, in order to appeal to a new generation of get-up-and-go 1960s hipsters.

BELOW: Model TPS-L2 Walkman® personal music player (1979) by Sony – the very first Sony Walkman®, this compact cassette player with matching headphones changed listening habits forever thanks to its unprecedented portability.

produce and easier to transport. This made them more affordable to buy, and in so doing contributed enormously to the wider dissemination of modern **democratic design**.

By the 1960s, the **Pop** zeitgeist was all about more nomadic lifestyles, which in turn led to an even greater focus on portability in design – with both Mario Bellini's Minerva GA45 record player (1968) and Ettore Sottsass's lightweight Valentine typewriter, with its bright red carrying case (1969), being veritable Pop icons of design portability. Even now, portability continues to be a major theme in product design because when something can be efficiently transported, it is far easier to distribute and sell in today's globalized marketplace. ■

RIGHT: Model Nos. 4965-6-7 Componibili storage units (1967) by Anna Castelli-Ferrieri for Kartell – these stackable ABS modular 'components' can be used with or without their sliding doors.

BELOW: 606 Universal Shelving System (1960) by Dieter Rams for Vitsoe – arguably the best shelving system ever designed, which demonstrates the outstanding adaptability of modular systems.

'Modular designs have an almost chameleon-like, multi-application aspect.'

*Design that is more than
the sum of its parts*

IDEA № 3
MODULARITY

Modular systems are found throughout the natural world, whether in the individual cells of a leaf, or in the cellular structure of bees' honeycomb. The reason for this is that modularity provides an extremely efficient way of building things and offers huge scope for constructional flexibility.

*Black Gold porcelain range (2000)
by Ineke Hans – 'a kind of
ceramic LEGO' collection that
was based on the use of five
modular elements.*

The Finnish architect-designer Alvar Aalto once famously remarked, 'The best **standardization** committee in the world is nature itself, but in nature standardization occurs mainly in connection with the smallest possible units: cells. The result is millions of flexible combinations in which one never encounters the stereotyped.'[3] Throughout the biological world, modular systems are used for constructive purposes – from pathogen structures to gene networks – and generally what works best in nature, having been honed through a process of evolution, often has significant design relevance for the development of man-made things. Modularity is frequently found in nature because it provides material and building efficiency, as well as constructional and functional flexibility – which is just what most designers are looking for in any particular design solution.

Modularity is an approach to design that rests on the idea of making multiple individual sub-units, or modules, that can be combined to form various design outcomes. By using this approach, a designer is able to break a complex system down into smaller components that can either be used as standalone objects, or combined to

form other design solutions. A modular system does not have to feature just one type of sub-unit, either, but can have several – modular office-furnishing systems, for example, are usually made up of different types of sub-units that can be mixed and matched in order to attain multiple applications that can also be reconfigured if needed.

The history of modularity in design stretches back to the ancient world, with the advent of standardized bricks and tiles, which literally built civilization. Today, modularity in design is found most notably in the construction of buildings and the manufacture of office furniture. Within the world of man-made things there are two kinds of modularity: one involves the creation of 'finished' objects, such as cars and computers, that are made up by a manufacturer using a combination of sub-units; the other involves objects made up of sub-units that consumers can configure and reconfigure themselves, such as Lego bricks or Vitsoe shelving units. The latter type gives a degree of creative control to the user because it offers an all-important degree of do-it-yourself **customization**.

The inherent flexibility offered by modularity is its greatest asset, for it not only provides significant efficiencies

within the production process, but also optimizes the functional capabilities of a design. Modular designs have an almost chameleon-like, multi-application aspect that allows them to be more readily adapted to specific changing needs, which in the long run can help increase their functional longevity over non-modular solutions.

Ultimately, modularity is a highly rational approach to design that is based on **simplicity**, standardization and **systemization**, with individual modules functioning as building blocks within a greater overall scheme. It is, however, the quality of the **connections** between these individual units that, in the end, almost always determines the success of a modular design – they are effectively the glue that enables a design to become greater than the sum of its parts. ∎

Setting standards to enable precise mass replication

IDEA № 4

STANDARDIZATION

Standardization is a vital aspect of designs intended for industrialized **mass production**, for it allows the components that make up a product to be fitted together with very little or no adjustment.

Standardized components also allow for a higher degree of interchangeability between products, meaning that components from one product can be swapped to another with little or no need for adaptation.

The first instances of standardization can be traced back to the ancient world of China's first emperor, Qin Shi Huang, who reigned from 221BC to 210BC, instigating an early system of standardization for the production of weapons. Later, the Romans widely employed standardized elements for the mass production of arms and armour. Likewise, during the Middle Ages, European craftsmen used a significant degree of standardization in order to serially manufacture items ranging from weapons to floor tiles. It was, however, during the early 1800s that standardization began to be used more widely and systematically in the design of mass-manufactured objects, most notably at the Royal Navy's Portsmouth Block Mills, from 1803. At this quayside manufactory, precision tools designed by Marc Isambard Brunel were used to achieve a remarkably high degree of standardization in the production of wooden and metal rigging blocks, which were needed in vast numbers during the Napoleonic Wars.

During the early 1800s, a number of precision machine tools were introduced, including various lathes, milling machines and planers, all of which helped to increase the ability of manufacturers to achieve previously undreamt-of levels of standardization. And with greater standardization came a better degree of manufacturing consistency, which in turn enabled manufacturers to realize the much-longed-for dream of component interchangeability. One of the greatest pioneers of standardization was the engineering genius Joseph Whitworth, who during his lifetime was known as 'the world's best mechanician [sic]'. It was Whitworth who established the standards for screw threads, while his design of incredibly accurate instruments, such as micrometers that could precisely measure to one millionth of an inch, heralded unprecedented levels of standardization.

In America, the most notable pioneers of standardization came from the world of small-arms production, with Eli Whitney and Thomas Blanchard both helping to evolve this concept through their manufacture of guns. The latter famously designed a copying lathe that could manufacture multiple gunstocks at the same time, all to a precise set of standard measurements. This highly innovative machine, known as Blanchard's lathe, accelerated production rates considerably and ultimately helped to usher in the industrialization of warfare.

Manufacturers of all kinds, including most notably those making sewing machines and bicycles, soon picked up the standardization techniques found in the armouries of 'the North'. Indeed, standardization, together with the concomitant interchangeability, eventually became known as the **American System of Manufacture**, and was the means by which large-scale mass production became a fact of life both in America and elsewhere. Even today, standardization is an important factor when it comes to the design of goods for industrial production, for it ultimately allows things to be made better, faster and cheaper. ∎

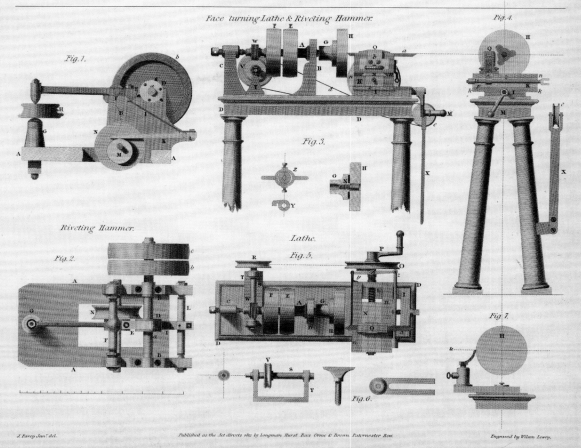

ABOVE: Block machinery at Portsmouth (1820) engraving by Wilson Lowry, illustrating the face-turning lathe and riveting hammer devised by the engineer Marc Isambard Brunel, among other machinery, which revolutionized the manufacture of pulley blocks for the Royal Navy.

RIGHT: Ship's pulley block made on Portsmouth block-making machinery – the manufacture of blocks had previously involved over twenty separate operations, but Brunel's series of machines were able to perform these without the need for skilled labour.

FAR RIGHT: Pulley blocks shown in the rigging of a tall ship.

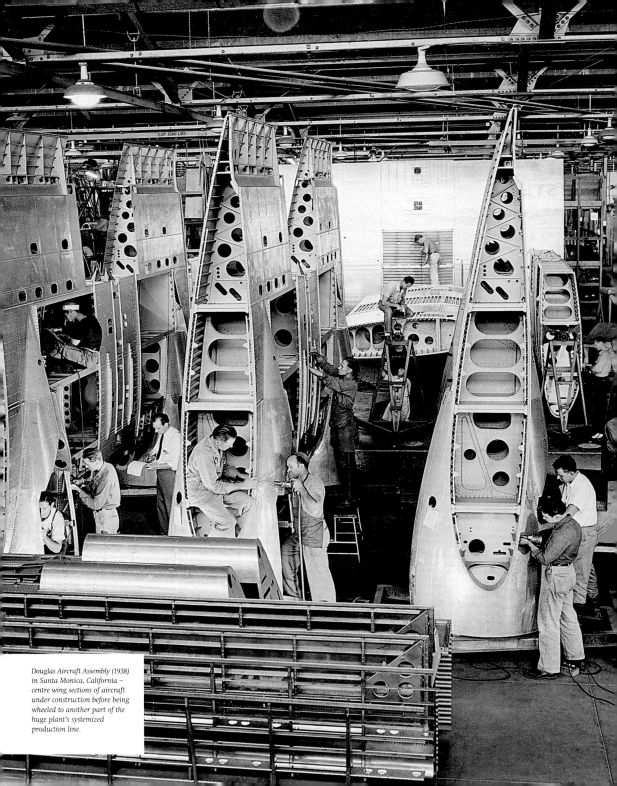

Douglas Aircraft Assembly (1938) in Santa Monica, California – centre wing sections of aircraft under construction before being wheeled to another part of the huge plant's systemized production line.

Managing the design process logically

SYSTEMIZATION

Roman wine amphorae found in the ruins of Bodrum Castle on the Aegean coast of Turkey.

Systemization in design practice is a way of methodically and analytically managing the workflow of various specialists collaborating on a design project in order to achieve the best outcome in the most efficient manner.

Although we often think of design creativity as something that involves an element of spontaneity and imaginative independent thinking, in certain areas of design, such as **industrial design** or transportation, the high degree of teamwork required negates this notion of design being driven by personal creative inspiration. Such projects are often very complex and capital-intensive, and inevitably require the skills of numerous specialists – not only different kinds of designers, production engineers and material scientists, but also marketing and **branding** experts. What these individuals do, when and how, all needs to be managed systematically within precisely scheduled project timetables and budgets.

As an idea, systemization can be traced back to the ancient world, when the first factories began the **mass production** of various types of objects – from coinage and weapons to amphorae and roof tiles – and ways were devised to manage how people involved on such large-scale enterprises worked together. This, however, was the systemization of the production process rather than the actual design process.   It was during the eighteenth century that Josiah Wedgwood – who had founded his ceramics factory in 1759 – became the first notable pioneer of 'modern' mass production based on systemization, which allowed him to replicate identical wares on an industrial scale. By contrast, systemization in design practice did not properly surface until the 1960s, when, influenced by the emergence of various design methodologies based on state-of-the-art design theory and research, companies began implementing organizational systems whereby their designers would work in a coordinated fashion with their engineering and marketing colleagues throughout the whole of the design process.

Today, systemized **design management** involves all sorts of practices that are generally, and often mistakenly, regarded as creatively constraining, from accountability systems and financial auditing to in-line reporting and continuous evaluation programmes. These controls, however, are absolutely essential for the successful realization of any sizable and technically complicated design project. In fact, systemization, when properly put into practice, offers one of the best frameworks for meaningful innovation in design – as anyone working at Apple or Dyson will tell you.

And, again, it would also be incorrect to think that creativity in the design process is the preserve of designers only, for engineers, material scientists and marketing professionals can also bring invaluable innovative thinking to a design project. Systemization in design practice ultimately provides a management framework for keeping charge of both processes and people, and provides three major benefits: it helps ensure that design strategy is part of a company's overall business strategy, that **quality control** is acted upon throughout the design process, and that a product from its conception is evolved from a user-friendly perspective – all key ingredients for the implementation of best design practice. ∎

IDEA № 6
STYLE

'Style' is the particular form a design takes, and at the same time is a useful way of distinguishing one design from another or, conversely, relating it to others that have similar characteristics.

The style or 'look' of a design is closely related to the concept of 'styles', which is one of design's biggest ideas, for it conveniently helps to define and categorize the different ideological and aesthetic approaches to problem-solving that have occurred in different countries and across the centuries.

This system of collective grouping helps us make sense of our material culture – it contextually places, in an easy-to-understand, linear order, the approaches to the design of man-made things in different eras. Ultimately, the styles-in-design scheme of classification not only assesses the outward appearance of an object or group of things, but also how it or they encapsulate the obsessions and aspirations, or zeitgeist, of the society that created them. Put simply, a style not only defines the underlying cultural attributes and **aesthetics** of a design or designs, but also helps codify it/them into the period and place in which it/they were created.

Throughout human history the designed artefact has served as an important barometer of social and cultural change. In every era, designed objects have their own distinct stylistic identity, with one style of design more often than not being motivated by the rejection of the one immediately preceding it. During the nineteenth

Armchair (c.1828) by Karl Friedrich Schinkel – with its Greek and Egyptian motifs, this sumptuous chair is a superb example of nineteenth-century Neo-Classicism and the late German Empire style.

'Designed objects have their own distinct stylistic identity.'

century in Britain, for example, this led to the so-called 'Battle of the Styles' between Classical Revivalism and Gothic Revivalism. In the twentieth century, the different major styles often swung back and forth between **rationalism** and Expressionism, universalism versus creative individualism. At times, different styles also coexisted – for instance, Art Deco was contemporaneous with early Modernism – yet sooner or later one style will inevitably gain the upper hand ideologically by being more in tune with the times and prevailing **taste**, and usurp its competitor. One of the most remarkable things about the twentieth century, at least in terms of design, was the pre-eminence of a single style for so long. This style was Modernism, which effectively dominated not only design

discourse, but also design practice, from around 1925 to the mid-1960s. Modernism was guided by a core belief that design could be used as a powerful tool for social change. Its adherents, with their slogans of '**form follows function**' and '**less is more**', sought to socially revitalize modern civilization through the application of rational design principles using the latest technological means. As Walter Gropius put it, 'Our guiding principle was that design is neither intellectual nor a material affair, but simply an integral part of the stuff of life, necessary for everyone in a civilized society.'[4] And it was this belief in the ethics of **democratic design** that made Modernism such a potent and long-lived style, for it was based on a moral argument that was hard to refute. Yet

Modernism was eventually undermined by the emergence of new international design styles (from **Pop** to Post-Modernism). These were motivated by new goals and thinking that rejected what had gone before, and sought better ways of doing things through the transformative power of design. ∎

The outward expression of affluence

LUXURY

The idea of luxury has always been associated with a level of comfort and beauty that is not strictly necessary, but rather an indulgence. Today, a whole sector of the design profession caters to the luxury market, which transcends national boundaries and is supported by a wealthy elite.

Chanel flap bag with top handle – this iconic handbag, made of fine quilted leather, epitomizes the exclusivity and craftsmanship associated with high-end luxury goods.

Yet the idea of luxury in design is open to interpretation – it might mean the 'bling-tastic' trappings of oligarchs, or it could refer to elegantly understated 'gentleman's essentials'. For some, luxury might be a diamond-encrusted mobile phone; for others it could be a perfectly handcrafted Japanese teapot. This is because luxury, like beauty, is ultimately a matter of personal **taste**. That said, the idea of luxury design is most usually associated with the rare, the expensive and the handmade.

Luxury has also long been tied to the art of pleasure, as well as excesses of wealth and power. As the design critic and cultural commentator Stephen Bayley has noted, 'luxury in some quarters has become a global Esperanto for certain expectations of what the world should be. This has a historical basis in degenerate Roman Emperors, Renaissance Popes, the neo-classical bling of "Le Gout Rothschild" and the nouveaux riches that followed.'[5]

In the Victorian era, various manufacturers were producing luxury goods aimed at the upper classes and aristocracy, as had been done for centuries, if not millennia. Very often, these goods incorporated precious materials, copious **decoration**, and relied on handcraftsmanship. But in parallel with this, other manufacturers, thanks to mechanization, were able to churn out lower-cost faux luxury wares that were marketed as 'fancy goods' to working-class and middle-class consumers. These sham wares were often described as 'deluxe', yet in reality they were the antithesis of real luxury. The shoddy fakery of these products, which pretended to democratize luxury in design, but in actuality catered to the lower orders' base desire for affordable extravagances, eventually provoked a cultural backlash that saw the rise of **design reform** in the mid- to late nineteenth century, which in turn laid the philosophical foundations of the **Modern Movement**.

Although the early pioneers of the Modern Movement were primarily concerned with **democratic design** and **utility**, in certain circles modernity was eventually connected to luxury, with the furniture and interiors by Le Corbusier and Eileen Gray, among others, epitomizing this modish appropriation. In the 1930s, the first generation of professional **industrial design** consultants in America, such as Raymond Loewy and Donald Deskey, went on to stylistically appropriate Modernism and began designing luxury Art Deco products within what became known as the Depression Moderne **style**.

Today, perceptions of what constitutes luxury in design are still highly subjective. However, the general consensus is that luxury design is dependent on either exceptional quality – especially in terms of design and execution – or exquisite handcraftsmanship. And while something that is luxurious does not necessarily have to be rare or expensive, it almost invariably is, with these two attributes being inextricably linked. But more than anything, luxury design functions as a tangible expression of status that can either whisper or shout about a person's economic and social standing. The idea of luxury is a very personal one, though, and whatever it might mean to someone, it will invariably have pleasurable connotations. As the architect Frank Lloyd Wright once quipped, 'I have always been willing to go without the necessities of life ... as long as I might enjoy the luxuries.'[6] ■

État cabinet (1922) by Émile-Jacques Ruhlmann, exemplifying the opulence of the French Art Deco style with its use of precious materials and superlative craftsmanship.

Juicy Salif citrus press (1990) by Philippe Starck for the Italian design company Alessi – Starck's highly idiosyncratic transformation of a common kitchen tool into an attention-grabbing design icon.

'Design, like art, is a powerful channel of personal creativity.'

Design as a means of conveying personality

CREATIVE EXPRESSION

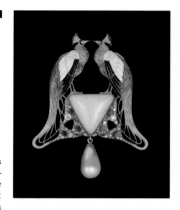

Peacock pendant (c.1901) by René-Jules Lalique – a signature piece by one of France's foremost Art Nouveau designers.

Creative expression in design has been about for as long as people have made things. The reason for this is that design, like art, is a powerful channel of personal creativity. As a result, a designed object often provides a unique insight into its creator's personality, including his or her way of looking at the world, and how they wish to represent themselves through their work.

While the channelling of personality has been a strong theme in design over the centuries, the notion of creative expression as an aim in itself only properly emerged in the early twentieth century. Up to that point, design had fallen primarily into two distinct categories – objects of pure **utility**, such as tools, and the decorative arts. The primary goal of the former was, and always has been, functional efficiency, which reduces but does not completely negate the possibilities for individual creative expression – for example, in a scythe, a plough or cooking pots. Objects falling into the decorative category, however, offered far greater scope for personal creative expression, whether they were craft-produced or factory-made. This might have taken the form of detail on a chair's back rail, or the decorative device found on a piece of silverware, or the distinctive pattern applied to a ceramic plate. Indeed, it is these telltale signs of design authorship that help differentiate one solution from another and have enabled individual designers to stand out from the crowd.

In the opening years of the twentieth century, however, the idea of **standardization** – based on a stripped-down **functionalism** suited to mechanized production – began to gain increasing currency among certain **design reform**ers in Austria and Germany, for it was realized that this was the only way that affordable, well-made **democratic design** could be brought to the masses. The subsequent machine aesthetic, derived from a process-driven approach to design, effectively eliminated personal creative expression from the design equation, at least when it came to the production of factory-made goods.

During the twentieth century there were two primary design-making pathways – mechanized industrial manufacture versus small-scale, craft-based manufacture. As the former became ever more denuded of **character** in the pursuit of **universality** through **mass production**, especially after World War II, so the latter became increasingly individualistic, with 1960s **Pop** and the 1970s Craft Revival reflecting a counterculture yearning for greater creative expression and individuality. This emerging tendency was transmitted through the iconoclastic work of the Castiglioni brothers, Gaetano Pesce and Verner Panton, among others, whose willingness to experiment signalled a fresh, creative self-assurance in design.

The subsequent rise of Post-Modernism in the late 1970s and early 1980s saw the questioning of Modernism's grip on progressive design and architecture, and reintroduced the idea of creative expression to the debate about what cutting-edge design could, or indeed should, be about. It was, however, the standout success in the 1990s of Philippe Starck, the world's first global megastar designer-as-brand that brought personal creative expression into the design mainstream. His distinctive signature **style** sold around the world, and its global commercial triumph sparked a new expressive confidence within the world of industrially manufactured goods.

Today, most high-profile designers have invariably built their careers on promulgating a recognizable signature style, which is based on their own distinct approach to design. And it is this ego-revealing design DNA, which is ultimately a form of creative expression, that imbues objects with a sense of personality – the emotional glue that binds people to products. ∎

The beauty of designed things

IDEA № 9
AESTHETICS

BELOW: Raku tea bowl (c.1800–50) – although the Kyoto maker of this Edo period tea bowl is unknown, it possesses the exceptional aesthetic refinement associated with the best Japanese design.

BOTTOM: Ferrari 250 TR (1957) racing car by Sergio Scaglietti – one of the most sublimely beautiful cars of all time, its aesthetics are derived from form following function.

Aesthetics, or the look of something, is an important factor in design because people are far more likely to be attracted to objects that are visually pleasing to them. And although it is widely acknowledged that the beauty of a design can enhance our experience of it, there is much less agreement as to what actually constitutes beauty.

Indeed, there is a modicum of truth in the oft-used proverb 'Beauty is in the eye of the beholder'. And yet, if you study the nature of aesthetics for long enough, it becomes clear that there are certain principles in design that lead to an undeniable beauty in an object.

In the mid-eighteenth century, the Scottish philosopher and economist Adam Smith noted, 'That **utility** is one of the principle sources of beauty ... the fitness of any system or machine to produce the end for which it was intended, bestows a certain propriety and beauty upon the whole, and renders the very thought and contemplation of it agreeable, is so very obvious that nobody has overlooked it.'[7] Indeed, there is a certain visual **rightness** or beauty in things that are designed from a **form follows function** perspective. The lines of a canoe or the curve of a scythe, or even the shape of a milk bottle, all have an incontestable beauty that is derived from a **purity** of form, a simple, straightforward expression of utility.

Despite this, over many centuries aesthetics has invariably been linked to the use of ornamentation – the embellishment of an object with applied **decoration**. It was not until the end of the nineteenth century that a proper ideological connection was established between ethics and aesthetics by **design reform**ers, such as Augustus Pugin and William Morris. This helped change **taste**, with the educated classes increasingly finding beauty in simpler, *more aesthetic* forms.

The aptly named Aesthetic Movement, which had its heyday in the 1870s, was a reflection of this trend, and looked Eastward for much of its inspiration. The technical and aesthetic refinement of Japanese design, which was first shown at the 'International Exhibition' of 1862, came as a complete revelation to many British designers, including Christopher Dresser, E.W. Godwin and Thomas Jeckyll, who subsequently attempted to channel its aesthetic spirit into their own work. The reason why Japanese design is so strongly associated with rarefied aesthetics can be attributed to the Shinto belief system, which deems inanimate objects, as well as people and animals, can have *kami* – a sacred essence or divine spirit. This goes some way

towards explaining why historically more aesthetic deliberation has been taken over the design and execution of everyday wares in Japan, so that they possess a definite sense of **character** or presence that accords with the Japanese **less is more** concept of *ma* (negative space).

The Aesthetic Movement also made inroads into the United States during the late nineteenth century, and it was there that eventually the full economic advantages of **styling** (imbuing a design with attractive aesthetics) was properly established by the first generation of American **industrial design** consultants in the 1930s. Among them was Raymond Loewy who, in his book *Never Leave Well Enough Alone* (1951), contemplated the nature of aesthetics in design and determined that it was not functionality per se that provided visual pleasure, but 'function

and **simplicity**' whereby there was a 'reduction to the essentials'.[8]

During the postwar era, the idea of aesthetics in design had generally moved on from the **Modern Movement**'s form follows function precept. Indeed, in 1951 the art and design historian Herbert Read observed: 'Aesthetics is no longer an isolated science of beauty; science can no longer neglect aesthetic factors.'[9] Nowhere was this truer than in Italy, where a new generation of architect-designers began focusing on the 'artistic' qualities of design. This heralded a new stylistic direction that became known as the *Linea Italiana* (Italian Line), which involved skinning products with seductively beautiful forms. Crucially for Italy, the aesthetics of its super-stylish products gave it an export advantage, and established un-equivocally the economic importance of beauty in the design of things. Indeed,

Ebonized sideboard (c.1867) by E.W. Godwin – this Anglo-Japanese design has a geometric elementalism that can be seen as being proto-modern in its aesthetic.

if something is visually attractive, then it is only human nature to emotionally engage with it – and we are also more likely to forgive its functional failings. When you get right down to it, we are suckers for beauty, whether it is displayed in people or in products. ∎

The adornment of design

IDEA Nº 10
DECORATION

Decoration is the means by which a design is embellished, and has nothing to do with functional purpose per se. This is because when ornamentation is added to a design's surface, in most cases it is intended to 'beautify' an object beyond its pure functional form.

Prior to the mid-twentieth century, the term 'decorative art' was commonly used to refer to what we now think of as designed objects, especially those that relate to the decoration of interiors – furniture, textiles, ceramics and so on. Indeed, the concept of decorative art is indicative of the central role ornamentation has played in these areas of design. Throughout history, decoration has been a defining feature of our material culture, from carved and painted Egyptian thrones and Greek black-figured pottery to ornament-encrusted Victorian tableware and swirling floral Art Nouveau textiles.

The reason for this is that the act of decorating is not only a form of **creative expression**, but also a way of imbuing a design with its own **character**, symbolism and meaning. Decoration has also, however, always been subject to the evanescence of fashion, with the decorative preferences of any one particular era encapsulating the **tastes** and cultural obsessions of the time. Decoration thereby helps define the **style** to which a design belongs – from the classicism of Regency furniture to the **streamlining** of Art Moderne radios.

The rich decorative traditions of folk art or even tribal art reveal that the embellishment of objects is an age-old human pursuit. Interestingly, the use of decoration in a society is a reliable barometer of its economic wellbeing, for if a population is having to scratch out a subsistence living, it is less likely to devote time to the embellishment of objects. If, on the other hand, a society is blessed with a buoyant economy, there is much more likelihood of decoration being applied to objects, thanks to a greater level of leisure time or economic patronage.

When craft-based manufacture was superseded by industrial manufacturing during the nineteenth century, the role of decoration in design fundamentally changed. Initially, decoration was often used either to hide shoddy quality or mimic handcraft production, with the showy, over-blown High Victorian style being the apotheosis of the use of excessive decoration. The reining in of applied decoration was one of the key goals of the early **design reform**ers, such as Henry Cole, and this idea was subsequently taken even further by the likes of Adolf Loos and Peter Behrens, who sought to expunge objects of wasteful decoration in their pursuit of truthful functional form.

The elimination of decoration was a key feature of Modernism, yet the **Modern Movement**'s dogmatic **form follows function** approach disregarded the symbolic value and emotional resonance that decoration can give a designed object. The Modernists' argument was that better value for money could be achieved if time and resources were focused on the intrinsic design of an object, rather than on its decorative surface treatment. And by eliminating adornment so that all effort was invested in a design's pure functional form, it became much better suited to mechanized industrial production. But what the Modernists failed to acknowledge was that when some objects have been stripped to their barest functional bones by being denuded of all decoration, they often possess a stark **utility** that can be difficult to engage with psychologically. Indeed, it was the inherent lack of intellectual, cultural and emotional **connections** within mainstream modern design during the mid to late twentieth century that ultimately led to the emergence of Post-Modernism, the adherents of which argued that the cultural value of decoration should not be disregarded, since it is a powerful way of imbuing objects with an emotional pull or intellectual hook.

Today, it is widely acknowledged among design practitioners that the primary function of decoration is to give connective meaning to objects, which in turn helps engender an emotional response. Yet despite this fact, often the highest level of aesthetic beauty is attained from pure form, rather than beautifying decoration, and it is this design attribute that is most likely to resonate with people, even on a subconscious, almost spiritual level. ∎

OPPOSITE: Fly chair (1834–35) by
Philip Hardwick and executed
by W. & C. Wilkinson –
originally created for the Court
Drawing Room at Goldsmiths'
Hall, London, it reflects the mid
nineteenth century taste for
flamboyant decoration.

BELOW: Altdeutsche cabinet
(2012) by Studio Jobs for the
Dutch design company Moooi,
referencing the form of a
traditional armoire, as well as
German 'folk' decoration, while
incorporating age-old symbols,
such as crosses, eyes, roses,
skulls, keys and feathers.

The momentary expression of aesthetic choice, from refinement to vulgarity

IDEA № 11

TASTE

The idea of 'taste' in design has always been a highly contentious issue, for it is heavily associated with education, and ultimately social class. And while the so-called 'taste police' have long been ridiculed for their elitism, it is an undeniable fact that good and bad taste do exist.

Although our concept of taste is subject to change, there are certain **ideal forms** and design principles that have a timeless **rightness**. For instance, **truth to materials**, **revealed construction** and **form follows function** are central pillars of **good design** and ultimately good taste, and imply a degree of integrity. By contrast, poor design and its badly dressed cousin, bad taste, are most often associated with artifice. As the design critic and cultural commentator Stephen Bayley once noted, 'The **Modern Movement** ... attempted to get beyond taste and define standards of design. ... There were many half-truths in Modern Movement theory, but no lies.'[10] Indeed, faux materials and structural deceit are, more than anything else, linked to poor design, and ultimately to bad taste.

In many ways, the idea of *bon goût* goes back to the Ancient Greeks, who through their sculptures established Western notions of the ideal human form – with the 'Greek statue' physique remaining an ideal today. Centuries later, the English artist William Hogarth attempted not only to identify the timeless principles of beauty, but those that govern good taste, too. In 1753 he published a seminal primer on the ethics of **aesthetics** entitled *The Analysis of Beauty*, which was subtitled thus: 'Written with a view of fixing the fluctuating IDEAS of TASTE'. And while this publication was concerned mainly

Hot Dog Sofa *(2017) by Studio Job for Seletti – this ironic Post-Pop design is intentionally kitsch, or is it?*

with how aesthetics relate to fine art rather than to the applied arts, it did make one important observation: 'So vague is taste, when it has no solid principles for its foundation!'

The idea of laying out principles of good taste as they relate to the design of objects, however, was later taken up by the organizers of the 'Great Exhibition of the Works of Industry of all Nations' (1851), who used £5,000 of the exhibition's profits to acquire objects deemed to be of high-quality design for an instructive study collection, which was housed in the

newly established Museum of Manufactures, now the V&A. Alongside these exemplars of good design/good taste, Henry Cole, the collection's first superintendent, also set up a display of poorly designed, tasteless objects, which was nicknamed the 'Chamber of Horrors' and was intended to inspire manufacturers and consumers to opt for more tasteful design choices.

A similar intention lay behind the English architect Charles Eastlake's publication of *Hints on Household Taste in Furniture, Upholstery and Other Details* (1868), which was highly influential in

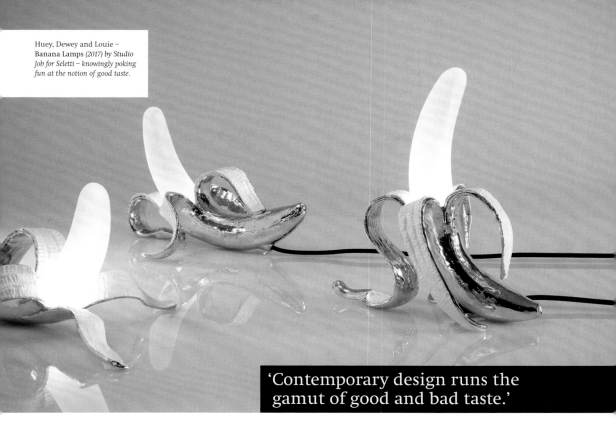

Huey, Dewey and Louie –
Banana Lamps *(2017) by Studio
Job for Seletti – knowingly poking
fun at the notion of good taste.*

'Contemporary design runs the gamut of good and bad taste.'

both Britain and America. By cleverly using the word 'hints' rather than 'rules' in the title of this how-to guide to tasteful interior design, Eastlake managed not to appear overly dogmatic in his advice. Yet in this text dedicated to modern design manners, he did not hesitate to name and shame those interior design practices he found to be a 'perversion of modern taste', such as petticoated toilet-tables and theatrical-**style** curtains. Indeed, his advice centred on how homes could be made more beautiful and sanitary through the adoption of greater **simplicity**, honesty and **morality**. No doubt Eastlake would have recoiled in horror at the **decoration**-festooned parlour furniture that was being produced contemporaneously by J.H. Belter in the United States.

During the twentieth century, the Modern Movement helped to solidify the association of good design with good taste. As Anthony Bertram noted in his book *Design* (1938), 'Are there, then, rules of taste, standards of beauty, tests of art? To some extent, yes. At least there are guiding principles. At least certain signposts and danger signals can be set up, certain blind roads indicated.'[11] And that was essentially the motivation behind MoMA's later 'Good Design' exhibitions (1950–55), which showcased designs that accorded with 'the progressive taste of the day'.[12]

Yet the associations of good taste with high culture, and bad taste with low culture, ultimately came to be seen as too prescriptive, and led to an **Anti-Design** backlash in the 1960s that saw kitsch being celebrated for its cultural authenticity, and good taste being admonished for being too boring. Today, contemporary design runs the gamut of good and bad taste because in our Post-Postmodern relativist times, what constitutes good or bad taste in design is supposedly all just a question of ... taste. ■

*Designed for the task in hand,
no more, no less*

IDEA № 12
UTILITY

'Utility' in design is about making something as useful as it can possibly be. This implies objects that are stripped down to their functional bare bones, whereby no superfluous **decoration** impedes their ability to do the job they were specifically devised to do.

Dining set (1927) by J.J.P. Oud for Schröer KG – this suite of furniture exemplifies the ideological adherence to utilitarianism by designers associated with the Modern Movement during its early years.

Indeed, the concept of utility in design has long been exemplified by the 'art' of tool-making.

Throughout human history, people have designed and made tools to assist them with tasks that they need to undertake, whether the ploughing of a field, the grinding of corn or the peeling of a potato. In fact, it is mankind's prodigious tool-making ability that has helped set us apart from the rest of the animal kingdom – it has enabled us to build civilizations and is ultimately responsible for the man-made world we live in today.

At its heart, tool designing and making is driven by the need for utility. A tool that is designed from a purely utilitarian standpoint will inevitably perform its job better than one that is not. With a pair of garden shears, for example, you only want them to be strong, lightweight and good at accomplishing their intended task. It is important, therefore, that they only comprise the parts that are absolutely necessary for their functionality, because if they were encrusted with ornamentation, not only would it be a waste of money and materials, but it would also quite possibly interfere with their usability, too.

Over the centuries, the design of tools used for agriculture and construction has been governed by utilitarianism, as has the creation of simple homewares – cooking pots,

teapots, mixing bowls and the like – which can be thought of as tools because they help people perform their daily chores without recourse to decorative embellishment. Such designs are far removed from the types of showy objects associated with the term 'decorative arts' because they have no real premeditated artistic aspect, having been designed to meet purely utilitarian needs.

The theory of utilitarianism is based on the idea of making useful things for the betterment of society at large – sometimes referred to as 'the greatest happiness principle'. Its origin can be

traced back to the English social reformer and philosopher Jeremy Bentham, who asserted that 'it is the greatest happiness of the greatest number that is the measure of right and wrong'. One of Bentham's students, John Stuart Mill, evolved his mentor's philosophy of happiness with the publication of a book entitled *Utilitarianism* in 1863. This liberal and positive philosophy, which focused on the belief that society's guiding ambition should be the promotion of happiness to the greatest number of people, inspired various members of the design avant-garde during the late

1910s and 1920s, who in turn attempted to realize this big idea in their work.

These designers adopted the strict **form follows function** approach that is common to traditional tool-making, for they understood that an adherence to utilitarianism in design was the best way of bringing well-designed everyday goods to the masses – the main social aim of the **design-reform**ers, beginning with those from Britain in the mid-nineteenth century, right up to those aligned to the **Modern Movement**. Their argument was that if a product was stripped of all **decoration** and designed purely as a means to a functional end, then all the materials and production value would go into the integrity of its construction and

functionality, rather than into how it looked. This, in turn, meant that it would, in all likelihood, not only be better by design, but probably more affordable, too.

The only problem was that, despite the Modernists' good intentions, the working-class consumers at whom these utilitarian wares were mainly aimed were not particularly receptive to their stark plainness. In 1927, the Dutch architect-designer Jacobus Johannes Pieter Oud, for instance, displayed furniture stripped down to its functional essentials at the Deutscher Werkbund's 'Die Wohnung' exhibition, which exemplified the Modern Movement's utilitarian stance, yet it was far too avant-garde for widespread public acceptance. Later, in

1942, the British Board of Trade introduced the Utility Furniture Scheme, which during wartime allowed only the production of standardized worthy-but-dull furniture items that were guided in design and manufacture by a rigorous adherence to utilitarianism. And while such designs were highly serviceable and met the needs of the time, when rationing came to an end most British consumers settled upon more stylish options. Ultimately, utility in design is a bit like porridge – it might be good for you, but its inherent blandness is very much an acquired **taste**. ∎

TOP: Big Ben alarm clock (1938), designed by Henry Dreyfuss for the Westclox Company – this streamlined Art Moderne product became a bestseller for Westclox, a division of General Time Instruments Corp.

LEFT: Bush TV22 television (c.1949–50) manufactured by Bush Radio – a popular British television model in the early 1950s, its Bakelite housing enabled it to be mass-produced on a large scale

Designing for the machine

INDUSTRIAL DESIGN

Industrial design relates primarily to the conception and planning of a product that is intended for multiple reproduction. While industrial design and product design often overlap, as terms they mean quite different things; the former almost always involves a process of machine manufacture, whereas the latter may or may not.

Brass and copper pitchers (c.1885) attributed to Christopher Dresser and manufactured by H. Loveridge & Co. – their simple geometric forms were perfectly suited for industrial manufacture.

The term 'industrial design' is also frequently used in relation to the design of machines themselves. Because of the complexity involved in the design of a machine or something intended for high-volume mechanized manufacture, industrial designers generally work as part of a larger team that often includes design engineers, production specialists and materials experts. So while industrial design is generally associated with product design and vice versa, it also encompasses other areas of design, from automotive and aerospace to weapons systems and **robotics**, which tend to have a fundamental mechanical aspect. For this reason, industrial design involves much more engineering – which can be summed up as problem-solving based on the practical application of the pure sciences and digital technologies – than straightforward product design.

The idea of industrial design came into being with the advent of the Industrial Revolution in the eighteenth century, which heralded new mechanized methods of production that ultimately necessitated a new approach to the design of objects – one that would allow exact, standardized replication on a previously unimaginable scale. The coining of the term 'industrial design' is generally credited to the industrial design consultant Joseph Sinel (in 1919),

although he refuted this himself. And while both Christopher Dresser and Peter Behrens were early pioneers of industrial **design consultancy**, it was only in the 1930s that the role of the industrial designer became widely celebrated outside design circles, with the likes of Henry Dreyfuss, Raymond Loewy and Walter Dorwin Teague becoming the first generation of industrial design celebrities. This cohort of super-talented design consultants commanded huge fees from corporations who were eager for them to create new products that were not only cheaper to produce, but looked better too, in order to capture a life-blood share of dwindling sales within a Depression-laden marketplace.

It was the actions of this first generation of American industrial design consultants that not only popularized this new profession but also ultimately helped define its practice. While today the vast majority of industrial design takes place within the design departments of manufacturing companies themselves, thanks to the increasing specialization in design, there are still a number of internationally renowned and independent multidisciplinary design consultancies who can bring an often hugely valuable external design vision to **the brief**, while working hand in hand with their client's production engineers and other specialists to

create innovative design solutions for industrial **mass production**.

Industrial design is fundamentally all about building into the design of an object a sufficient degree of **standardization** and enough interchangeability of its parts to enable efficient and cost-effective mass replication. But over and above this, it is also about fully understanding the manufacturing processes that will be used to make something and then allowing that knowledge to inform the conception and planning of the solution – or, in other words, **process-led design**. The practice of industrial design also frequently has to take in other factors, too, such as **ergonomics, packaging, quality control, recycling, sustainability, universality, IoT** and even **branding** strategy. ∎

Making products last longer to minimize waste and energy consumption

IDEA № 14
PRODUCT DURABILITY

The concept of product durability is one of the most important ideas relating to **sustainability**. Making products last longer not only minimizes waste and energy consumption, it also provides better value for money to consumers.

Dualit 2-Slot Classic toaster (2009) – this design is an evolution of a toaster first designed by Max Gort-Barten for Dualit around 1946. Built to last, it has heating elements that can be easily replaced when they wear out.

While **recycling** and **upcycling** can reduce energy consumption, they do not minimize it, and in some ways can be seen to actually perpetuate a throwaway culture. The benefits of product durability, on the other hand, are clear: if you double the useful life of a product, its environmental impact can be halved; if you triple its life cycle, then its ecological impact can be reduced by a third, and so forth. Product durability is simply one of the most effective ways of achieving more sustainable consumption.

Product durability is the polar opposite of **disposability**. Obviously some products by their very nature need to be readily disposable, such as syringes or food **packaging**. The vast majority of mass-produced goods, however – from cars to furniture – can be rendered much more durable by utilizing more thoughtful design, engineering and better-quality manufacturing. One of the ways a product can be made more durable is if it is made of high-quality materials, which are less likely to degrade and ultimately fail. Another way of enhancing durability is to design better serviceability into a product so that it is easier to mend when a part does eventually expire. In practice this means not using so-called closed systems, which have batteries or other parts that cannot be changed, and instead designing a product so that its component parts have more of a plug-in aspect; if they fail – say the element

of a toaster or a kettle – then they can be easily taken out and repaired or replaced. This negates the wasteful scenario of products ending up in landfill because just one part that has failed cannot be easily accessed, thereby making it impossible to be replaced or fixed.

In centuries gone by, most things were designed to last not for a few years, but for decades, and it was only in the 1930s that the idea of **planned obsolescence** became a strategy in the manufacturing industry. During this period, fashion-driven **styling** also began to be used cynically by manufacturers to render their last season's products stylistically obsolete. Thankfully times have changed, and

many manufacturers are now starting to realize the benefits that can be gained from adopting a culture of product durability.

Professor Tim Cooper of Nottingham Trent University has defined these benefits as:

(1) being able to charge a premium price for the higher quality reflected in a product's greater longevity;

(2) enjoying increased customer loyalty because customers are more likely to return to a manufacturer if they have had a positive experience relating to a product's durability;

(3) saving money, as more durable products tend to have longer design cycles, meaning tooling costs can be written off over a longer period of time;

Land Rover Series II (1958) styled by Tony Poole, a member of David Bache's legendary design team, for the Rover Company – generally regarded as 'the classic Land Rover', many Series II are still on the road, testifying to the remarkable durability of this off-road workhorse.

'Product durability is the polar opposite of disposability.'

and (4) improving strategic business foresight by thinking long term. As for the consumer, product durability invariably offers better quality as well as better value for money over the total lifespan of a product. More significantly, enhanced durability provides the best way of reducing the excessive throughput of energy and materials in our economy and of achieving both sustainable design and consumption.

Today, the cultural tide seems to be turning towards product durability, as suggested by the emerging millennial 'fixer' culture. More and more people are beginning to question whether it really is too much to ask that furniture can be passed down from generation to generation, or that white goods are

built to last for decades, as in the past, rather than the more customary three to five years. And with this new **green design** eco-awareness among consumers there are encouraging signs in the world of high-tech product design. Take, for example, Jake Dyson's CSYS task lights, which are the first LED lighting designs to boast an effective cooling system, ingeniously based on heat pipe technology. This means that not only is their emitted light more energy efficient and tonally stable, so easier on the eye, but their bulbs will also last for 144,000 hours – which equates to an astonishingly durable 37 years. This type of step-change product durability is sadly all too often the exception to the rule, but maybe

designs such as these will act as beacons of hope, inspiring other product designers, design engineers and manu-facturers in the future to harness the power of technology to design and manufacture more ethically and more durably. ∎

The economy of scale making things cheaper to produce

Matthew Boulton and James Watt's steam engine, elevation and plan of the beam floor (1776) – engraving by Wilson Lowry after an illustration by J. Farey and from Abraham Rees' Cyclopedia or Universal Dictionary, London, 1813.

IDEA № 15

MASS PRODUCTION

The term 'mass production' generally implies the high-volume, continuous manufacture of goods by mechanized means, and the implementation of various factory production systems, such as **standardization**, the **division of labour**, assembly lines and industrial **robotics**.

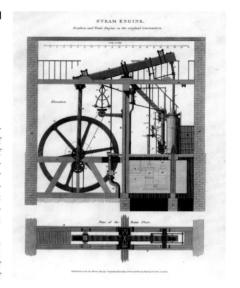

Although in ancient times a form of mass production was used to manufacture items such as bricks, weapons and coins, the real emergence of what could be described as modern mass production did not occur until the Industrial Revolution, in the mid- to late eighteenth century. This new idea of continuous industrial production necessitated a different way of thinking about design and its relationship to manufacturing. Rather than an object being crafted by hand in small batches, early steam-powered machines gave a degree and speed of exact replication that had been hitherto unachievable.

The realization of mass production hinged on two key concepts: standardization and interchangeability, both of which were achieved by the design, manufacture and implementation of precision machinery. Likewise, the very nature of industrialization, with different components of a design being made on different specialist machines before being assembled together to make a final product, prompted a new system of working that did not have to rely so heavily on highly paid skilled craftsmen, but instead was able to employ cheaper unskilled workers to supervise the machines that made the parts. This meant that workers were, for the most part, no longer involved in the creation of a whole product, but only a specific aspect of it. For instance, in a factory making ceramic teapots, a worker might now only be involved in the moulding of handles or spouts, or tasked with the teapots' glazing or painted **decoration**. This division of labour extended to the actual design of the objects themselves, with professionally trained designers being hired by companies to oversee the conceptualization and planning of products, but not their actual production development or, indeed, their eventual manufacture.

Another key aspect of mass production, which is rarely considered outside industry, is the engineering of mechanized systems and the layout of production lines so that the manufacture of designed goods is executed in the most rational, consistent and productive way possible. This was especially the case with the advent of the moving assembly line, which enabled enormous increases in manufacturing productivity.

More recent advances in **CAD/CAM** software and computing power – particularly those that have taken place in the last 10 to 15 years – have helped to reduce considerably the time required to take a design from initial concept to final prototype stage, and ultimately into mass production. The increasing automation found in factories today, thanks to advances in robotics technology, has also speeded up production rates exponentially – so much so that it is not unusual for a product to pass through an entire manufacturing process without ever coming into contact with a human hand.

Over the last two centuries, mass production has enabled well-designed goods to become ever more affordable for the masses by making them better, faster and cheaper. There is, however, a major environmental downside to mass production: when products are made too easily and, therefore, potentially too cheaply, their perceived value is downgraded, which in turn can lead to a throwaway mentality that promotes mindless waste.

Having started in the Coalbrookdale foundry, the Portsmouth Block Mills and Josiah Wedgwood's potteries in the mid- to late eighteenth century, mass production truly came of age in the American armouries during the nineteenth century as a way of making guns more quickly and efficiently. Later known around the world as the **American System of Manufacture**, mass production has always been about the beneficial economies of scale offered by wholesale replication. Over the decades, higher volumes of goods achieved from the implementation of

Preformed vehicle panels ready for assembly at the Toyota Motor Manufacturing plant in Sakarya, Turkey, 2014.

mass production have increasingly helped to drive down manufactured unit costs, which in turn has made designed objects more affordable to more people. And this has ultimately transformed not only our shared material culture but also all of our lives for the better in so many different ways. ∎

'The moving assembly line enabled enormous increases in manufacturing.'

Workers assembling one of the bestselling cars in the world – the Toyota Corolla – vehicles on the moving production line at Toyota's state-of-the-art plant in Sakarya, Turkey, 2014.

Production line of the F-Type sports car at the Jaguar car plant in Castle Bromwich, Birmingham, 2013.

36
LINE 3

BELOW: Potter at Wedgwood's Etruria Works in Stoke-on-Trent, Staffordshire, while an assistant turns a pulley to spin the potter's wheel. From 'Scenes of England' by Rev. Isaac Taylor, London, 1822.

BELOW RIGHT: Workers painting ceramic wares at Wedgwood's Etruria Works in Stoke-on-Trent, Staffordshire, 1936.

Breaking down the manufacturing process into compartmentalized actions

IDEA № 16

DIVISION OF LABOUR

From ancient times a modicum of departmentalizing had always taken place within workshops, and early factories had employed workers who specialized in different aspects of the production process, but this had never been particularly systemized.

In the eighteenth century, however, by harnessing the power of rational design planning in the pursuit of **mass production**, the British ceramicist Josiah Wedgwood changed the nature of design practice through his introduction of the division of labour – which effectively systemized the workflow in his potteries.

Wedgwood twinned this new idea with another initiative that comprised separating out the different processes involved in the making of his ceramic wares into dedicated work zones. First introduced at his new factory in Burslem, which opened in 1763, taking over from his previous pottery, Ivy House, his **rationalized** factory system compartmentalized the whole design and making process into separate tasks carried out by different specialists. The benefits of this system were twofold: quality was improved and productivity substantially increased.

By the 1790s, Wedgwood's later state-of-the-art Etruria factory was using an early form of assembly-line production, with each workshop having its own specialists – including, among others, modellers, painters, decorators, mould-makers, seal-makers, lathe-turners, spout-makers and engravers. This new systemized form of manufacturing meant that designers were now largely separated from the act of making, and workers entrusted with a design's production were specially trained for the execution of very specific tasks.

Wedgwood's instigation of this division of labour was one of the driving forces behind the Industrial Revolution in Britain. Prior to this, most objects had been handcrafted or serially produced by individuals in small-scale workshops, and although a degree of specialization might have existed among the craftsmen in a workshop – for instance, in a furniture-making enterprise, one craftsman might be a skilled cabinet-maker, while another might be more adept at gilding or French polishing – such roles were usually quite loosely defined. Often craftsmen, especially in smaller workshops, took on the role of designer-maker, being solely responsible for not only the original design concept but then its execution, too. By taking ownership of the whole design-making process, skilled craftsmen such as these were much more likely to take pride in their work and to find joy through a job well done.

By contrast, within factories that implemented a division of labour, standardized goods could be mass-produced by machines with specialist workers effectively acting as trained machine-minders, undertaking repetitive tasks that helped to increase manufacturing productivity. Thanks to the linking of mechanization with the division of labour, all kinds of objects could now be produced faster and cheaper, and consequently in much higher volumes, which in itself introduced an unprecedented economy of scale that effectively helped to democratize design, at least for the middle classes.

Significantly, after the introduction of the division of labour, designers were left with two distinct career pathways – they could either work for industry and devise product solutions that strove for **universality** for the sake of mass appeal, or they could continue working as designer-makers, creating objects in much smaller volumes that provided more opportunity for personal **creative expression**. ∎

One design that fits all

*Official Swiss Railways Clock
(1944) by Hans Hilfiker for Swiss
Federal Railways (SBB) – this
iconic design reflects the bold
directness of the Swiss School's
universal language of graphic
design.*

IDEA № 17
UNIVERSALITY

The concept of universality in design has been subject
to different interpretations over the years, but is
fundamentally about creating a solution that can
be used by as many people as possible.

Since the Industrial Revolution in the eighteenth century, designers have been faced with two very different design pathways: either to create designs for the benefit of the many by harnessing industrialized systems of **mass production**, or to create designs for the enjoyment of the few using primarily handcraft methods of manufacture. The former approach is guided by the idea of the universal solution, while the latter relates more to the pursuit of individual **creative expression**, or the fulfilment of personal needs through either highly limited or bespoke designs.

During the early years of the **Modern Movement**, the pros and cons of universalism versus individualism were endlessly debated. Members of the Deutscher Werkbund, for instance, fell into two distinct camps. On the one side were those such as Hermann Muthesius, who argued the case for universalism, which involved the acceptance of greater **standardization** so that designed goods would be easier to produce industrially. And on the other side were those like Henry van de Velde, who continued to stress the benefits that individualism (personal creative expression) could have on design practice. The argument, in other words, was machine-made goods designed from a rational standpoint versus Arts and Crafts-inspired **art manufactures** made mainly by hand.

This long-running debate, however, was ultimately decided by the outbreak of World War I, which necessitated the adoption of an industrial approach to design and manufacturing. But after the conflict ended, a battle of **styles** – Expressionism versus **rationalism** / individuality versus universality – was effectively played out at the Staatliches Bauhaus in Weimar, which was founded in 1919. Initially, the school's director, Walter Gropius, was sympathetic to the Expressionist cause, yet he soon changed tack and eventually went on to become an influential champion of universalism in design. As the editor of *Architectural Forum* magazine Peter Blake once noted, under Gropius's leadership 'the Bauhaus was enamored with a new vocabulary of forms: the forms of machines, the forms of *our* century'.[13] And those shapes, based on pure geometry – cylinders, cubes, spheres and cones – would go on to establish the formal 'universal' vocabulary of Modernism. The theory of the Modern Movement was that if a design or a building was stripped of all ornament and possessed a geometric **purity**, then its appeal would be universal. In many ways this was true, as was demonstrated by the emergence of the subsequent International Style in design and architecture during the 1920s and 1930s, which was effectively a universal expression of Modernism that was able to transcend regional cultural constructs.

The idea of universality in design has also been closely linked to the notion of **democratic design** – in other

Färgrik mug (c.2015) by IKEA – this universally appealing stoneware design is the Swedish homeware giant's bestseller and was created for maximum stackability.

words, creating well-designed things for the many rather than the few. It was also expressed in the development of product families during the postwar era with, for example, a range of chairs having a single 'universal' seat shell that could be used in conjunction with various types of interchangeable bases so that many different combinations and applications were possible – such as Charles and Ray Eames' Plastic Shell Group (1948–50), Arne Jacobsen's Series 7 (1955) and Robin Day's Polyprop range (1963–64, page 72). Another seating design that speculated on universality was Joe Colombo's appropriately named Universale chair (1965–67), which was based on the concept of **modularity**, whereby different heights of legs could be plugged into a universal seating module to create either a low lounge chair, a dining chair or a bar stool, depending on functional requirement. It was only the dining version, however, that made it into mass production.

By the 1970s the concept of universality had moved on considerably and into the realm of **inclusive design**, whereby designs are created not for 'Joe or Jane Average' but for as wide a range of people as possible, regardless of age or physical ability. Today, the terms 'universal design' and 'inclusive design' are often used interchangeably, and ultimately they mean the same thing: finding all-embracing design solutions that have the broadest possible appeal. ∎

Standardization and interchangeability of components for increasing manufacturing productivity.

IDEA Nº 18

AMERICAN SYSTEM OF MANUFACTURE

Pioneered in the early to mid-nineteenth century the 'American System of Manufacture' was fundamental to the birth of modern industrialized production. Quite simply, it changed how products were designed in the United States, and eventually across the world.

The American System of Manufacture was predicated on the use of specially developed precision machinery that enabled the accurate **standardization** of a product's components so as to facilitate their mass replication and interchangeability. This new manufacturing approach required products to be conceived specifically for machine production. This meant that the product's design had to be simplified and **rationalized**, with the component parts making up the product designed in such a way that they enabled highly accurate replication. With the appropriate degree of accuracy achieved by means of mechanization, component parts could be standardized. And only with the standardization of component parts could they then be truly interchangeable, from one product to another. Machine-aided standardization and interchangeability enabled massive increases in manufacturing productivity, which ultimately spawned the development of assembly-line production.

The first attempts to realize a mechanized manufacturing system based on these twin ideals of standardization and component interchangeability can be traced back to the late eighteenth century, when Eli Whitney won a contract from the US Government in 1798 to produce 10,000 muskets within a period of 28 months.

Whitney's original claim was that by using water-driven precision machinery he could mass-manufacture small arms to such a degree of standardized accuracy that when one of their parts broke, a replacement could be easily swapped in from a cache of identical spare parts – the benefit on a battlefield being that it would render a broken musket entirely serviceable again within a matter of minutes. At a stroke this negated the time-consuming hand-fitting of replacement parts, which were all slightly different having been ostensibly handcrafted. Although it eventually took Whitney ten years to complete the government order, and his muskets never actually achieved the level of component interchangeability he had hoped for, his new system of manufacture was hugely influential as an idea.

In fact, the Portsmouth Block Mills in England was the first large-scale manufacturing enterprise to successfully batch-produce standardized objects using machine tools: wooden rigging blocks for ships (page 15), which had previously been laboriously made by hand by skilled craftsmen. Set up by the Royal Navy, which needed a supply of 100,000 pulley blocks per annum in order to keep afloat, this large quayside manufactory installed in 1803 a series of precision machines devised by the British engineer Marc Isambard Brunel.

These machines accelerated production rates to such an extent that within five years the Portsmouth Block Mills were producing an astonishing 130,000 blocks per annum, and at a fraction of the previous cost because now lower-paid unskilled labourers could be used to oversee the blocks' production.

Yet despite this momentous achievement, it was the Springfield Armory in Massachusetts that propelled the industrial techniques of standardization and interchangeability to new levels. It was here that Thomas Blanchard invented two ingenious copying lathes that allowed the precise replication of gunstocks and rifle barrels in 1818 and 1822 respectively. Using these together with a dozen other specialized Blanchard-designed shaping and inletting machines, the armoury was able to streamline and accelerate the process of making rifled muskets – with over 1 million Model 1861 examples being produced by the Springfield Armory and 20 other subcontractors for use in the American Civil War. Eventually, the mechanized high-volume manufacture of all kinds of standardized products, from clocks to bicycles, became known as 'armoury practice'.

Model 1861 rifled muskets at the Springfield Armory in Springfield, MA – mass-produced on an unprecedented scale using Blanchard's revolutionary lathe.

An original Blanchard lathe at the Springfield Armory National Historic Site, Springfield, MA, one of the great birthplaces of the American System.

This system of industrial production became so widespread in the United States that it inspired manufacturers overseas to take it up, too. As the idea caught on across the world, it became known as the American System of Manufacture, and it would inevitably have huge ramifications for how products were conceived and planned – or, in other words, designed – for industrial manufacture. ∎

Legally protecting designs from intellectual property infringement

IDEA № 19
DESIGN RIGHT PROTECTION

Honda staff and government officials smash fake Honda spare parts at a Honda plant in the Philippines as part of a campaign against counterfeit goods, 2004.

OPPOSITE: Incandescing Electric Lamp patent (1882) filed by Thomas Edison.

Patents, copyright, design right and trademarks enable designers to legally protect the intellectual property (IP) that resides in their designs from being infringed or misused. Design right protects three-dimensional designs, whereas copyright protects two-dimensional work.

As such, the notion of IP in relation to a designer's work has been crucial to the development and expansion of design practice and **innovation** over the decades.

Designs that are truly innovative often require a large investment of both time and money to bring them to market. For designers and manufacturers, there would be very little motivation to go to all this trouble if, as soon as their designs were launched, they were copied with no legal recourse for infringement. Indeed, the introduction of patent, copyright, design right and trademark laws was one of the great driving forces of design innovation during the eighteenth and nineteenth centuries.

In America, it was the Patent Act of 1836 that accelerated innovation in design and industry, for it established the principle of a search to ensure that no previous claim already existed in relation to an invention before a patent was granted. Prior to this, patents had been granted to all claimants and the onus was on them to battle it out in the courts as to who had the rightful claim to originality. The upshot of the 1836 Patent Act was that within 20 years, the number of patents granted in the United States increased threefold – from 702 'utility' patents in 1836 to 2,315 'utility' patents plus a further 107 'design' patents in 1856.

Other countries subsequently introduced similar legal provisions. It was not until 1967, however, that the World Intellectual Property Organization (WIPO) was created as an agency of the United Nations in order to promote the protection of intellectual property throughout the world, including that which relates to the design of things. Under WIPO's auspices, the Patent Cooperation Treaty was formally ratified by 18 countries in 1970, and brought into force eight years later, thereby helping to protect designs that fall into the realm of inventions. It is, however, design right, rather than patents, that protect the look and feel of products.

In 1979, the People's Republic of China began acknowledging and protecting intellectual property rights, and the following year it also became a member of WIPO. However, to this day there is still a problem in China with the implementation and enforce-ment of design copyright. But this may well change as the country inevitably transforms itself into a high-value, design-led economy and its homegrown design innovators require the robust IP protection enjoyed in other parts of the world. This in turn will also help designers and manufacturers in other countries.

While larger companies can generally afford the legal fees involved in going after their competitors who infringe their IP, it is harder for smaller concerns because of the associated financial risks. That said, they do have the umbrella protection of ACID (Anti Copying in Design), which is a membership and campaigning trade organization that was set up by designers for designers in 1996. By raising awareness of IP and encouraging respect for it within design and manufacturing, ACID is proactively helping to stamp out the abuse of IP rights by copyists, who will only be deterred when the full weight of IP law is brought against them. ACID is an advocate of registering design rights with the Intellectual Property Office, but many cannot afford this, so ACID offers an alternative solution – a Copyright and Design Databank for the lodgement of new designs, offering dated evidence of their existence held by an independent third party. For designers working in today's international marketplace, it is critical to be as 'IP savvy' as possible so they can formulate a proactive and effective IP strategy. The effective global protection of design-related IP is absolutely essential for the development of tomorrow's meaningful design innovations because the investment stakes are just too high for anything less. ∎

(No Model.)

T. A. EDISON.

INCANDESCING ELECTRIC LAMP.

No. 268,206.

Patented Nov. 28, 1882.

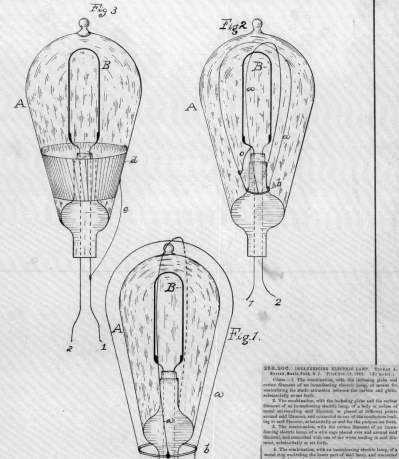

Fig 3

Fig 2

Fig. 1.

268,206. INCANDESCING ELECTRIC LAMP. Thomas A. Edison, Menlo Park, N. J. Filed Oct. 17, 1882. (No model.)

Claim.—1. The combination, with the inclosing globe and carbon filament of an incandescing electric lamp, of means for neutralizing the static attraction between the carbon and globe, substantially as set forth.

2. The combination, with the inclosing globe and the carbon filament of an incandescing electric lamp, of a body or bodies of metal surrounding said filament, or placed at different points around said filament, and connected to one of the conductors leading to said filament, substantially as and for the purpose set forth.

3. The combination, with the carbon filament of an incandescing electric lamp, of a wire cage placed over and around said filament, and connected with one of the wires leading to said filament, substantially as set forth.

4. The combination, with an incandescing electric lamp, of a metal ring encircling the lower part of said lamp, and connected to one of the conductors leading to the lamp, and two or more wires bent over the top of the lamp, with their ends attached to said ring, substantially as set forth.

WITNESSES:

Edw. C. Rowland

A. W. Seely

INVENTOR:

Thomas A. Edison

By Richd N. Dyer,

Atty.

'Designers will frequently look at historical archetypes for inspiration.'

Comback rocking chair (2012) by Patricia Urquiola for Kartell – its form harks back to a well-known antique furniture archetype: the spindle-backed Windsor chair.

History repeating itself stylistically in design

IDEA № 20

HISTORICISM

Throughout history, there has been a tendency among designers to look back to the past in order to find inspiration for the present and the future. This is known as 'historicism', and to this day designers will frequently look to historical archetypes for inspiration, just as they have done over the centuries.

Paper Chandelier L (2010) by Studio Jobs for Moooi – a quirky Post-Post-Modern take on an antique chandelier.

The elegant Neo-Classicism of a Robert Adam interior from the mid-eighteenth century incorporated, for example, ideas taken from the designs of Ancient Greece and Rome, but in no way slavishly copied them. Similarly, a Gothic Revival table by Augustus Pugin might well be based on an antique model and therefore deemed historicized, yet it is also very much of its own time, being essentially a Victorian interpretation of the Gothic **style**. Indeed, during the mid- to late nineteenth century, the decorative arts were in the frenzied grip of a veritable revival mania, as designers, magpie-like, drew inspiration from a host of different historic styles, ranging from Etruscan and Renaissance to Rococo and Queen Anne. With hindsight, the historicizing revivalism of this period was not only prompted by National Romanticism, which saw countries across Europe, Scandinavia and the Americas exploring their indigenous design roots in order to find an authentic cultural expression of their nationhood, but was also a form of rose-tinted escapism in the face of rapid industrialization.

The emergence of the Art Nouveau style in the *fin de siècle* period marked a break from historicism, for instead of looking to the past, it sought inspiration from the natural world. In fact, the defining ahistoricism of Art Nouveau led it to become generally regarded as the world's first truly modern style. This break from the past was also instrumental in the subsequent founding of the **Modern Movement**, which sought to purge design of any backward-looking historicism and **decoration**. Indeed, historicizing ornament was seen as culturally regressive, and it was widely believed among modernizing **design reform**ers that form should only follow function.

Yet despite the Modernists' rejection of historicism per se, during the twentieth century there were sporadic outbreaks of looking back in time for creative inspiration. For instance, the Art Deco style of the 1920s and 1930s frequently made reference to Ancient Egyptian and Rococo motifs, from ziggurat forms to stylized roses. Then, in the 1960s, there was a strong Art Nouveau revival, which saw swirling William Morris-style textile patterns printed in lurid colours. The emergence of Post-Modernism in the late 1970s and early 1980s as a full-blown major international style saw an ideological reassessment of historicism within both design and architecture, with designers such as Charles Jencks and Michael Graves famously making direct tongue-in-cheek references to previous historic styles.

Today, the use of historicism in design is far more subtle, with the Belgian design group Studio Job, alongside many of the designers associated with the New Dutch Design movement, creating interesting work that channels the past – whether through form, materials, decoration or craft process – while at the same time embracing the use of cutting-edge technologies. ∎

The artful creation of well-designed products

ART MANUFACTURES

Galleon brass charger (1892) by John Pearson, possibly for the Guild of Handicraft – a quintessential example of the type of art manufactures associated with the British Arts and Craft Movement.

In Britain, the advent of the Industrial Revolution brought in its wake the **mass production** of machine-made domestic wares that were intended mainly for middle-class consumers. Many of these goods were of questionable quality and **taste**, often being overly decorated to disguise their shoddy manufacture.

To confront this tide of dross, **design reform**ers came up with the idea of better-designed 'art manufactures'.

Even by the mid-eighteenth century, concerns had begun to be raised in Britain about the low standards of design in manufactured consumer goods. This prompted the establishment of the Society for the Encouragement of Arts, Manufactures and Commerce in 1754 (now known as the Royal Society of Arts). It was, as the artist William Hogarth, one of its leading members, noted, 'A Society for the encouragement of art manufactures and commerce' – with the term 'art manufactures' meaning wares designed by professionally trained fine artists, such as those who would later be employed by the likes of Wedgwood and Coalbrookdale. Despite the Royal Society's best efforts, however, as industrialized manufacturing increased over the coming decades, so did the number of poorly designed products.

Eventually, in 1835 the British Government established the Select Committee of Arts and Manufactures 'to inquire into the best means of extending a knowledge of the Arts and the Manufacturing Population of the country; also to inquire into the constitution, management and effect of Institutions concerned with the Arts'. Or in other words, how to best promote the design and production of art manufactures over what were referred to as 'artless manufactures' – badly designed goods.

The committee, inspired by the advanced **design education** system in Germany, recommended in its resulting report a two-pronged approach, involving the establishment of a new instructive museum dedicated to the applied arts (a term that covered various categories of designed artefacts, from metalwork and glassware to textiles and furniture) that would eventually morph into the Victoria and Albert Museum, and the founding of an aligned design-teaching institution, the National Art Training School, which was later renamed the Royal College of Art. The content of the museum was chosen by a subcommittee 'composed of artists and connoisseurs of taste and judgement' that included, among others, the design reformer Henry Cole, who under a pseudonym set up Felix Summerly's Art Manufactures in 1847 – one of the very first enterprises to produce consumer goods designed by established artists.

Cole's art-manufacturing endeavours inspired the next generation of designers – most notably William Morris, whose own company, Morris & Co., helped to publicize the concept of art manufactures to the wider public. The term 'art manufactures' was widely understood as meaning objects that were not only better designed, but that were also of higher-quality manufacture. Indeed, the whole notion of art manufactures was one of the main inspirations behind the Arts and Crafts Movement in Britain and America, and the impetus for the founding of various design-reforming groups and institutions in Europe, including the Weimar Bauhaus, which sought from its outset to improve design standards through the production of art manufactures that reconciled art, craft and industry. As the first successful and instructive attempts at design reform, art manufactures were an important progenitor of **good design** in that they demonstrated practically a better way of doing things in terms of design and manufacturing, and so helped to raise standards considerably for future generations of design practitioners. ∎

'Art manufactures were an important progenitor of good design.'

Jack-in-the-Pulpit vase (c.1900–20) by the Quezal Art Glass and Decorating Company of Brooklyn, NY, using the same iridescent glass-making techniques as used by the Tiffany factory.

Staatliches Bauhaus building (completed 1926) in Dessau, Germany, designed by Walter Gropius.

'A design institution that sought to better reconcile the teaching of art and technology.'

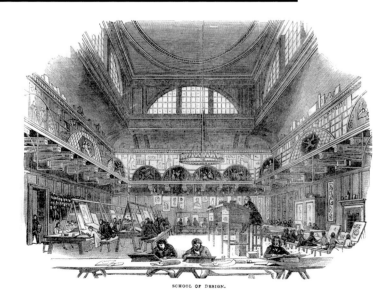

SCHOOL OF DESIGN.

Government School of Design at Somerset House in London, established in 1837.

The teaching of all facets of design

Diagram of the teaching syllabus
at the Staatliches Bauhaus
in Weimar (1922) devised by
Walter Gropius.

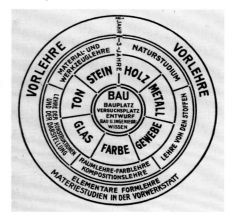

IDEA № 22
DESIGN EDUCATION

For centuries, the act of designing was inextricably linked to craft production, with designer and maker often being one and the same. This meant that design was for the most part learnt on the job. However, the onset of the Industrial Revolution brought the need for better design training, which eventually led to the founding of dedicated teaching institutions across the world.

Over time, design education broadened its terms of reference beyond simply practice to include design history, theory, criticism, communication and promotion. Historically, there really was no distinction between the fine and applied arts, with both being more or less viewed as pursuits of the artisan class. During the Italian Renaissance, for instance, the sculptor Benvenuto Cellini designed metalwork and jewellery, while Leonardo da Vinci designed all manner of mechanical inventions. It was within the context of specialist workshops that master craftsmen taught the fundamentals of design to apprentices. The Industrial Revolution in the late eighteenth century, however, broke the long-held connection between designing and making, and as a result a new kind of designer was needed – one who understood how to design articles for industrial production. Initially, formally trained fine artists stepped into the breach. However, it soon became apparent that this was not the answer and that a new type of design education was needed that would produce a much-needed cohort of professionally trained specialists, who would be better able to work within the constraints of machine production.

By the early nineteenth century there were a number of design-led trade schools operating in Continental Europe, and this prompted the establishment in Britain of the country's first dedicated design-teaching institution in 1837. Known as the Government School of Design, it had a curriculum based on the 'merits' and 'operations' of these earlier European schools, and was originally located in London's Somerset House. The course taught there was initially split into two, with its 'Elementary' pathway involving drawing, modelling and colouring, while its 'Instruction in design for special branches of industry' pathway not only included the study of materials and processes, but also 'the history of **taste** in manufacture, the distinction of **styles** of ornaments and such theoretical knowledge as is calculated to improve the tastes of the pupils, and add to their general acquaintance with art'.[14] The usefulness of the school's teaching methods is borne out by the fact that it was where Christopher Dresser, one of the first-ever professional design consultants, learnt how to design for industry. Eventually, the school was moved to South Kensington and renamed the Royal College of Art,

which to this day is recognized as one of the world's leading design-teaching institutions.

It was, however, the founding of the Staatliches Bauhaus in 1919 that pulled design education into the modern age. Borne from the amalgamation of Weimar's two existing art schools, it was a new interdisciplinary type of design institution that sought to better reconcile the teaching of art and technology. Indeed, its founding remit was to 'provide artistic advisory services to industry, trade and craft'.[15] Of greatest significance to the evolution of design education was the school's one-year preliminary course, which became a blueprint for other art-and-design foundation courses.

Over the last century, as the practice of design has increasingly expanded its scope, the need for greater specialization in design education has grown. As a result, a multitude of specialist design courses are now being taught across the world, with each design discipline having its own renowned centres of excellence. ∎

The reform of design through the promotion of good design principles

IDEA № 23

DESIGN REFORM

The idea that design needed to be reformed first emerged in the late eighteenth century as a reaction to the plethora of shoddy wares that were being mass produced thanks to the new steam-driven wheels of the Industrial Revolution.

One of the very first people to put forward the notion of design reform was the British satirical artist William Hogarth, who in his book *The Analysis of Beauty* (1753) argued that functional considerations should guide the design of objects rather than the use of applied **decoration**, as that would more likely endow them with a discernible aesthetic beauty. Over the next century, however, manufacturers by and large flagrantly disregarded this early entreaty for products of more purposeful design, and increasingly used mechanization to mass-produce wares of questionable value – both aesthetic and monetary.

Indeed, the 1851 'Great Exhibition of the Works of Industry of All Nations' held in London became, much to the chagrin of its organizers, a veritable showcase of overblown decoration. For although the tools and machinery on show exemplified a **form follows function** approach, the same could not be said for the tens of thousands of fussily decorated domestic products, the vast majority of which were encrusted with superfluous ornament in a host of revivalist **styles**. It was such a sorry state of affairs that the exhibition's design-reforming organizers later set up an instructive museum at Marlborough House in Pall Mall in 1852, the purpose of which was to improve the standards of **design education** in Britain. One of the ways it did this was by having a display that compared and contrasted examples of 'dishonest' design with exemplary objects of **good design**. This easy-to-understand, spot-the-difference exhibit ultimately helped to promote the merits of well-conceived designs with an inherent functional logic and material honesty to both the general public and manufacturers alike. This design-reforming initiative formed the genus of an important study collection that would eventually evolve into London's Victoria and Albert Museum – one of the world's greatest museums of decorative and applied art.

The concept of an instructive good-versus-bad design museum was also taken up by the Deutscher Werkbund, which was founded in Munich in 1907. Two years later this influential German design-reforming association co-established the Deutsche Museum für Kunst in Handel und Gewerbe (German Museum of Art and Trade Works) in Hagen with the industrialist collector Karl Ernst Osthaus. It similarly exhibited exemplars of good design alongside poor-quality, often kitsch objects so that designers, manufacturers and consumers could easily see for themselves the differences that existed and thereby make more informed choices. This collection went on to form the basis of the later Werkbund Archive's Museum der Dinge (Museum of Things) in Berlin, which is still in operation.

Sweden's Svenska Slöjdföreningen (Swedish Society of Crafts and **Industrial Design**) was also a noteworthy design-reforming force with its promotion of 'More Beautiful Everyday Objects' in 1919, and its later staging of the landmark 'Stockholm Exhibition' in 1930, which was an influential showcase of Scandinavian **functionalism**. Later organizations, such as Britain's Council of Industrial Design (subsequently known as the Design Council), Germany's Rat für Formgebung (German Design Council) and the Industrial Designers Society of America, as well as other like-minded organizations across the world, eventually took up the torch of design reform, and to this day continue to promote and encourage the values of good design in order to stem the tide of poorly designed, poor-value, wasteful products. ∎

Design

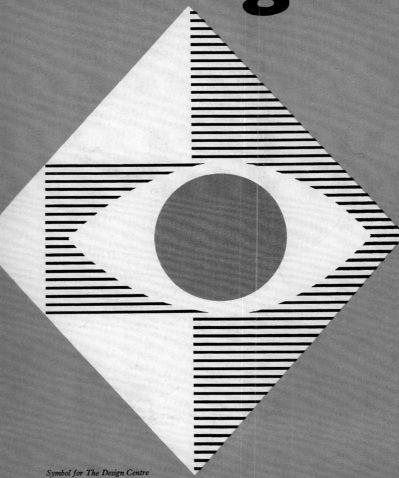

Symbol for The Design Centre

The Council of Industrial Design October 1955 No 82 Price 2s 6d

'All ornament should consist of enrichment
of the essential constructions of the building.'
– *Augustus Pugin*

*Centre Georges Pompidou, Paris (1971–77) by
Renzo Piano and Richard Rogers – this
building is a masterpiece of revealed
construction with all its structural elements
and services sited externally and then
colour-coded according to function.*

Honestly exposing structure

IDEA № 24
REVEALED CONSTRUCTION

The great British architect, designer and writer Augustus Welby Northmore Pugin believed that only a 'good' and caring society could possibly create designs that were both honest and beautiful – with beauty being a natural outcome of honesty in design.

To this end, he famously advocated not only being 'truthful to materials' but also exercising 'revealed construction', by which he meant allowing the structure of a building or an object to be shown honestly, rather than concealed by falsifying ornamentation.

Pugin's book *The True Principles of Pointed or Christian Architecture* (1841) can be seen as the wellspring of ideas from which nineteenth-century **design reform** evolved, first in the guise of the Victorian Gothic Revival and later in the form of the Arts and Crafts Movement. The latter in turn laid many of the philosophical foundations of the early **Modern Movement**. One of the most influential key concepts put forward by Pugin in this seminal text was 'revealed construction', which he explained thus: 'The two great rules for design are these: 1st, that there should be no features about a building which are not necessary for convenience, construction, or propriety: 2nd, that all ornament should consist of enrichment of the essential constructions of the building.'

Pugin was not calling for the total elimination of **decoration** per se, but rather that any embellishment on a building or object should 'have a meaning or serve a purpose'. This resulted in a reduced use of and vocabulary of ornament – or, in other words, a marked decorative **simplicity**.

Pugin's idea of revealed construction went on to become a major theme in British Arts and Crafts furniture design, with pegged joints on

Ducati Monster 797 (2017) – a superb example of revealed construction, this bike employs the firm's signature tubular steel trellis frame, which makes it light yet rigid.

tables and incised heart-shaped hand-holds on chairs being its most obvious manifestations. American Arts and Crafts designs similarly relied on this type of constructional honesty, such as the lamps by Dirk van Erp and the furniture by Gustav Stickley, with their no-nonsense handcrafted constructions having no element of superfluous decoration. Likewise, some designers associated with the Art Nouveau **style** on the Continent also took on board the idea of revealed construction, with Victor Horta incorporating exposed ironwork in his design of the Hôtel Tassel (1892–93), and some of Henry van de Velde's furniture designs having an almost engineered quality, with any sense of the decorative deriving solely from structural function.

The idea of revealed construction would later become a cornerstone of the Modern Movement – with Marcel Breuer's furniture or Christian Dell's lighting designs exemplifying a struct-ural truthfulness and **rightness** that was the outcome of a process-driven approach to problem-solving. Indeed, the notion of revealed construction can be seen as the conceptual progenitor of another big design idea: **form follows function**, and as a result it had an enormous influence on how Modern design developed over the course of the twentieth century. ■

Design well suited
to the job in hand

Fiskars PowerGear cutting tools (2017) – purposefully designed for various tasks.

IDEA № 25

FITNESS FOR PURPOSE

The idea of 'fitness for purpose' is one of the key pillars of Modern design, and implies both an obligation and a responsibility to create objects that fulfil their intended functions as appropriately and worthily as possible.

Fitness for purpose implies not only form following function, but also a certain level of **rationalism**, straightforwardness and **rightness**. Obviously, in some areas of design the idea of fitness for purpose is more critical than in others. For instance, would anyone want to be a passenger in a car that was not fit for purpose? Historically, the idea has been most relevant within the realm of military design, where in the midst of a battle a soldier's life very often depends on weapons that work properly.

The concept of 'purpose', however, is mutable, for what is considered purposeful might change from era to era. Indeed, there is some degree of potential obsolescence in virtually all man-made objects, especially those that have a mechanical or electronic aspect. The shifting nature of purpose is ever accelerating in line with inevitable technological progress and social change. You only need to go into an antiques market to see product types that have been rendered obsolete by new patterns of living brought about by advances in technology.

While today the term 'fitness for purpose' is most often associated with products and manufacturing industry, the ideological origins of the concept can potentially be traced as far back as Aristotle and Aquinas.[16] In the eighteenth century, the British artist William Hogarth dedicated the first chapter of his seminal work *The Analysis of Beauty* (1753) to the concept of fitness in man-made things. Here he penned, 'Fitness of the parts to the design for which every individual thing is formed ... is first to be considered, as it is the greatest consequence to the beauty of the whole,' and further on, 'in nature's machines, how wonderfully so we see beauty and use go hand in hand!'.

The idea that the natural outcome of functional design is beauty was a powerful driver for **design reform**, as it helped validate the belief in greater fitness for purpose in both design and architecture. In 1836, Augustus Pugin wrote that 'the great test of architectural beauty is the fitness of the design to the purpose for which it was intended'. Such was Pugin's influence that among later design reformers,

fitness for purpose became a rallying cry; in Britain, the Design and Industries Association (DIA) adopted the phrase as its motto in 1915.

For much of the twentieth century, the concept of fitness for purpose guided **design education**, and to this day, the vast majority of professional designers adhere to its principles. Designing from a purposeful perspective is not only the best guarantee of successfully fulfilling a brief, but also of attaining a design solution that embodies and clearly communicates functional integrity.

The concept of fitness for purpose has also been instrumental in shaping product liability legislation and has consequently made products safer by design. Nowadays a design that does not fulfil its purpose can be deemed defective, and its manufacturer held legally liable for any resulting damages. This has, perhaps more than anything else, contributed to the raising of design standards throughout the world. ∎

Miura barstool (2005) by Konstantin Grcic for Plank – this stackable polypropylene design became an instant hit thanks to its remarkable functionality, being comfortable, washable and highly durable.

*Akari Light Sculptures (1951+)
by Isamu Noguchi for Ozeki Co.
(later Vitra) – this lighting
range gave the traditional
lantern-making industry in
Gifu, Japan, a much-needed
sales boost, and perfectly
expressed the properties of the
mulberry bark paper it was
made from.*

Honesty, not artifice, in design

IDEA № 26
TRUTH TO MATERIALS

The concept of 'truth to materials' was one of the great founding tenets of the **Modern Movement**. It means using materials in an appropriate manner and allowing them to nakedly express their inherent physical properties. But more than this, it implies that no material should be used in such a way that it pretends to be something it is not.

Cultura double serving dish (1953) by Sigurd Persson for Silver & Stål – made of high-grade stainless steel, this design's crisp lines express perfectly the intrinsic hardness and optical brilliance of this then-revolutionary new material.

The origins of this idea can be traced to the nineteenth-century writings of the great Gothic Revivalist architect-designer Augustus Pugin. In his seminal book *The True Principles of Pointed or Christian Architecture* (1841), he wrote the following: 'the smallest detail should have a meaning or serve a purpose and even the construction itself should vary with the material employed, and the design should be adapted to the material in which they are executed.'

This idea of being truthful to the intrinsic properties of the materials used in a building or a design was further championed by the critic John Ruskin in his influential volume *The Seven Lamps of Architecture* (1849). Indeed, his second 'lamp' – or principle – was 'Truth', and in the chapter dedicated to it he argued that the false use of materials was inherently wrong and 'as truly deserving of reprobation as any other moral delinquency' for it was a sign 'of a singular debasement of the arts'.

Thanks to the writings of both men, throughout the latter half of the nineteenth century and into the early twentieth century the use of faux materials was rejected by more progressive architects and designers, especially in mass-produced 'fancy goods' that gave the illusion of being made of more expensive and luxurious materials than they actually were. In consequence, under the auspices of the Arts and Crafts Movement, they applied the principle of truth to materials to the production of furnishings and many other types of homewares so that their designs would embody an easily recognizable material integrity and structural **rightness**.

Although it is not widely recognized, the ideas put forward by members of the British Arts and Crafts Movement, such as William Morris, C.R. Ashbee and Charles Rennie Mackintosh, had a seminal influence on the formation of the later Modern Movement, with one of its principle founding ideals being truth to materials. Indeed, members of the Bauhaus in Germany, such as Marcel Breuer and Walter Gropius, and Modernist pioneers in France, such as Le Corbusier, Charlotte Perriand and Jean Prouvé, in their pursuit of **functionalism** and **purity** rigorously adhered to this ideological principle, with their buildings and furniture designs truthfully employing modern industrial materials.

Yet while they were following this fundamental principle of **good design**, plastics manufacturers were developing new polymers that were increasingly able to mimic **luxury** materials, such as tortoiseshell, ivory and onyx. Over the succeeding decades, other plastics – including plastic laminates, which could be patterned to give the appearance of wood grain – superseded these earlier faux materials. Such 'untruthful' materials were widely associated with cheap manufacture and kitsch, and as such were admonished within the lexicon of good design. However, when the precepts of Modernism began to be challenged by the **Anti-Design** movement in late 1960s, so began a re-evaluation of the idea of truth to materials. Could faux materials themselves be used truthfully? The answer was an unequivocal yes, as demonstrated by the kitsch-referencing Safari seating unit (1968) by Archizoom Associati, among many other Radical designs by the Italian avant-garde. ∎

Eliminating the unnecessary

Ulm stool (1953) by Max Bill, Hans Gugelot and Paul Hildinger for the Hochschule für Gestaltung (HfG) in Ulm – this minimalist design was created for HfG students at the school that was the Bauhaus's spiritual successor.

IDEA Nº 27

SIMPLICITY

In centuries gone by, the idea of simplicity was often linked to notions of poverty. However, these associations were turned on their head when William Morris began championing simplicity as a goal in design.

Through his earnest and practical endeavours at Morris & Co., Morris did much to counter the overblown fussiness of the High Victorian **style** with his advocacy and manufacture of simpler designs for the home. As he famously stated, 'Simplicity of life, even the barest, is not a misery, but the very foundation of refinement.'[17] Morris made the concept of simplicity fashionable, and as a result helped it to become a defining feature of later **Modern Movement** designs.

Another early **design reform**er who likewise helped to focus attention on the benefits of simplicity in manufactured goods was Christopher Dresser, who was the first designer to undertake an official design-research tour of Japan in 1876. This expedition left a lasting impression on him and he subsequently recommended that designers 'try and acquire the Japanese power of delineating natural forms with simplicity'.[18] Indeed, the whole aesthetic of Japanese design is based on simplicity and refinement – or in other words, a Zen of pure form.

Japanese architecture and design also exerted an enormous influence on the work of Frank Lloyd Wright, whose **Gesamtkunstwerk** (total artwork) buildings were marked by a highly considered simplification of form and spatial elements, which became increasingly emphatic in the work of later designers aligned to the Modern Movement – from Marcel Breuer and Le Corbusier to Eileen Gray and Jean Prouvé. It was, however, the Danish mid-century designer Jens Quistgaard who perhaps best encapsulated one of the goals of Modern design with his credo, 'Simplicity without poorness'.

While at the helm of Braun's design team, Dieter Rams was also instrumental in making the concept of simplicity desirable. The resultant body of work, guided by Ram's 'Omit the unimportant' mantra, demonstrated how aesthetically refined consumer electronic products could become when simplification, or **clarity of layout**, was a primary aim. Described by Rams as 'a return to the simple basic aspects',[19] this approach was about simplifying a design down to its most essential elements. Another design that shared a similar aesthetic purification was a wooden stool designed in 1955 by Max Bill, Hans Gugelot and Paul Hildinger for their students at the Ulm School of Design. This elemental, stripped-down design was an early precursor of Minimalism, which emerged in both art and design during the late 1960s and early 1970s as an extreme interpretation of simplicity. A reaction to the overblown excesses of **Pop** design and 1960s rampant consumerism, Minimalism was all about decluttering – whether one's spirit or one's home – and focused on the creation of simple objects with a **purity** of form.

It was this type of Zen-like simplicity in design that later inspired the creation of Apple's products. As Apple founder Steve Jobs once noted, 'That's been one of my mantras – focus and simplicity. Simple can be harder than complex: You have to work to get your thinking clean to make it simple. But it's worth it in the end because once you get there, you can move mountains.'[20] ■

'Simplifying a design down to its most essential elements.'

PC 3 record player (1955) by Dieter Rams, Gerd Alfred Müller and Wilhelm Wagenfeld for Braun – a masterful exercise in design simplification.

Hitting the design sweet spot

RIGHTNESS

Supermarine Spitfire Mk IXB (first flight 1936) by R.J. Mitchell – this legendary warbird is a testament to Bill Lear's observation: 'If it looks good, it will fly good.'

The renowned American engineer and businessman William 'Bill' Lear, who founded the Learjet Corporation, famously observed of aeronautical engineering, 'If it looks good, it will fly good'.

With this statement – which is oft misquoted as 'If it looks right, it flies right' – Lear was referring to the intrinsic 'rightness' of a design; how when something has been developed to be as functionally efficient as possible, it invariably possesses an inherent beauty. The Supermarine Spitfire is a classic example of this, at least in the world of aviation. Nevertheless, Kelly Johnson, who was manager of Lockheed's legendary Skunk Works, disagreed with Lear's observation and would frequently tell his subordinates, 'If it looks ugly, it will fly the same'.

The concept of 'rightness', as linked to the **aesthetics** of an object, is widely accepted in the world of design. Many professional practitioners see it as a natural outcome of pursuing a **form follows function** approach to problem-solving. Even as far back as 1845, William Smith Williams noted in *The Art Journal* that, 'In the commonest, rudest, and oldest implements of husbandry – the plough, the scythe, the sickle – we have examples of simple yet beautiful curves. The most elemental and simple of forms ... are the most pleasing.' It is the laid-bare functionality of such utilitarian designs that gives them an identifiable sense of rightness. The British **design reform**er William Morris also believed that if something was designed in accordance with the principles of **simplicity** and honesty, and in harmony with nature, then it would have a natural rightness. An example of this is Shaker furniture, for it was designed purely from such a premise.

In art history, the so-called 'theory of rightness in composition' is studied in order to understand the different factors that give an artwork visual impact and balance. Likewise, throughout the decades, there have been many instances of designers consciously employing harmonious proportions and mathematically precise forms, often based on Euclidean geometry, as a way of engendering a visual **purity** and rightness in an object – from Ludwig Mies van der Rohe's Barcelona chair (1929) to Arne Jacobsen's Cylinda stainless-steel hollowware range (1967). And it is no coincidence that the vast number of designs that have achieved iconic status possess an inherent rightness that is derived from carefully worked-out mathematical proportions and an appropriate response to functional considerations – whether it is Poul Henningsen's PH Artichoke pendant light (1957–8) or a T-34 Soviet medium tank (1937–40).

The notion of **ideal forms** in design is closely related to the concept of rightness – indeed, an ideal form could be said to be a three-dimensional realization of it. But the virtue of rightness in a designed object is relative; what is considered functionally appropriate and a rational solution to any given problem in one period is likely to change over time and be seen differently in another. That said, when a design is stripped of all superfluous **decoration** to reveal its most essential form, it is far more likely to possess an inherent rightness and an underlying authority, which can lead to functional and aesthetic longevity and, ultimately, 'classic' status. One could even go so far as to say that when a designer chooses to follow the righteous path of **good design**, then he or she is far more likely to create something that has an innate design rightness and moral worth. ∎

Shaker rocking chair (c.1820–50)
probably made by the Shaker
community in New Lebanon,
New York – the design of this
chair was completely informed
by practical concerns, giving it
an undeniable aesthetic and
functional rightness.

Design with a social conscience

IDEA Nº 29
MORALITY

Many of the world's biggest problems, from global warming to coping with an ageing population, can only be addressed by harnessing the transformative power of design. Indeed, many believe there is a moral compulsion to use design thinking positively for the benefit of society as a whole.

The modus operandi of designers has always been to improve on what has gone before in order to make people's lives better. In terms of morality in design, there is a general consensus among practitioners that a set of design ethics does exist, yet these have never been properly codified. While one designer might happily accept **the brief** to design a new weapons system, another might find this type of commission completely unacceptable from a moral standpoint. That said, there is nevertheless widespread general agreement about what constitutes **good design**, which is based on a set of ethical principles – **truth to materials**, **fitness for purpose**, **quality control** in construction, value for money, **universality**, and so on. The roots of many of these ideas can be traced back to the nineteenth century and the first generation of **design reform**ers.

Indeed, the idea of linking design with morality first emerged in 1836, when the British architect Augustus Pugin published his book *Contrasts, or a Parallel between the Architecture of the 15th and 19th Centuries*, which was effectively a manifesto. A Catholic convert, Pugin championed the Gothic **style** as the embodiment of 'true' Christianity as well as an indigenous national style, and vehemently attacked the stucco-fronted artifice of Neo-Classicism, which he admonished as being both foreign and pagan. The idea that a design style could have a moral under-pinning was strengthened by John Ruskin, who likewise saw an inherent morality 'which composed the inner spirit of Gothic architecture'.[21]

It was, however, the British Arts and Crafts designer William Morris who, inspired by the writings of Ruskin and Karl Marx, sought through the implementation of design reform 'a holy crusade against the age' that would stem 'the flood of philistinism in ... Victorian life'.[22] But more than this, Morris attempted to put ethical design theory into moral design practice with his founding of Morris & Co. (established 1861), which was essentially an experiment in design as social mission. Through this enterprise he attempted to offer workers not only better working conditions, but also more creatively meaningful work based on the handicrafts, in contrast to machine-minding in a factory. In 1899, the Swedish feminist writer Ellen Key also helped bolster the idea of morality in design with the publication of her influential pamphlet *Skönhet för alle* (Beauty for All), which argued that if design standards were improved, then the lives of ordinary people could be bettered.

Founded in Germany in 1906, the Deutscher Werkbund attempted to infuse both products and their manufacture with greater moral value. It was, however, after World War I that the moral impetus in design became increasingly emphatic, with **rationalism** being seen as the best means of building a new society for the benefit of the many rather than the privileged few – and this meant the acceptance of industrial mechanization. The 1930s witnessed mass slum clearances in Britain, Sweden, Germany and else-where in Europe, and the building of

OLPC XO-1 laptop (2006) by Yves Béhar for One Laptop Per Child (OLPC) – although the cost versus benefit of this non-profit educational initiative has been questioned, none can doubt its underlying moral intentions.

well-equipped new homes from modern materials that had been designed from a functionalist perspective to be both healthy and hygienic. Fundamentally, this was a moral design crusade to redress the stark inequalities in society.

After World War II, Britain's Council of **Industrial Design** (later the Design Council) and the Industrial Designers Society of America, as well as a host of like-minded design associations in other countries, did much to promote the moral cause of good design through **design education**, as well as numerous publications and exhibitions. These earnest design-reforming efforts were, however, perhaps best summed up by the German-born art historian Nikolaus Pevsner in a BBC broadcast of 1946, in which he said,

'What matters is that a life-enhancing quality can emanate from a really good design. This is what justifies my plea to manufacturers to take design[ing] morally as seriously as good materials or good relations to workmen.'[23] And the sentiment of that statement – that good design can be life-changing – rings more true today than ever, especially now that we understand the waste caused by and environmental impact of its alter ego: poor design. Currently, the non-profit One Laptop Per Child (OLPC) design initiative, which has distributed over 3 million laptops to children in developing countries since 2005, is perhaps the best contemporary example of how morally driven design can make a hugely positive impact on people's lives. ■

The persuasive argument behind a design

IDEA № 30
DESIGN RHETORIC

Edison's incandescent lightbulb (1880s) – ever since its introduction in the late nineteenth century, the filament lightbulb has been symbolic of technological progress, scientific genius and the spark of a great idea.

OPPOSITE: Special New Year pullout poster from Puck magazine (1879) showing the 'rhetoric' underlying Thomas Edison's incandescent lightbulb.

Within the academic world of design there is the widely held view that design is a means of non-verbal and unwritten communication. While this might be blatantly obvious when evaluating a work of graphic design, other types of design also communicate ideas and values through their inherent rhetoric.

All man-made objects are the result of some modicum of forethought, a certain degree of conception and planning, and because of this they all express innately the beliefs, aspirations and values of their creators. While the primary argument of a design is usually upfront and centre – normally, 'Buy me and I will make your life better' – it also postulates a secondary, less obvious argument, that is in many ways equally important, which is to persuade its intended audience to buy into the ethos of its creator.

Although loosely related to product **semiotics**, which is all about the transmission of ideas through signs and symbols, design rhetoric is, by contrast, focused on the idea of how a design can pose a form of argument based on its persuasiveness. This persuasiveness is normally predicated on four central attributes, or a combination of them: better-performing functionality, technological advantage, intellectual engagement and/or **aesthetics**. The communicative eloquence of an object, and the strength of its embedded design argument, can help change the attitudes and beliefs of an audience of potential users. A Tesla Model S automobile (introduced 2012) is an outstanding example of how a design's functional, technological and aesthetic persuasiveness can radically change people's

perceptions – in this case, of what an electrical vehicle can be like; its viability and thereby its desirability.

In much the same way, 150 years ago, Thomas Edison's first practical incandescent light bulb had a similar impact on people's acceptance and understanding of electricity. As one of the world's leading design theorists, Professor Richard Buchanan has written extensively on the subject of design rhetoric. He notes, 'By presenting an audience of potential users with a new product – whether as simple as a plow or a new form of hybrid seed corn, or as complex as an electric light bulb or a computer – designers have directly influenced the actions of individuals and communities, changed attitudes and values, and shaped society in surprisingly fundamental ways. ... Most important, however, is the idea of argument, which connects all of the elements of design and becomes an active engagement between designer and user or potential user.'[24]

Indeed, the **character** of a design is not only a reflection of the persona of its designer, but also an outward expression of the underlying rhetoric it embodies – for instance Studio 65's Baby-Lonia modular seating (1972) mocked the pervasive reverence of Classicism within Modernist circles, while Jonas Bohlin's Concrete chair (1981) was a forthright rebuttal of

Modernism's influence on Swedish design. While some designs possess a flamboyant spirit, others might have a subtler demeanour. Yet wherever a design sits on the personality scale, each will be a projection of the ideals it ultimately stands for, and will be making a case for you to accept these values. And through the act of acceptance – by means of use or purchase, or even just viewing – you are ultimately casting a vote for those values. ■

Total Eclipse of the Sun by the Earth.

The Northern Lights pack valise and move on.

A NEW LIGHT TO THE WORLD

AMERICA

The Moon goes into mourning.

MAY THEY FULFILL THEIR PROMISES—THE NEW YEAR AND THE NEW LIGHT!

Local, need-based designs functionally honed over time

Ciacapo teapot (2000) by Kazuhiko Tomita for Covo – a contemporary interpretation of a traditional cast-iron Japanese teapot, known as a 'tetsubin'.

IDEA № 31

VERNACULARISM

Just as specific regions have their own distinct spoken dialects and building **style**s, so different places have evolved over time their own particular language of design for objects of everyday use. This is known as 'vernacularism'.

Objects of local design are often evolved over many generations and influenced by the availability of raw materials, prevailing climatic conditions and regional customs. These are design solutions that can be deemed 'provincial' in the truest sense of the word. By their very nature they invariably possess a well-honed functional honesty, while at the same time displaying an endearing and distinctive homespun **character**.

The idea of vernacularism in design has long fascinated designers, for ultimately such 'folk' designs demonstrate how an evolutionary approach to design can facilitate the creation of **ideal forms**. Design archetypes such as these are quite simply the outcome of a hands-on response to real needs. They are not driven by commercial imperative, or even necessarily **aesthetics**.

One of the first to realize the worth of such designs was William Morris, who manufactured a number of chairs based on vernacular antecedents under the auspices of Morris & Co. – most notably the Sussex chair, the design of which is attributed to the architect Philip Webb, but which was based on a Georgian-period vernacular rush-seated model found in an antiques shop in Sussex. Indeed, later members of the British Arts and Crafts Movement celebrated the authenticity of the

vernacular and tirelessly sought to channel it into their designs. This led to the 'discovery' of Philip Clissett – a Herefordshire-based rural maker of vernacular chairs – by the Arts and Crafts architect James MacLaren. The Arts and Crafts designer-maker Ernest Gimson, subsequently took lessons from Clissett, and then designed his own Arts and Crafts versions, including a ladder-back model that is normally referred to as the Clissett chair (1895). Indeed, the general reassessment of the vernacular that took place in Britain and elsewhere during the late nineteenth and early twentieth centuries was very much part and parcel of the National Romantic movement, which sought authentic expression of national identity through design.

It was in Scandinavia during the twentieth century, however, that the idea of vernacularism in design found the most fertile ground. The Nordic countries not only had a rich folk tradition, with many craft skills still remaining intact, but they were also politically progressive nations with social agendas that focused on the concept of 'the national home'. Motivated by the related idea of **democratic design**, Scandinavian designers often sought inspiration from their indigenous folk-design roots, as well as those of other countries, in order to create

'better everyday things'. Indeed, there are numerous examples of well-known Scandinavian design icons that are based on vernacular precedents – Hans Wegner's Peacock chair (1947 – based on the earlier English 'Windsor chair'), Børge Mogensen's Hunting chair (1950), Timo Sarpaneva's teak-handled cooking pot for W. Rosenlew (1960) and Tapio Wirkkala's Puukko hunting knife (1961), to name but a few.

Inspired by such famous and long-lived designs as these, and in particular by the authenticity they so clearly embody, the idea of vernacularism is resurfacing in design. Designers are now reassessing the inherent values found in local craft production and attempting to channel these principles into their own contemporary work – for vernacularism equals identity, identity equals character, and character equals **connections**. ∎

> 'An evolutionary approach to design can facilitate the creation of ideal forms.'

Cast-iron casserole with teak handle (1960) by Timo Sarpaneva for W. Rosenlew (later Iittala) – a stunning Mid-Century Modern reworking of a traditional Nordic cooking pot.

Three-legged stool (2004) by Ingvar Kamprad for Habitat – designed by the legendary founder of IKEA, this simple design channels the form of the age-old milking stool.

The pursuit of the quintessential

'Brown Betty' teapot (c.1680–1840s) – the form of this iconic yet anonymous British design was evolved over centuries in the pursuit of functional perfection.

IDEA № 32
IDEAL FORM

One of the biggest ideas that designers have pursued over the centuries is the notion of the 'ideal form'. What could be more tantalizing for a designer than the realization of the ultimate design solution that cannot be improved upon?

One country that has pursued the notion of the ideal form in design more thoroughly than any other is Japan. The Japanese design aesthetic is based on ancient ideals, including among others: *wabi* (rustic **simplicity** and quiet refinement), *sabi* (age-old patina and elegant **simplicity**) and *Yūgen* (subtle gracefulness and hidden beauty). These ideals are utterly entrenched in Japanese culture and, as a result, design **aesthetics** form an integral part of everyday life in Japan – whether it is the patterning of a silk kimono, the arrangement of food in a bento box, or the shape of a vase for an Ikebana flower arrangement.

In 1876, the British **industrial designer** Christopher Dresser became the first Western artistic adviser to be officially invited to Japan in order to assess its architecture, art and **art manufactures**. While there, he identified that in Japan 'things of beauty' were produced when there was 'perfect appropriateness' in relation to 'the application of the material'.[25] Indeed, one of the key attributes of a design deemed to have an ideal form is its ability to channel the inherent **character** of the material from which it is made through the exploitation of its physical properties – be it a silver pitcher, a glass vase or a wooden chair.

In China, there is also a long history of ideal forms having been evolved and perfected over time, especially in the design and manufacture of ceramics.

Here design excellence is expressed through an understated aesthetic derived from the development of extremely refined shapes and subtle glazing techniques, which have been repeated over and over again, and as a consequence have undergone a process of refinement across many generations. Similarly, in Western cultures there are many examples of vernacular designs that have ideal forms, which have likewise been functionally honed over time – from farming tools to Brown Betty teapots to various region-specific chair designs. Indeed, it is the basic functional **purity** of such vernacular designs that makes them so 'ideal'.

The search for ideal forms has also long been a defining aspect of Scandinavian design. This is not as surprising as it might first seem, for both Sweden and Denmark as seafaring nations established trading links with Japan and China in the early eighteenth century, and through the import of wares from the East, Scandinavian designers became well aware of oriental ideal forms. During the early to mid-twentieth century, for example, various Scandinavian ceramicists based their designs on earlier oriental vessel forms and ceramic glazes.

It was, however, the Danish architect-designer Kaare Klint who firmly established the notion of ideal forms within Danish furniture design. In 1924, he became lecturer at the Royal Danish Academy of Fine Arts, and

under his exacting tutelage students analysed the ideal forms of various antique furniture paradigms. This involved the study of historic models' constructions, proportions and functional shapes so that students – many of whom went on to forge highly successful design careers – could then create their own modern interpretations of these ideal designs. The fruits of this training include some of the most iconic chairs of all time, from Hans Wegner's Peacock chair (1947), based on the earlier English Windsor chair, to Børge Mogensen's Spanish chair (1958), which was inspired by a vernacular Iberian model.

Today, there are a number of designers, most notably Naoto Fukasawa and Jasper Morrison, who continue to search for ideal forms, and to this end have created contemporary interpretations of age-old design archetypes. The success of such designs lies not just in their honed functionality but also in their sense of familiarity, for ideal forms are by their very nature timelessly appealing. ∎

BELOW: Polyprop chair (1960–63) by Robin Day for Hille – twinning a universal seat shell with a variety of interchangeable bases, this chair became one of the most democratic seating designs of all time.

RIGHT: Habitat carrier bag (1960s) – Terence Conran's first Habitat store opened in London's Fulham Road in 1964 and heralded the advent of affordable modern design in Britain.

*Good design for the many
rather than the few*

DEMOCRATIC DESIGN

IKEA's founder Ingvar Kamprad
holding up the Thonet-inspired
Ögla chair alongside some of
his company's other affordable
and democratic furniture
designs, 1961.

For nearly 150 years 'democratic design' has been a goal for design practitioners, reformers, theorists, entrepreneurs and manufacturers, for it is about the creation of well-designed, well-made products that offer value for money. The notion is underpinned by a sense of social **morality** and a belief in the transformative power of design.

It was the British Arts and Crafts designer and reformer William Morris who first mooted the idea of democratic design through his promotion of 'Good Citizen's Furniture' – by which he meant 'work-a-day furniture' that was simply constructed, well proportioned and less expensive than more elaborately **styled** furnishings. The problem was, however, that Morris's ideological adherence to hand-making over machine production meant that he was unable to reconcile high-quality craftsmanship with true affordability for the masses. Yet as a socially motivated idea, it was a potent one, for the concept of democratic design centres on the belief that the lives of ordinary people can be significantly improved through the use of better-designed everyday things.

In Scandinavia the idea of democratic design found especially fertile ground, with the Swedish feminist writer Ellen Key publishing an influential collection of essays in 1899 entitled *Skönhet för alla* (Beauty for All). One of these tracts, 'Beauty in the Home', functioned as a practical how-to guide for people of modest means to create simple yet attractive living spaces. Key encouraged the use of light colours and natural materials, and admonished the use of 'pointless **decoration**' and the collecting of 'knickknacks'. Key's big idea was that

'Beauty can be achieved by simple means and without great expense ... [while] observing the need for **utility**'.[26]

This belief that an improvement in design standards could enhance the lives of the working classes inspired Gregor Paulsson, the director of the Swedish Society of Crafts and **Industrial Design**, to write a seminal pamphlet in 1919 on democratic design entitled *Vackrare vardagsvara* (More Beautiful Everyday Objects). The title of this publication became a sort of rallying cry for those supporting **design reform** in Sweden, and it was directly responsible for the subsequent manufacture of various low-cost yet high-quality functional wares aimed specifically at working-class consumers. Unsurprisingly, therefore, it was a Swedish company – IKEA (founded in 1943) – that would later bring the idea of democratic design to a global audience with affordable homewares that encapsulate the long-held social ideals of Swedish design. In the words of the company's founder, Ingvar Kamprad, the goal of democratic design is 'To create a better everyday life for the many people'.

The founding of Habitat in 1964 by Terence Conran similarly helped to democratize **good design** in Britain through the stylish and **taste**ful promotion of the plain, the simple and

the useful. Indeed, Conran has spent much of his long career, both as a designer and design entrepreneur, helping to simplify everyday life for the everyman through his advocacy of democratically affordable, well-designed wares. As he once noted, 'I passionately believe that good design is of fundamental importance to our quality of everyday life.' Ultimately, it is that sentiment that has motivated the socially progressive march of democratic design over the last century and a half, with most of us – at least in the developed world – having reaped untold benefits from this ideological revolution in design. ∎

Design as professional practice

DESIGN CONSULTANCY

The late nineteenth-century British **industrial design**er Christopher Dresser was one of the very first professional practitioners to run a fully fledged design consultancy. His London-based design studio worked for a host of different manufacturers across a wide product range, from metalwork and glassware to furniture and textiles.

Henry Dreyfuss in his office with maquettes of his design for a bus and a locomotive, 1946.

Since then, professional design consultancy has expanded well beyond the realm of physical products and into the world of services and systems design.

Although Dresser was a highly prolific design consultant, who became the first designer to have his signature emblazoned on his products, he must really be considered somewhat of a jobbing outlier. In fact, it is the German architect-designer Peter Behrens who is generally credited with being the first 'modern' industrial design consultant. The reason for this is that in 1907 he was appointed artistic consultant to the Allgemeine Elektricitäts-Gesellschaft (AEG), and subsequently instigated the first-ever programme of **total design**. To this end, he not only designed the company's electrical products and even a factory building, but also developed the world's first integrated corporate identity, which comprised various logos, posters, advertising materials and company publications – all of which were executed in a visually unified house **style**. Behrens's influential total design scheme at AEG led other companies over the ensuing years to begin hiring professionally trained designers as consultants in order to bring a greater consistency and rationality to their industrially manufactured product lines.

It was, however, not until the 1930s that the true worth of design consultancy was widely revealed, espec-ially in the United States. During the Great Depression, manufacturers there – who were increasingly vying against each other in a shrinking marketplace – realized that one of the most cost-effective ways of surviving was to use the allure of attractive modern **styling** as a means of differentiating their products from those of their competitors. To this end they hired, often at vast expense, members of the first generation of American professional industrial design consultants, notably Raymond Loewy, Henry Dreyfuss, Lurelle Guild and Walter Dorwin Teague.

Having cut their career teeth as stage designers or as commercial artists in advertising agencies, these so-called 'industrial stylists' were perfectly skilled at giving products that all-essential streamlined 'eye appeal'. They also often helped raise manufacturers' profits by designing into products greater manufacturing efficiencies. At the behest of these consultants, slight design tweaks or material swaps – for example, metals to plastics – could make a significant difference to a company's margins and overall survivability.

Today, the concept of design consultancy is firmly established, and numerous multidisciplinary agencies, from IDEO and Pentagram to Smart and Teague, bring their expertise to

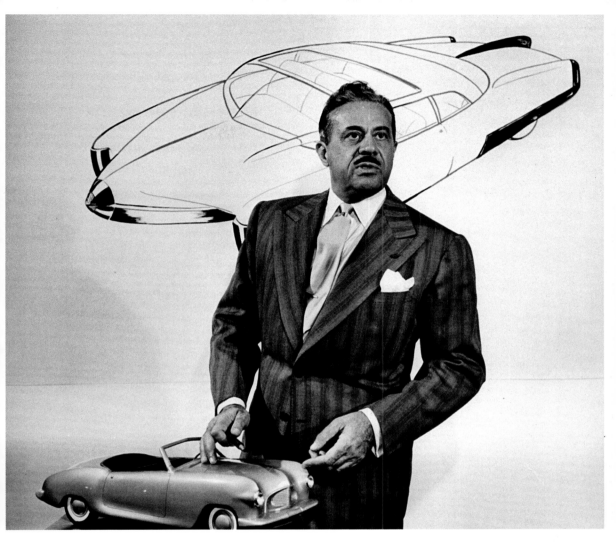

bear globally on the creation of better-performing design solutions for their clients. Often these agencies work hand in hand with their clients' own in-house design teams and production engineering and materials specialists because, more than anything else, design – at least in the realm of large-scale industrial manufacture – increasingly involves the teamwork of specialists rather than the creative input of a single design genius.

Over the last 20 years, design consultancy has also become more and more embedded into overall business strategy, which has led a number of global interdisciplinary consultancies

to become what can only be described as design think tanks. These types of agency now not only develop design-smart products for their clients, but are also becoming increasingly involved in the development of human-centred services and experiences. ■

Raymond Loewy standing in front of a concept sketch and alongside a scaled model of another of his streamlined designs, 1948.

Laying out the guidelines for design success

IDEA № 35
THE BRIEF

Model 3A dining chair from the Chiltern range (1943) by Edwin Clinch and Herbert Cutler – this standard model was manufactured under the Utility Scheme from 1943 to 1948.

The brief is an essential road map for any design project, for it lays out intended goals and establishes parameters that are crucial to a successful outcome. As a statement of intent as well as action, it is a hugely important first step on the journey that takes a design idea and transforms it into a physical reality.

And while a brief may be transmitted verbally in a casual way when, for example, someone is commissioning a piece of bespoke furniture from a designer-maker, within the world of **industrial design** the brief will often be a very detailed, multi-page document, or even a multi-document manuscript.

The brief is crucial in design practice because it makes sure everyone is on the same page at the beginning of a project. It clarifies key roles (what is expected from whom) and lays out a schedule of actions according to a carefully worked-out timetable and budget (when deliverables are deliverable, and how much they are going to cost). If a design brief is properly drafted and signed off by the various stakeholders, it should at least in theory, help avoid any confusion between parties that could derail the process over the course of a design's development.

Just how prescriptive a brief needs to be is entirely dependent on the nature of the design being developed – for instance, a robotic vacuum cleaner will be a far more complex project in terms of research and development than, say, a specially commissioned one-off piece of silver, and therefore will need a much more worked-up brief.

The brief is all about establishing constraints: What materials should be used? What production technologies should be employed? What is the market-entry price point that needs to be achieved? And so forth. Contrary to popular belief among many designers, constraints are actually a good thing for the development of innovative design because they promote left-field thinking. Put simply, they challenge designers to come up with innovative and intelligent solutions, which is what every manufacturer is aiming for, no more, no less. And while being given a brief-lite or brief-free carte blanche on a project might sound appealing to certain designers, it is the most sure-fire way for a project to drift off course and flounder – because the most successful designs invariably flourish within a framework of predetermined functional, material, technological, economic and marketing constraints. If a brief is well thought through it will undoubtedly accord with the legendary American design consultant Raymond Loewy's pragmatic concept of 'MAYA' (Most Advanced, Yet Acceptable). Basically, any mass-manufactured product needs to hit the sweet spot of popular **taste**, understanding and acceptance if it is to become a breakout success – as Apple's innovative but user-friendly designs, for example, have demonstrated time and again over the last two decades.

But that said, a brief also needs to have enough in-built flexibility to accommodate any additional issues that might come into play during the research and development phase of the design process; too much rigidity in sticking to the plan can at times stifle **innovation**. An effective design brief is, therefore, one that keeps a project moving forward intelligently through its transformative journey from good idea to saleable product. When it achieves this, a brief is one of the most critical elements for ensuring the ultimate success of any design commission. ∎

LIVING ROOM

SIDEBOARD : Second Section—Model 1a
Price £10 . 7 . 0

The living room furniture is
in oak. The dining chairs have
loose, padded seats covered
with leather cloth, in a variety
of colours.

SIDEBOARD : Second Section—Model 1b
Price £10 . 7 . 0

DINING CHAIR :
Second Section—Model 3a
Price £1 . 9 . 0

Sideboard, with doors open, showing
inside shelves. The sideboards are
4 ft. wide, 2 ft. 9 ins. high and 1 ft.
6 ins. deep.

DINING CHAIR :
Second Section—Model 3c
Price £1 . 9 . 0

'The brief is all about establishing constraints.'

*ABOVE: Page from a Utility
Furniture catalogue (1943–48)
– featuring furniture models
that had all been designed in
accord with the brief set by the
Utility Design Panel.*

*RIGHT: 'CC41 188' mark on the
frame of the Model 3A dining
chair – signifying it had been
made under the Utility Scheme.*

The drive for improvement, prompted by dissatisfaction with the status quo

THERE IS ALWAYS A BETTER WAY OF DOING THINGS

Most designers believe that there is room for improvement in what has gone before. As the American designer-sculptor Harry Bertoia once noted, 'The urge for **good design** is the same as the urge to go on living. The assumption is that somewhere, hidden, is a better way of doing things.'[27]

myVision LED light bulb (2012) by Philips – this new generation LED light bulb consumes 80 per cent less energy that traditional incandescent bulbs and lasts up to 25 times longer.

In fact, no matter what specific approach design practitioners subscribe to, they all tend share this belief in the possibility of creating better solutions to any number or type of problems, needs and concerns. This could mean just coming up with their own 'better' take on a product, or might mean the realization of a highly significant step-change **innovation**. This common trait reveals a very positive mindset, for designers tend to be pretty optimistic people, at least in their own abilities. Certainly, they normally have enough self-belief to suppose that they have the wherewithal to enact the design change they want to see and make it a reality.

Often this belief that something can be improved upon is also borne of an underlying frustration and dissatisfaction with the status quo – the can opener that does not work properly, the task light that gets too hot, the milk **packaging** that is difficult to open, and so forth. Famously, it was James Dyson's utter frustration with the dismal performance of his vacuum cleaner nearly 30 years ago that led him to completely reinvent this product category with his revolutionary Dual Cyclone technology. It is this desire for more perfect design solutions that drive other designers, too – whether it is the design team at Apple, who painstakingly hone each successive

generation of the iPhone to perform better than the last, or the Smart **design consultancy** researching **ergonomics** in order to create the best **inclusive design**s they can for the ever-expanding OXO Good Grips range.

This quest to find new and better solutions to specific problems within given constraints was once described by the German architect and designer Ludwig Mies van der Rohe as the urge to 'create form out of the nature of our tasks, with the methods of our time'. Indeed, for him this was the absolute key driving force of the architect-designer. As he put it, 'This is our task.'[28]

The motivating belief that there is always a better way of doing things is often helped in practice by the writing of a detailed design **brief** that acts as a guiding document for all the participants involved. The brief sets out the objectives and goals of a design project, while also establishing budgets and schedules and defining its intended audience, among other things. As the design thinker and **branding** expert Dana Arnett recently noted, 'Designers are aspirational. They want to make things better. Now we have better data to help that aspiration and create a better brief.'

As existing technologies are constantly being improved, and new ones are being invented, so the designer's arsenal of

tools is ever expanding. This means that upon the introduction of any particular new design – inevitably shortly thereafter – new materials and techniques become available that enable it to be superseded. And thanks to this endless march of technological progress, there is always, *and probably always will be*, a better way of doing things. It is just an irrefutable design fact of life. ∎

'Designers are aspirational. They want to make things better' – *Dana Arnett*

Model X (2017) by Tesla – this all-electric vehicle featuring falcon wing doors has a much lower centre of gravity than traditional SUVs, making it safer, the largest cabin space in its class and giving it a range of 351 miles per charge.

Purposeful function shaping practical designs

FORM FOLLOWS FUNCTION

'Form follows function' was the favourite catchphrase of the **Modern Movement**, and as an undoubtedly potent design idea it has, over the decades, inspired the creation of countless useful products and well-designed buildings. Even to this day it remains a defining tenet of **good design**.

Although the phrase is sometimes ascribed to the early nineteenth-century American sculptor Horatio Greenough, who waxed lyrical about the primacy of function, it was effectively coined by the American architect Louis Henry Sullivan, who stated, 'Form ever follows function. This is the law.' Included in an article in *Lippincott's Magazine* in 1896, this observation was made in consideration of nature, with Sullivan noting that the form of animals, plants and even geology is dictated by their purpose. He felt that the design of the modern office building should be approached in exactly the same way.

This idea as it relates to design was not a new concept, but it had never been so emphatically expressed before. The making of tools and weapons, for instance, has always been guided by form following function. So too were the simple yet purposeful designs created by the Shaker communities in America during the late eighteenth and nineteenth centuries. The Shakers considered functional efficiency in design a crucial means of enhancing their productivity, so as to allow themselves more time dedicated to prayer. Indeed, the way a Shaker community was planned was a lesson in purposeful design; walls were fitted with pegged rails on which to hang chairs in order to keep them out of the way when floors were swept, cooking pots had hinged lids so they were easier to use, and the Shakers' round barns were meticulously thought-out from a functional point of view.

Sullivan's idea that a building or an object should reflect its purpose through its form was taken up in the early twentieth century by the Deutscher Werkbund, which accentuated **utility** in design and promoted the idea of form following function through its various publications showcasing simple functional wares. Around the same time, the Hungarian-born architect-designer Marcel Breuer also began designing seating that employed state-of-the-art tubular steel and was conceived using a strict form follows function approach. But what might seem practical from a manufacturing perspective, might not be so functional in practice; and so it was with Breuer's furniture, which, with its hard-edged Modern aesthetic, was generally too far ahead of popular **taste** for widespread acceptance.

Today, with digital technology increasingly being built into products, designs often have multiple functions that are not reflected in their overall form. The outward appearance of an iPhone, for example, does not express that beyond it being a mobile telephone it also functions as a music player, a compass, a map, a calendar and so on. However, that is not to say that there has been a complete departure from the form follows function mindset among designers, but rather a migration from the physical to the digital, as it is still a strong consideration in the design of user interfaces. And, of course, there is still a host of product categories, from office chairs to signage, that work better when their creators have followed a form follows function approach. ∎

TOP AND LEFT: Fuel Ice Tool by Black Diamond (2014) – in use by Heike Schmitt climbing waterfall ice in Rjukan, Norway (photo: Thomas Senf).

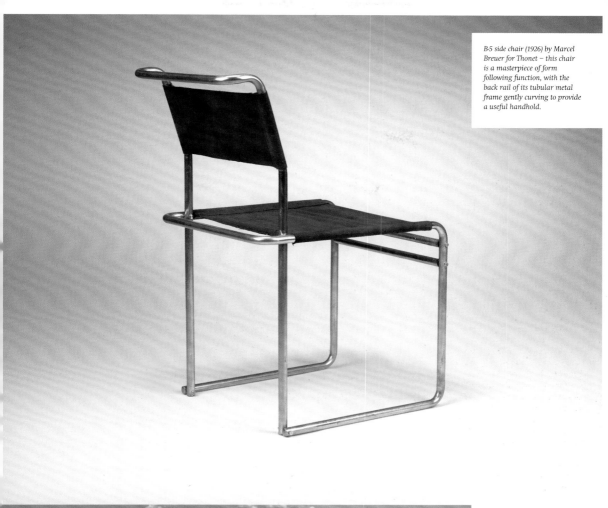

B-5 side chair (1926) by Marcel Breuer for Thonet – this chair is a masterpiece of form following function, with the back rail of its tubular metal frame gently curving to provide a useful handhold.

Lockheed Martin F-22 Raptor (first flight 1997) – a tour de force of purposeful design, this advanced tactical, single-seat, twin-engine fighter combines stealth technology and state-of-the-art aerodynamics to provide unparalleled performance in the air.

The prioritizing of purpose in design

FUNCTIONALISM

It is the functional aspect of a thing that determines whether it is art or design. Yet in many ways design could be described as 'functional art' for it straddles the worlds of **aesthetics** and engineering to a greater or lesser extent, depending on the thing being designed.

The Frankfurt Kitchen (1926) by Margarete 'Grete' Schütte-Lihotzky – conceived like a laboratory, this exercise in progressive kitchen planning centred on the idea of maximizing functionality, which was intended to enhance workflow and hygiene.

Design is essentially the synthesis of form and function, and their exact balance ultimately shapes how rational a design solution ends up being. The idea of functionalism, which stresses purposeful **utility** (the function of a design), can be traced back to the Roman architect and author Vitruvius, who defined *utilitas* (utility) as one of the three cornerstones of architecture.

It is, however, the American architect Louis Henry Sullivan who is widely regarded as the 'Father of Functionalism'. In 1896, he wrote an essay entitled 'The Tall Office Building Artistically Considered', in which he stated that, 'It is the pervading law of all things organic and inorganic, of all things physical and metaphysical, of all things human and all things superhuman, of all true manifestations of the head, of the heart, of the soul, that the life is recognizable in its expression, that form ever follows function. *This is the law.* Shall we, then, daily violate this law in our art? Are we so decadent, so imbecile, so utterly weak of eyesight, that we cannot perceive this truth so simple, so very simple?'

By unequivocally stating that form was a natural outcome of function and identifying it as a law of nature, Sullivan established what would become the Modernists' favourite slogan: **form follows function** (based on his original quote). But over and above this, he also helped form the ideo-logical bedrock of the **New Objectivity** – a new Modernist approach to design based on functionalism, which subsequently emerged in the early 1920s.

But even before this, Walter Gropius and Adolf Meyer's Fagus Factory (1911) had heralded the pro-industrial ethos of functionalism with its severe geometric brick construction and innovative glass facades. Likewise, from 1916, the Deutscher Werkbund had begun promoting via its *Deutscher Warenbücher* (German Production Directories) utilitarian wares with a faultless form follows function **simplicity** that accorded with this new emerging spirit. After the devastations of World War I, however, the argument for funct-ionalism gained considerable ground within design and architecture circles, as it appeared to offer a way of solving the severe social-housing crisis across Europe.

In 1925, the mayor of Stuttgart, Karl Lautenschlager, and the president of the Deutscher Werkbund, Peter Bruckmann, outlined the functionalist think-ing behind an exhibition they were planning as follows: 'Efficiency measures in all areas of our lives do not stop where housing is at issue. The econo-mic conditions of today prohibit any kind of waste and demand the maxi-mum effect with minimum amount of means, requiring the implementation of such materials and technological appliances which will lead to lower building and operational

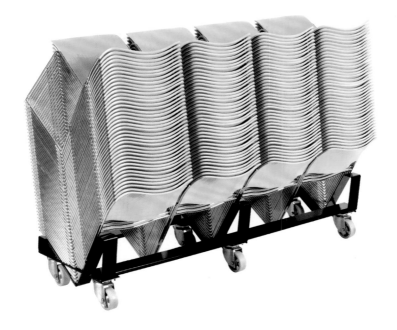

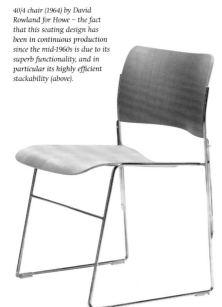

40/4 chair (1964) by David Rowland for Howe – the fact that this seating design has been in continuous production since the mid-1960s is due to its superb functionality, and in particular its highly efficient stackability (above).

costs, and will lead to a simplification of house-holds, and to improvements of living itself.'[29] The resulting landmark 'Die Wohnung' (The Dwelling) exhibition held in Stuttgart in 1927 comprised a model housing estate of houses and apartments designed by an inter-national roster of avant-garde architects in sync with the functionalist *Neue Bauen* (New Building) trend.

It was, however, the Frankfurt Kitchen (1926) designed by Margarete Schütte-Lihotzky for a social-housing project that perhaps best exemplified **Modern Movement** functionalism. Devised for maximum efficiency, its rational layout was strongly influenced by the scientific management studies associated with **Taylorism**. In Sweden, the pressing need for better social housing during the interwar period also led to functionalism – or *Funkis*, as it is known in Swedish – being adopted by the country's avant-garde architects and designers. Indeed, the 'Stockholm Exhibition' of 1930 was a high-profile showcase of this new purposeful language of design, which reflected a new social idealism, and celebrated technology and **standardization** as a means of realizing a progressive welfare state. Yet it was the prescriptive nature of functionalism that ultimately led to its ideological downfall, for as the Danish artist and author Asger Jorn once noted, 'It is a basic weakness of functionalism that it cannot tolerate the idea of freely creative art.'[30] ∎

Managing the business side of design

DESIGN MANAGEMENT

RIGHT: Electric wall clock (c.1910) by Peter Behrens for AEG.

BELOW: Lithographic poster (1910) by Peter Behrens for AEG, advertising the company's metal filament lightbulbs.

Design management is primarily about systematically implementing design thinking into a business framework. It involves not only managing design-led projects, but also devising and maintaining strategies that will lead to a culture of creative problem-solving within an organization.

Design management is foremost a business-orientated discipline used by companies as a means of ensuring that the research, design and development side of their operations run as smoothly as possible. The role of a design manager is multifold, for it not only entails the day-to-day management of design-related projects – running the whole gamut of the different design disciplines – but also involves strategic mid- to long-term planning and the development of organizational structures that will enable design to flourish throughout a firm's activities. Put simply, design management is used as a way of linking design, **innovation** and technology with business strategies and marketing concerns so as to create economic, social, cultural and/ or environmental advantages.

In-house or agency design teams will often be headed up by a director of design, assisted by a design manager who ostensibly functions as their right hand. They act principally as both an enforcer and a facilitator, making sure that throughout the duration of a project everything adheres to **the brief** as much as possible so that, among other things, schedules and budgets are met. A design manager, though often coming from a design or engineering background, does not normally undertake a hands-on design role, but will often make helpful and insightful suggestions that affect the overall development of a product. In essence,

they help orchestrate the upstream side of a project – the research, design and development – by overseeing the work of designers, engineers, production specialists and materials experts, while also liaising with their employer's more commercially orientated teams.

Design management is about integrating multiple work streams so as to ensure a project's overall success, while keeping all the related stakeholders updated on progress and ensuring that any potential difficulties can be addressed before they become major obstacles. Or in other words, anticipating problems before they have a chance to blow a project off-course.

A design manager is also responsible for keeping an eye on **safety** and reliability issues, and assessing the different risks involved in bringing a design to market so that quick responses can be implemented should any issues of this nature arise during the design, research and development of the product. Wide-ranging and multidisciplinary in its remit, design management also incorporates accountability systems, financial auditing, inline reporting and continuous evaluation programmes – all of which help to provide the best guarantee of a design project not collapsing into disarray through lack of leadership. Nowadays, any large-scale design project involves a high degree of teamwork, and it is the design manager's responsibility to make sure each player

remains focused on the common goal.

The origins of modern design management go back to 1907, when Peter Behrens was appointed artistic director of AEG, and began implementing a **total design** strategy. It was, however, in the 1960s that design management began to make serious inroads into design practice, as large corporations began realizing the gains that could be achieved through a more systemized approach to design. Having demonstrated its efficacy over the last 50 years, design management now has a far broader portfolio than ever. Indeed, today it is one of the most vital roles within any design-led organization. That is because the realm of creative problem-solving currently goes well beyond the straightforward development of physical products and into all aspects of business activity. ∎

Implementing unified design solutions that take in the big picture

IDEA № 40

TOTAL DESIGN

The idea of 'total design' has for most of the last 100 years had an enormous bearing on design thinking. In the late nineteenth century it inspired many of the leading architect-designers to create exquisite, harmoniously unified **Gesamtkunstwerk** buildings.

And throughout much of the twentieth century, total design influenced the development of comprehensive and integrated corporate design programmes for a variety of well-known manufacturing companies, from AEG and Olivetti to IBM and Philips.

Total design is an over-arching vision of design implementation whereby, for example, a building is designed holistically so that its structure, interiors, lighting, furniture and fixtures work as one harmonious entity – the aim being to create a fully integrated design **unity** in such a way that the whole is greater than the sum of its parts. Sublime examples of this approach to design include the *Gesamtkunstwerk* residential projects of Frank Lloyd Wright, Victor Horta, Charles Rennie Mackintosh, Gerrit Rietveld and Arne Jacobsen.

In terms of corporate design, total design means taking a similarly integrated approach, but one that deals with all aspects of design relating to a business's activities – from the architecture and interiors of its factories and headquarters, to the design of its products, its **branding**, marketing and communications materials, and so forth.

The origins of total design in relation to industrial companies can be traced back to 1907, when Paul Jordan, the technical director of Allgemeine Elektricitäts-Gesellschaft (AEG), com-missioned the German architect-designer Peter Behrens to design and help implement what became the world's first truly comprehensive corporate identity programme. Acting as AEG's 'artistic adviser' (design director), Behrens masterminded a total design policy, which involved him overseeing every design decision relating to the company. This led to his redesign of the company's entire product line, ranging from electric kettles and desk fans to toasters and light fixtures, as well as drawing up plans for the firm's new factories and workers' housing. He was also responsible for the creation of a new AEG brand identity and related **packaging** designs. Behren's total design programme was highly instrumental in the creation of AEG's strong brand identity, and helped to firmly establish the company's modern design credentials.

The British transport administrator Frank Pick famously pioneered a similarly early programme of total design at London Transport. During his legendary tenure there, from 1906 to 1940, Pick oversaw the implementation of an integrated house **style** that not only covered the design of London Transport's signage and branding, but also its Underground stations and staff canteens, as well lamp posts, bus seats, bus shelters and so on. In fact, Pick believed nothing was so small as to fall

Park Royal Underground Station, London (1936) designed by Welch & Lander for London Transport – this Art Deco building features a stained glass Underground roundel and reflects the comprehensiveness of the firm's total design policy.

London Underground map (1933) by Henry Beck for London Transport – a hugely influential masterpiece of visual communication design that was part of Frank Pick's total design initiative at London Transport.

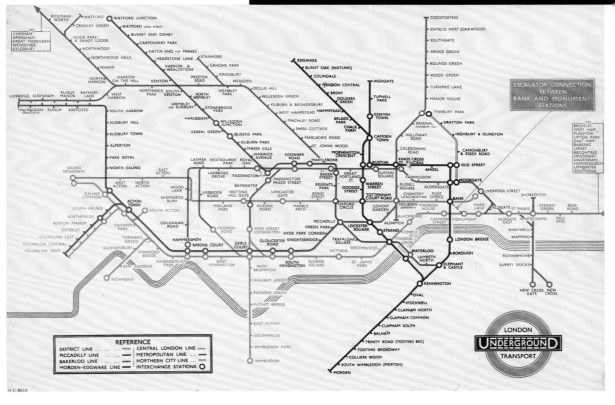

outside his exacting remit. Even today, the legacy of Pick's design policy can still be detected in the look of the latest generation of London buses.

Another great champion of total design was the architect Rein Veersema who, as head of design at the Dutch electronics company Philips from 1960 to 1964, oversaw the establishment of a highly influential systematic design strategy. As Philips notes, 'Veersema understood that when **mass production** becomes a company's core business, design could no longer be the individual expression of an individual personality, but should be the anonymous outcome of collaborative team

work, involving many different kinds of expertise.'[31] The outcome was a completely integrated house style that was recognizable the world over. Under the inspired design directorship of Dieter Rams, the German consumer-electronics company Braun correspondingly implemented a total design policy that saw a similarly distinctive house style developed that was immediately identifiable.

The concept of total design today is part and parcel of any serious manufacturing company's core business strategy. In fact, it is so much a given that no one really talks about it anymore. Nevertheless, it is one of the

main reasons why Apple and Dyson products, for example, are so easy to distinguish from those of their competitors, for ultimately they are the result of a highly considered and holistic 'total' approach to design. ■

Fallingwater, Mill Run, Pennsylvania (1935) by Frank Lloyd Wright – designed as a weekend residence for Edgar J. Kaufmann and family, this extraordinary organically designed building is completely unified with its surrounding landscape.

'The built and the natural worlds are exquisitely connected.'

Harmony and wholeness in design

IDEA № 41

UNITY

Panton chair (1959–60) by Verner Panton for Vitra – a masterful expression of design unity, it was the first-ever single-material, single-piece chair to be injection-moulded in plastic.

Over many decades the idea of unity has been a recurring theme in design. The reason for this is that it implies a synthesis of form, function and materials, whereby a visual and structural harmony is created.

Beyond this, when a design possesses a constructional 'oneness', it is also generally easier to produce because the fewer components something has, the easier it is to replicate.

One of the earliest champions of unity in design was the British **industrial design**er Christopher Dresser who, during his studies at the Government School of Design at Somerset House in London, chose to specialize in a new area of design research known as Art Botany. He subsequently published a book entitled *Unity in Variety, as Deduced from the Vegetable Kingdom* (1859), which was, as its subtitle explained, 'An attempt at developing that oneness which is discoverable in the habits, mode of growth, and principle of construction of all plants.' In the preface to this book Dresser wrote: '... while we trace a unity amidst all the works of creation, the mind, by an effort of its own, informs us that *one* system resulted from *one* intelligence, and thus the heart is led up from the manifold works of the beauteous creation to the one God who rules over all.' For Dresser, the fact that unity was found in the 'designs' of nature, meant that it had an inherent God-given **rightness**, and was therefore something to strive for in the design of man-made goods. And certainly many of Dresser's designs reveal a far greater sense of structural and visual unity than the work of other contemporaneous designers, which ultimately gives them a compelling proto-Modernist aesthetic.

During the late nineteenth century, this interest in design unity was also expressed in a number of masterfully conceived **Gesamtkunstwerk** buildings by, among others, Victor Horta, Charles Rennie Mackintosh and Frank Lloyd Wright. These remarkable 'total work of art' buildings were a complete unity of architecture and design, where each and every element of the harmoniously integrated composition was the work of a single design visionary. It is, however, Wright's later *Gesamtkunstwerk* house, Fallingwater (1935), that perhaps best expresses his goal of an organic wholeness, whereby the built and the natural worlds are exquisitely connected.

The idea of unity also found fertile ground at the Bauhaus, which was founded in 1919 to unite the teaching of art and craft. When the emphasis of the institution's teaching shifted from Expressionism to **rationalism** in 1923, the Bauhaus's director Walter Gropius came up with the new slogan *Kunst und Technik – eine neue Einheit* (Art and Technology – A New Unity) for its modified educational programme, which was more geared towards design for industrial **mass production**.

The concept of unity has also been a particularly strong theme in chair design over the decades. One of the very first designs to achieve formal and material unification was a lounge chair created in 1933–34 by the British designer Gerald Summers. This seating design conceived for use overseas was constructed from a single piece of cut-and-bent birch plywood so as to overcome the effects tropical heat and humidity had on traditionally joined and upholstered seating.

During the late 1950s and 1960s, numerous furniture designers aimed for the holy grail in seating design – the first single-form, single-material adult-sized chair made of plastic. Eventually, this milestone was successfully realized by Verner Panton in partnership with the Vitra furniture company. Originally made in fibreglass, the Panton chair (1959–60) was later made out of moulded polyurethane (1968–71), before being modified in 1971 so that it could be injection-moulded in a thermoplastic. This wholly unified cantilevered design was the world's first single-material, single-form, injection-moulded chair, and as such was the antecedent of the ubiquitous monobloc garden chair.

Today, unity in design continues to find fresh and technically innovative applications, from immersive gaming environments to **IoT** products that seek a flawless unification between the digital and the physical. ∎

The unification of architecture and design

IDEA № 42

GESAMTKUNSTWERK

Detail of the interior of Hill House in Helensburgh (1902–04) by Charles Rennie Mackintosh – both the light fixture and wallpaper shown here feature the 'Glasgow rose', a Mackintosh motif found throughout the house.

The term *Gesamtkunstwerk* was first coined by the German philosopher and writer Karl Friedrich Eusebius Trahndorff in 1827. It describes 'a total work of art' that seeks to bring together elements of various artistic disciplines in order to create a harmonious and unified whole.

The concept of *Gesamtkunstwerk* was subsequently popularized by the composer Richard Wagner, who believed that the fragmentation of the arts since Ancient Greek times had been a stultifying influence and that the only remedy was the synergetic integration of the different artistic disciplines. Practising what he preached, Wagner's epic four-opera cycle *Der Ring des Nibelungen* could, for instance, be described as a *Gesamtkunstwerk*, for it integrated music, singing, costume, set design and drama into a revolutionary new and monumental art form.

Various architect-designers during the latter half of the nineteenth century and the opening years of the twentieth century also took the *Gesamtkunstwerk* philosophy on board. This resulted in a number of buildings being designed as 'total works of art', whereby their architects designed site-specifically the majority of their contents, including furniture, fixtures and fittings. Victor Horta's house and studio (1898–1901), Charles Rennie Mackintosh's Hill House (1902–04), Josef Hoffmann's Palais Stoclet (1905–11), Frank Lloyd Wright's Robie House (1908–09), Gerrit Rietveld's Schröder House (1924), Rudolf Steiner's Goetheanum (1925–28) and Le Corbusier's Villa Savoye (1928–31) are among the most important and extraordinary examples of *Gesamtkunstwerk*

residential projects, their unified compositions providing exquisite three-dimensional realizations of their creators' singular architectural visions.

Wright was the most prolific *Gesamtkunstwerk* architect of all time; he created an impressive portfolio of totally unified buildings for private clients, corporations and public organizations alike, with each one painstakingly composed and lovingly detailed so that the whole was a sublime **unity** of its constituent parts. Wright even went as far as designing stylistically appropriate clothing for some of his female clients so that they would be in harmony with the **aesthetics** of their Wright-designed interiors.

The economic downturn of the 1930s, twinned with increasing mechanization and industrialization, saw the concept of *Gesamtkunstwerk* buildings eroded. In the postwar period, Arne Jacobsen notably and almost exceptionally continued to practise this approach to architecture and design in order to create several of highly unified public buildings, while both Joe Colombo and Verner Panton created a number of futuristic *Gesamtkunstwerk* interior environments – with the latter's *Visiona 2* installation (1970) even featuring auditory and olfactory elements.

Today, the only contemporary examples of *Gesamtkunstwerk* buildings

are usually architect-designer's own homes. As for other contemporary expressions of *Gesamtkunstwerk* schemes, perhaps the closest we get to realizing the concept in totality is within the immersive and illusory worlds of gaming and virtual reality, where creative-design imaginations are not constrained with anything as mundane as physicality. ∎

'The whole was a sublime unity of its constituent parts.'

ABOVE: The drawing room at Hill House in Helensburgh (1902–04) – devised by Charles Rennie Mackintosh as a completely harmonious composition.

LEFT: Hill House in Helensburgh – Charles Rennie Mackintosh's 'domestic masterpiece' created for the publisher Walter Blackie.

Ornamentation as a sign of cultural degeneracy

IDEA № 43

ORNAMENT AND CRIME

During the mid- to late nineteenth century a number of prominent **design reform**ers, including John Ruskin and William Morris, had admonished manufacturers for making goods that relied too heavily on ornamentation in order to hide shoddy manufacture and poor-quality materials.

It was, however, the Austrian architect-designer Adolf Loos who went a step further, positing the idea that decorative embellishment equated to criminality in his famous 'Ornament and Crime' essay – written in 1908, but first delivered as a lecture two years later.

The genus of his big idea can actually be traced back to the three years (1893–96) that he spent in the United States directly after graduating from the Technical University of Dresden. It was during this American sojourn that Loos became profoundly influenced by the ideas of the American architect Louis Sullivan. Sullivan had earlier written an article for *The Engineering Magazine* (August 1892) entitled 'Ornament in Architecture' in which he wrote, 'it would be greatly for our aesthetic good if we should refrain entirely from the use of ornament for a period of years, in order that our thought might concentrate acutely on the production of buildings [and products] well formed and comely in the nude'.

Loos took on board this notion of stripped-down **utility**, and on his return to Vienna designed a number of buildings that were, over the years, increasingly characterized by a strict aesthetic **purity** – most notably the Looshaus (1909–12). He also designed simple, unadorned furniture, lighting and fittings site-specifically for his architectural projects, such as those for the interior of the Café Museum (1899). His ideas for design reform through the elimination of decorative embellishment, however, were perhaps most eloquently expressed in his 'Ornament and Crime' essay.

Waxing lyrically about Papuan tribesmen covered in tattoos, and linking contemporary inking to im**morality**, Loos famously ranted, 'The modern man who tattoos himself is either a criminal or a degenerate. ... The tattooed who are not in prison are latent criminals or degenerate aristocrats. If someone who is tattooed dies at liberty, it means he has died a few years before committing a murder.'

Yet despite his fulminating tone, Loos made a strong case for the idea that 'the evolution of culture is synonymous with the removal of ornament from utilitarian objects', for he intelligently reasoned that there was a direct correlation between **decoration** and wasted material, labour and wealth, both on a private and national level. His was a rallying cry that struck a chord among other progressive designers who similarly realized that the emerging modern world would evolve its own industrial aesthetic, where superfluous ornament could be eliminated and in its place a purity of functional form would reign supreme. Spurred on by his teachings and his belief that, 'Freedom from ornament is a sign of spiritual strength', this younger generation of designers would put Loos's radical ideas into practice over the coming decades, thereby laying the ascetic foundations of the **Modern Movement**. ∎

Villa Müller in Prague (1930) by Adolf Loos – this residence's white cubic facade exemplifies Loos's theories regarding the elimination of superfluous decoration.

'Freedom from ornament is a sign of spiritual strength.' – *Adolf Loos*

Cha kettle/teapot (2014) by Naoto Fukasawa for Alessi – with its minimalist aesthetic, this design reflects its designer's quest for 'complete harmony'.

'For Rams, design purity equals
good design.'

The distillation of function through the purification of form

IN-50 coffee table (1947) by Isamu Noguchi for Herman Miller – the purity of this table's aesthetic can be attributed to its designer's belief that 'every garden is a landscape, and every garden can be considered a table, too, especially Zen gardens'.

IDEA № 44
PURITY

The concept of purity has long been associated with cleanliness and virtue, and certainly within the world of design, physical purity has in the past often been equated with **morality**.

The idea of design purity tends to centre on the purification of form through the purging of any superfluous ornament, and, as a result, objects that display a structural purity invariably possess a strong stripped-down, elemental quality.

Purity in design as a consequence has a strong aesthetic dimension and is generally associated with particular types of formalism. Classicism, for instance, has an innate formal purity derived from its mathematical sense of order, while the **aesthetics** of purity have also long been a defining feature of traditional Japanese design and architecture. The purity of form found in Japanese design had a major influence on the early foundations of the **Modern Movement**, with Christopher Dresser being the first **industrial design**er to create Western designs intended for mechanized production based on Eastern purifying aesthetics, for when an object has a purity of form, it is invariably easier to manufacture, whether using handcraft or industrial means.

Frank Lloyd Wright was also highly influenced by the stripped-down quality of Japanese design and architecture, as his numerous Arts and Crafts **Gesamtkunstwerk** buildings attest; these possess such a strong sense of aesthetic purity both inside and out that they have a spiritual quality. Indeed, Wright defined what he described as 'pure design' as 'the abstraction of nature-elements in purely geometric terms'.

It was, however, the Austrian architect-designer Adolf Loos who most memorably linked the idea of design purity with moral decency in his seminal 1908 essay 'Ornament und Verbrechen' (**Ornament and Crime**), in which he argued that decorative embellishment was indicative of cultural degeneracy. Later, taking up Loos's lead, and in response to the horrors of World War I, there was a strong desire within the international design community for a forward-looking purification of design, which was first expressed in the elemental designs of the De Stijl movement, and later in the reductivist language of Modern design pioneered at the Bauhaus. The linking of social morality with design purity was also part and parcel of the interwar obsession with health and hygiene. Certainly there was a strong case to be made for creating designs that had a purity of line because they were so much easier to keep clean. But beyond this practical concern, purity of design also had connotations of industrial progress and social progressiveness, which lay at the very heart of the Modern Movement.

Design purity was also seen as an attribute of **good design** during the postwar period, with Isamu Noguchi's IN-50 coffee table being a perfect example of formal purity expressed through the language of **organic design**. Similarly, Dieter Rams channelled a purity of form with his designs for Braun; his SK4 Phonosuper combination radio and record player,

designed in collaboration with Hans Gugelot, was an influential tour de force of design purity and **clarity of layout**. For Rams, design purity equals good design, and accords with his desire for 'as little design as is possible'.

The pursuit of structural purity is also related to Minimalism, which emerged in design in the early 1970s, most notably in the furniture of Donald Judd. This was fundamentally a **style** based on design purity that relied on stripped-down geometric forms and usually a restricted colour palette. Today, purity in design is most often found in objects where functional considerations are paramount, such as in medical equipment or weaponry. It can also, however, be detected in the work of essentialist master form-givers, such as Ross Lovegrove. ∎

Design governed by reason

RATIONALISM

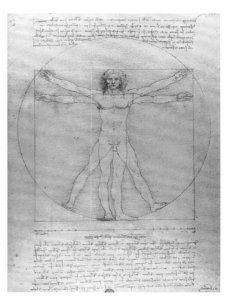

Vitruvian Man *(1492) by Leonardo da Vinci, a drawing that demonstrates the measurements of the ideal human body according to the rules of classical proportions laid out by Vitruvius in his* De Architectura *treatise.*

Rationalism is a philosophy that views scientific reason as the only true source of knowledge, and over the centuries it has had a strong bearing on the evolution of design thinking.

Indeed, it was one of the main driving forces behind the **Modern Movement**, which sought to bring a more rational approach to design practice so that it could provide the most benefit as efficiently as possible to the greatest number of people.

The origins of rationalism in design can be traced back to the Roman military engineer and architect Vitruvius and his famous treatise *De architectura* (On Architecture), written c.27 BC, which laid out the arguments for why the status of architecture should be raised to that of a scientific discipline. This idea of design having a stronger, rationally based scientific footing was furthered in the Renaissance and also during the Age of Enlightenment, eventually leading the French Neo-Classical architects Claude-Nicolas Ledoux and Étienne-Louis Boullée to adopt pure geometric 'rational' forms in the designs of their buildings and monuments, which were essentially proto-Modern.

During the early twentieth century, the cause of rationalism was taken up by the Austrian architect-designer Adolf Loos in his seminal essay of 1908 entitled *Ornament und Verbrechen* (**Ornament and Crime**), which made a strong economic case for greater rationalism in design, arguing that **decoration** constituted a criminal waste of labour, money and materials. Meanwhile, at the German electrical goods company AEG, the **industrial design**er Peter Behrens had already begun putting rationalist theory into practice after his appointment as the firm's artistic director in 1907. Through his pion-

eering work for AEG, Behrens introduced a new level of pragmatism to the design of products intended for industrial **mass production**, which was based on solid technological reasoning. For instance, a number of his designs were conceived so logically for maximum efficiency in manufacture that they shared common components across entirely different product types. Developed 'from the spirit of the machine', Richard Riemerschmid's standardized *Typenmöbel*, or 'Type Furniture' (1906), for the Dresdener Werkstätten für Handwerkskunst (Dresden Handicraft Workshops) similarly reflected a new rationalism in design that was coming to grips with the demands of mechanized industrial manufacturing.

It was, however, in America during the 1910s that rationalism within the realms of design and manufacturing really took off, thanks to the adoption of both **Taylorism** and **Fordism**, which saw the **systemization** of factory production in order to increase output exponentially. This adoption of rationalized manufacturing systems was accelerated during World War I, with factories in both Europe and America geared up for munitions and other wartime materiel production. After World War I, the argument for greater rationalism in design became hotly debated within avant-garde design circles, as it seemed to its adherents to offer a purposeful way of constructing a more just postwar society.

The founding of the Bauhaus in 1919 for the purpose of bringing a more industrial slant to **design**

education was an indication of this, as was the rise of the **New Objectivity** movement in Germany during the 1920s, which adopted a rationalist approach as a means of building a better and fairer society. A new trend in Italian design and architecture known as Rationalism also emerged during the 1920s and 1930s, which attempted to synthesize a machine aesthetic with Italy's classical tradition. A hybrid Modernistic **style**, Italian Rationalism was typified by the utilization of state-of-the-art materials, such as tubular steel and plate glass, and the adoption of a strict geometric vocabulary of form. Initially favoured by the Fascists for the progressiveness of its **aesthetics** and imperial disposition, Italian Rationalism soon fell from political grace, yet left an enduring legacy that includes a number of acknowledged Italian design icons, such as the Sant'Elia chair (1936)

by Giuseppe Terragni and Gabriele Mucchi's Genni lounge chair (1935).

During World War II, a new form of rationalism emerged by necessity, which was dictated by the use of rationed materials. While this helped the war effort on all fronts, by the cessation of hostilities most people were heartily sick of rationalism and yearned for designs that were not quite so starkly utilitarian in nature. Indeed, it was not until the 1970s that rationalism in design came to the fore again in response to the economic downturn precipitated by the 1973 oil crisis. But as soon as the global economy recovered in the early 1980s, rationalism was ditched in favour of Post-Modernism, which was essentially anti-rational. Yet since then, rationalism has been revisited in the guise of Late Modernism and remains a highly valid approach to problem-solving because it provides designers with the intellectual framework for delivering the maximum function with the minimum means, which is an important aspect of **sustainability**. ∎

ABOVE: Pipe table and chair (2009) by Konstantin Grcic – this furniture was inspired by the highly rational language of design pioneered by Marcel Breuer and the Bauhaus.

BELOW: 'Project for a Country Lodge' (c.1790) by Claude-Nicolas Ledoux, a visionary Enlightenment architect whose various seemingly quirky building proposals were based on a forward-looking rationalism.

Designing production lines to optimize the efficiency of machines and workers, while also maximizing profitability

IDEA № 46
TAYLORISM

'Taylorism' is the term used to describe a production-efficiency methodology that is based on the industrial-management ideas of the American mechanical engineer Frederick Winslow Taylor (1856–1915). These ideas resulted from a series of scientific time-and-motion studies that Taylor undertook in the early 1880s to determine the most efficient layout of assembly lines in factories.

This in turn had an enormous bearing not only on how production lines were subsequently designed, but also on how products were conceived to be mass-produced within such work-planning systems.

When thinking about design, all too often it is the final product that takes centre stage. Outside the manufactory, little if any thought is given to the 'invisible' design and engineering of the machinery and production-line system used to make the product. Yet in the world of making things on an industrial scale, the design of specialist machines and production lines is absolutely critical to successful design outcomes and commercial profitability. In many ways, Taylor can be seen as the founding father of modern assembly-line design. He was the first to develop and implement the concept of time-and-motion studies, having realized that productivity could be enhanced if the tasks that individual workers performed were scientifically analysed using, among other things, early time-lapse photography, and then broken down into constituent parts so as to eliminate any redundant motion or wastage of time.

In 1911, Taylor published his seminal book *The Principles of Scientific Management*, which set forth his precepts for high-volume manufacturing within the context of assembly-line factories. Although his approach was initially criticized for alienating workers by making them mere cogs in a machine, Taylor believed that his scientific approach would finally bring 'the elimination of almost all causes for dispute and disagreement' between manufacturers and workers, for it would afford 'maximum prosperity' for both. And while Taylorism famously helped to inspire Henry Ford's invention of the moving assembly line, it was originally regarded as a dehumanizing force – as was so memorably parodied by Charlie Chaplin in the film *Modern Times* (1936). Yet ultimately it led to greater automation within factories, which in turn gave rise to a new generation of skilled machine operators who were, in many ways, much more empowered than their unskilled jobbing predecessors.

Today, the design legacy of Taylorism still resounds in factory production lines across the world. Yet increasingly these factories are not populated by humans, but instead are highly – or in some cases, completely – automated, thanks to ever-advancing **robotics**, which are among the most sophisticated design-engineered machines on the planet. In such state-of-the-art manufacturing facilities, scientific-management systems based on Taylorism are still used to analyse the work done by each 'worker' (in this case a robotic machine, rather than a human) and then using this data, each machine is programmed to operate to its maximum efficiency alongside its fellow 'workhorses' in a production line.

There is also a modern evolution of Taylorism – known as Digital Taylorism – that uses digital surveillance tools to monitor employee productivity in workplaces and the operation of workflow systems. Like its namesake, this new form of Taylorism has attracted much criticism because it is based on quantitative research, so is geared to the improvement of manufacturing efficiency. As a consequence, Digital Taylorism usually does nothing to enhance the job satisfaction of employees, and in fact its implementation can at times have a negative impact on workers' wellbeing. ∎

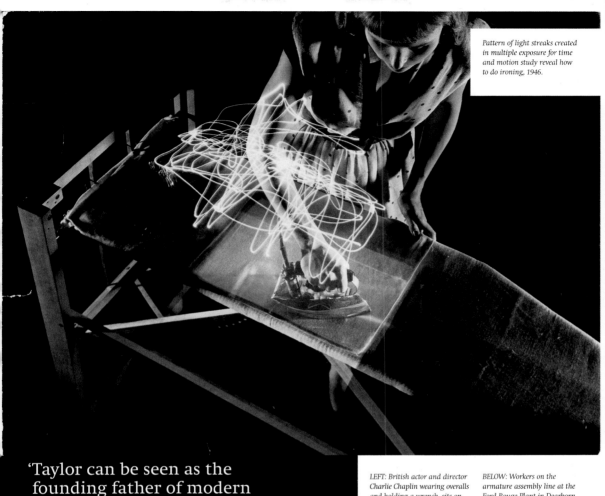

Pattern of light streaks created in multiple exposure for time and motion study reveal how to do ironing, 1946.

'Taylor can be seen as the founding father of modern assembly-line design.'

LEFT: British actor and director Charlie Chaplin wearing overalls and holding a wrench, sits on an enormous set of gears in a still from his film Modern Times, 1936

BELOW: Workers on the armature assembly line at the Ford Rouge Plant in Dearborn, Michigan, 1934.

A manufacturing philosophy based on the moving assembly line

IDEA № 47

FORDISM

The term 'Fordism' is used to describe a system of industrial **mass production** that incorporates the process of moving assembly lines. It originated from its inventor's name, Henry Ford, who devised it to make his car manufacturing plants more productive.

Henry Ford, c.1910, who revolutionized industrial production techniques by inventing the moving assembly line, which led to dramatic increases in factory output.

Like other innovative manufacturing techniques before it (namely **standardization**, interchangeability and the **division of labour**), Fordism had profound ramifications for design because it enabled all kinds of products to be made faster, cheaper and on a previously unimaginable scale.

In 1908, Henry Ford launched the legendary Model T, which was the first automobile to successfully democratize car ownership. He described it as 'a motor for the great multitude', and it was an instant success, thanks to its reliability and affordability. The only problem was that although the Ford factory in Dearborn, Michigan, was run according to the **American System of Manufacture**, it still could not keep up with the overwhelming demand for the automobile.

What Ford needed was a method of speeding up production flow at his plant so that the Model T could be manufactured at a much faster rate. Fortuitously, Frederick Winslow Taylor's *The Principles of Scientific Management* (1911) had just been published, and it proposed an analytical approach, based on time-and-motion studies, as a way of increasing the throughput efficiency of factory assembly lines. Ford took the principles of **Taylorism** fully on board and began implementing them at his plant in Highland Park. He also took related ideas from Frank Bunker Gilbreth and Robert Thurston Kent's *Motion Study: A Method for*

Increasing the Efficiency of the Workman (1911), which claimed that the aim of motion study as applied to 'standardized practice' was to increase output or decrease 'the hours of labor'. In combination with this, Ford carefully studied the production flow of his factory. He realized that an inordinate amount of time was being wasted by having to manhandle and physically pull components from one work desk to the next along the assembly line, and that it was this type of stop–start practice that was affecting the overall speed at which cars were produced.

Casting around for a new production process that would increase his output, Ford was inspired by the use of a mechanized conveyor system in operation at a grist mill – an early automated technology invented in 1787 by Oliver Evans, who has been described by the curator of the Henry Ford Museum as 'early America's foremost technological innovator'. Ford was also inspired by an innovative system of electrically powered overhead pulleys that was being used by the meatpacking factories in Chicago and Cincinnati to move animal carcasses efficiently through their 'disassembly' lines.

In essence, Ford merged these two clever systems – moving conveyors and pulleys – to create the world's very first moving assembly line, which he introduced into his Highland Park factory in 1913. As he would later explain, 'Every piece of work in the

shop moves … there is no lifting or trucking of anything other than materials.'[32] Productivity was dramatically increased, with the assembly times of magnetos, for example, being reduced from 20 minutes to just 5. The astonishing efficiency that Ford's moving assembly line achieved ultimately reduced the overall time it took to make a Model T from 12.5 hours in October 1913, to just 93 minutes the following year. A consequence of this time saving was that Ford was able to slash the price of the Model T from $850 in 1910, to $360 in 1916.

Having seen the remarkable success of Ford's moving assembly line, the editors of *The Engineering Magazine* subsequently published *Ford Methods and the Ford Shops* (1919) in order to outline its principles to 'students of metal-working economies the world over'. This book helped to promote the adoption of

Ford Model T assembly line at the Highland Park Plant, Michigan (1914) – showing the filling of radiators and the starting of engines.

Fordism in factories across the globe, thereby heralding the advent of truly large-scale modern mass production. But more than this, Fordism led to a complete rethinking of how products were conceived, for this new state-of-the-art manufacturing system relied on a product being designed holistically and much more systematically so that its components were optimized for efficient assembly in order to achieve maximum productivity. ■

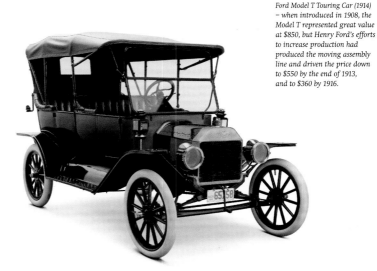

Ford Model T Touring Car (1914) – when introduced in 1908, the Model T represented great value at $850, but Henry Ford's efforts to increase production had produced the moving assembly line and driven the price down to $550 by the end of 1913, and to $360 by 1916.

The message maketh the design

Proust's Armchair (1978) by Alessandro Mendini for Studio Alchimia – the decoration of this 'antique' chair was inspired by Pointillism and was an intentional attempt to blur the boundaries of art and design.

IDEA Nº 48
SEMIOTICS

Semiotics is the study of signs and symbols set within the context of communication and social interactions. Given this, semiotics has huge relevance in graphic design and corporate identity design, which are all about visually communicating ideas to an audience. The use of semiotics also comes into play within the realm of three-dimensional design, though perhaps not in such an obvious way.

Semiotics is concerned with the analysis of non-linguistic communications and can trace its origins back to the English physician, writer and classical scholar Henry Stubbe, who coined the term 'semeiotics' [sic] in 1670 to describe a very specific branch of medical research involved with the interpretation of signs. The English philosopher and physician John Locke (1632–1704) later defined semiotics as 'the doctrine of signs'. Then, in 1903, American philosopher, logician and mathematician Charles Sanders Peirce – who is sometimes credited as 'the father of pragmatism' – gave a series of semiotics lectures at Harvard University and the Lowell Institute in which he put forward the idea that 'A sign ... is something that stands to someone for something in some respect or capacity'.

It was, however, the Swiss linguist Ferdinand de Saussure – who coined the analogous term 'semiology' – who went on to evolve this early research of signs and symbols into a definable modern social science in the late nineteenth and early twentieth century. In his influential book *Course in General Linguistics*, first published in 1916, Saussure put forward the idea that a sign is the unity of two matched components: the signifier (the sign embodied in a symbol or word) and the signified (the actual concept of the sign).

Over the following decades, further research was undertaken into semiotics, but it was not until 1957 that the Argentine design theorist and educator Tomás Maldonado formally introduced semiotics into the teaching of design for the very first time at the Ulm School of Design (Hochscule für Gestaltung, or HfG), having replaced Max Bill as the school's rector the previous year. By doing so, Maldonado enriched the repertoire of **design education** with the introduction of various previously untaught subjects, notably operations research, mathematical decision theory, systems analysis, planning techniques and even game theory. The aim of this new kind of design teaching was to give students valuable strategic knowledge, which meant they could now take a greater role at the front end of the design process, being able to provide crucial inputs and insights relating to the initial planning and early-stage development of products and services. This in turn brought greater professionalism to design practice.

The same year that semiotics was introduced into the curriculum at the HfG, Roland Barthes's *Mythologies* was published in French. This collection of essays helped popularize the idea of semiotics through its exploration of myth creation and its analysis of the signed message's communicative power. Barthes's book was subsequently published in English in 1972, and, as a result, led to much greater awareness of semiotics within design discourse. This ultimately helped to lay some of the philosophical foundations of Post-Modernism in design during the late 1970s and early 1980s, which as a definable anti-**Modern movement** sought to bring 'meaning' back into architecture and design through the

use of historicizing motifs and **decoration** – or, in other words, signs and symbols. It was not until 1984, however, that the term 'product semantics' first appeared in the heading of an article penned by Reinhart Butter and Klaus Krippendorff for the **Industrial Design**ers Society of America's journal, *Innovation*. They defined it thus: 'the study of the symbolic qualities of man-made forms in the context of their use and the application of this knowledge to industrial design'. As Krippendorff would later observe, it was 'the starting point for the proposal to redesign design'.[33]

Today, the act of problem-solving (for that is what design is) is widely seen as a form of semiotic discourse, for it allows designers to communicate their thoughts and feelings through their creations. But over and above the impact that semiotic research has had in relation to both the teaching and practice of design, as an idea it has also helped to spawn a new area of academic research: design studies. And while this relatively youthful discipline covers many other design-related topics, the semantic aspect of objects – often referred to as their **design rhetoric** – is one of the key areas of examination and research. ∎

Patriot (Model FC-400) radio (1940) by Norman Bel Geddes for Emerson Radio and Phonograph Corp. (NY) – this iconic Catalin plastic radio intentionally referenced the American flag.

Design guided by the theory and psychology of colour

COLOUR THEORY

The power of colour to shape our perceptions of a design should never be underestimated. That is why today manufacturers of all kinds hire fashion forecasters to identify the next on-trend hues.

The idea of colour theory, however, has a much longer history than colour forecasting and was originally based on the use of colour wheels, which are essentially diagrammatic rainbows of hues that demonstrate whether colours contrast or complement each other.

From Renaissance times onward, colour theory was developed primarily in regard to painting, but the new discipline of 'colour psychology' that eventually evolved out of it sought to explain the way different hues affect human behaviour and mood. The German philosophers Goethe and Schiller famously created a diagram in 1798/99 that colour-matched 12 hues to the four temperaments and, rather bizarrely, 12 associated occupations. Colour theory and colour psychology's application to design practice, however, took quite a while to catch on. It was the Swiss painter Johannes Itten who was the first proper pioneer within this field.

While a master at the Bauhaus in Weimar, Itten devised the curriculum for the school's *Vorkurs* (foundation course), which included colour theory – a subject dear to his heart because he believed that colours had 'a mystical capacity for spiritual expression'. In 1921 Itten also developed his own star-shaped *Farbenkugel* (colour ball) teaching aid, while his colour researches are often credited with inspiring later seasonal colour analysis whereby certain colour groupings are associated with specific seasons.

One of the first modern designs to put avant-garde colour theory into practice was Gerrit Rietveld's Red/Blue chair (1917–18/1923), the slatted form of which got its famous primary-colour makeover in 1923. This gave it an enhanced spatial aspect and transformed it into *the* defining design of the De Stijl group.

The calculated use of colours as a means of making a design more alluring to consumers was, however, first systematically exploited by the American car industry. At the helm of this 'Color Revolution', as hailed by *Fortune* magazine in 1930, were the trend-setting colourists of DuPont's Duco Color Advisory Service. These forecasters advised manufacturers across a range of sectors what the next season's fashionable colours would be. One of their most high-profile clients, General Motors, used the company's True Blue paint as an important sales differentiator in its battle for market share with Ford. This in turn prompted the launch in 1927 of the Ford Convertible Cabriolet, which was offered in a range of colours that were intended to entice 'the Woman Motorist'. General Motors, however, went a step further by setting up its Art and Color Section in 1928 to develop a programme of annual cosmetic changes to its automobiles in order to accelerate their stylistic turnover rate – with colour forecasting being at the forefront of this new trend in design.

More recently, the pulling power of colour in design was dramatically demonstrated with the introduction of Apple's gumdrop-hued first-generation

BELOW: Red/Blue chair (1917–18/1923) by Gerrit Rietveld, executed by G.A. van de Groenekan – having first appeared in 1918, this design was radically transformed in 1923 with a colour makeover.

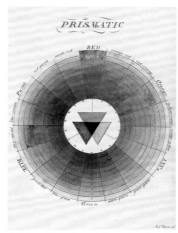

BOTTOM: Diagram from Moses Harris's book The Natural System of Colour (1776) – this 'prismatic' colour wheel was devised to show complimentary facing colours.

iMac (1998) and iPod Mini (2004), both revealing how the use of colours can have a massive impact on brand awareness and sales.

Today, while many manufacturers still use colour as a way of superficially updating their products, a more in-depth understanding of colour psychology has come to the fore, with most designers being all too aware of how colour can influence people's emotional perception of both products and services. The symbolism of colour, however, varies according to cultural context. For instance, in China red is linked with good luck, whereas in South Africa it is associated with mourning. It is therefore crucial for designers to be mindful of these differences in colour association so that any design solution can be optimized for the intended audience. ∎

iMac computer (1998) by Jonathan Ive and the Apple Design Team – this first generation iMac playfully injected colour into the world of desktop computing, which hitherto had been dominated by beige boxes.

Revolutionizing design for a better society

Bölgeblick jug (1932) by Aino Aalto for Karhula (later Iittala) – this pressed glass design embodies the softer-edged formal vocabulary of the Modern Movement as it was expressed in the Nordic region.

IDEA № 50

MODERN MOVEMENT

In the early twentieth century a new and progressive philosophical movement emerged – Modernism, the aim of which was to reshape society through experimentation and the innovative application of scientific knowledge and technology.

Designers and architects aligned to the Modern Movement were inspired by the same moral imperative as the **design reform**ers of the previous generation: to improve society through **democratic design**. But rather than looking back nostalgically to preindustrial craft for inspiration, they instead accepted industrialization, seeing it as a *fait accompli* of the Modern Age. For them, mechanization was a vital means of bringing about the social change they desired, so they fully embraced the manufacturing potential of 'the machine', and outwardly celebrated industrial progress, while vehemently rejecting any form of **historicism**.

One of the key features of the Modern Movement was the tireless pursuit of ever-greater efficiency – making things better, faster, cheaper. To achieve this aim, new modern materials and industrial processes were utilized, which in turn gave Modernist designs a definable machine aesthetic. Indeed, it was the purification of form resulting from this drive for a new language of design, manufacturing efficiency and functional effectiveness that set Modern designs apart stylistically from anything that had gone before.

This new Modern spirit first emerged in the work of the Italian Futurists and the Russian Constructivists, and was then followed up by the De Stijl group in the Netherlands. After the devastation of World War I, the impetus for a more progressive type of design that embraced the realities of the modern industrialized age grew exponentially from, on the one hand, a desire to expunge the memories of the recent past, and on the other, as a means of promoting better health and hygiene among war-decimated populations.

It was in Germany, thanks to the efforts of the Deutscher Werkbund and the later Staatliches Bauhaus, that Modernism finally coalesced into an international design movement, which was defined by the pursuit of what became known in Germany as *Die Neue Sachlichkeit* (the **New Objectivity**) – in other words, **functionalism** based on **standardization** and **rationalism**. It was felt by its adherents that this new approach could potentially cleanse society of all its ills – from rampant nationalism to social inequality – and ultimately lead to a fairer world order based on a new avant-garde spirit of international solidarity. The Swiss architect Le Corbusier subsequently stated that the house was now a *machine à habiter* (machine for living in), while furniture was 'equipment for living', which perfectly summed up the Modernists' wholesale embrace of functionalism efficiency.

Utilizing industrial methods of production and state-of-the-art materials, such as tubular steel and plywood, the Modernists pioneered a reductivist approach to design based on functionalist goals that was invariably expressed through the use of rectilinear forms and an elemental **simplicity**. The Modernists' overriding ambition was to achieve **universality** in design. This, they believed, would be born from the aesthetic **purity** gained from a rational approach to problem-solving, whereby **form follows function**.

In 1928, the CIAM (Congrès Internationaux d'Architecture Moderne) was founded, and over the next 30 years acted as the de facto mouthpiece of the Modern Movement, the influence of which spread so far that it eventually became known as the International **Style**. During this period, however, the ideological stance of the Modernists became increasingly dogmatic – so much so that by the late 1950s, its vice-like grip on the design and architectural establishment began to be questioned in certain more youthful quarters, which led to the incremental erosion of its influence. By the 1970s Modernism was seen as a bit passé – it was no longer the dominant 'new' aesthetic and its philosophical shortcomings were becoming increasingly apparent. Nevertheless, many designers in practice today remain true to its rationalist principles, especially within the industrial process, where in most cases manufacturing efficiency still rules. ∎

B34 armchair (1928) by
Marcel Breuer for Thonet
– an exemplary Modern
Movement design, stripped
down to its bare functional
bones while using a then
state-of-the-art material
– tubular metal.

'This new approach could potentially
cleanse society of all of its ills.'

7

congrès international
d'architecture
moderne   22–31 juillet 1949

ciam

bergamo   palazzo della ragione

Poster designed by Max Huber
for the seventh CIAM congress
held in Bergamo, Italy, 1949.

A rational approach to designing a better society

IDEA № 51
NEW OBJECTIVITY

In the 1920s a new anti-Expressionist art and design movement arose in Germany, which coalesced under the banner of *Die Neue Sachlichkeit* – the English translation being the New Objectivity. In many ways, this new approach to design represented a desire for order after the ghastly upheavals of World War I.

The term was coined from the title of an art exhibition held in Mannheim in 1923 and was, as one of its organizers noted, 'a new realism bearing a socialist flavour'.

The founding of the Staatliches Bauhaus in Weimar in 1919 can be seen to have presaged the anti-Expressionist spirit of the New Objectivity movement. Indeed, the Bauhaus's avowed aim was to cultivate a greater sense of purpose and contemporary relevance in the teaching of design. As its first director, Walter Gropius, explained, the intention behind its establishment was to 'provide artistic services to industry, trade and craft'. As a way of achieving this goal, the Bauhaus innovatively unified the teaching of art and technology. Even the school's name, which can be translated as 'building house', smacked of a new objective direction in **design education** that involved equipping students with the construction skills they needed to design successfully for industry.

Yet, despite its initial 'objective' intentions, the Weimar years of the school were heavily influenced by the tutors Johannes Itten, Lyonel Feininger and Gerhard Marcks, whose teachings were aligned to the Expressionist movement. In fact, it was only after the departure of the charismatic Itten in 1923 that the school wholeheartedly embraced the New Objectivity, thanks in large part to increasing contact with the Russian Constructivists and the De Stijl group in the Netherlands. Both of these avant-garde design groups produced work that expressed a new form-purifying aesthetic based on geometric abstraction, which would go on to become a defining characteristic of the **Modern Movement**'s New Objectivity. Around the same time, the Bauhaus began emphasizing in its teaching a more rational and industrialized approach to design, which saw the introduction of field trips to factories so that students could learn first hand about the manufacturing processes used for **mass production**. This more objective design-teaching route became even more emphatic when the Bauhaus relocated to Dessau in 1925. Dessau was a much more industrialized city than Weimar, so offered greater potential for achieving the school's original mandate: collaborative design ventures with industry.

Two years later, the model dwellings, interiors, furniture and lighting that were shown at the Deutscher Werkbund's 'Die Wohnung' exhibition, which featured the Weissenhof housing estate, reflected an increasing adherence to the **rationalism** of the New Objectivity. Significantly, these exemplars of progressive modern design based on **form follows function** principles had been created by an international roster of avant-garde architect-designers – including Marcel Breuer, Mart Stam, Ludwig Mies van der Rohe and Le Corbusier – revealing that the New Objectivity had now become the defining idea within contemporary design practice in Europe. As a result, its political radicalism and utopian goals would go on to shape the Modern Movement ideologically as it transitioned into the so-called International **Style**. Crossing national borders and cultural boundaries, this new internationalized form of Modernism became the dominant force in architecture and design throughout most of the world from the 1930s onwards, and its influence is still very much felt today. ∎

'The Bauhaus innovatively unified the teaching of art and technology.'

RIGHT: Walter Gropius's Director's Office at the Dessau Bauhaus (1925–26) – reflecting the institution's new formal sobriety.

'It employs minimal materials to the maximal effect.'

Biosphère geodesic dome in Montreal, Canada – now a museum dedicated to the environment, but originally designed by Richard Buckminster Fuller as the United States Pavilion for the 1967 World's Fair, Expo 67.

The simpler, the better

IDEA № 52
LESS IS MORE

MR10 chair (1927) by Ludwig Mies van der Rohe for Thonet – the most elegant of all tubular metal cantilevered chairs.

Although 'Less is more' is one of the most used aphorisms in the world of design, and perfectly sums up the philosophy of the **Modern Movement**, its precise origins are somewhat unclear.

The first known use of 'Less is more' can be found in Robert Browning's poem 'Andrea del Sarto' (1855). However, this is probably a bit of a red herring as it was used in a context that had nothing to do with architecture and design. It was, in fact, the architect Ludwig Mies van der Rohe who famously popularized the maxim. In a recorded interview with some architecture students in 1960, however, when he was asked about the origins of the phrase, Mies declared, 'I think I first said it to Philip [Johnson] ... [but] I think where I heard it first was from Peter Behrens. Yes. You know it is not original but I like it very much.'[34]

Indeed, the author of an early biography on Behrens, Alan Windsor, acknowledged that 'Wenig ist mehr' (Less is more) was one of Behrens's oft-used sayings. This catchy aphorism certainly accorded with Behrens's desire to strip away the superfluous in order to reveal the essential – which is exactly what he did on many of the electrical appliances he designed for AEG. Likewise, the adage worked well in describing Mies's own architectural and product designs, which were similarly reductivist in nature and, like Behrens's work, possessed a modern classicism based on simple geometry – his Barcelona Pavilion of 1929 being an exceptionally fine example.

The underlying premise of 'Less is more' is that if you do away with all **decoration** and strip a design down to its most elemental functional form the savings gained through manufacturing efficiency will result in the product being less expensive to manufacture. These savings can then potentially be reinvested in the intrinsic design, the use of higher-grade materials or better manufacturing processes – or a combination of all three – so that the end result is of superior quality and provides better value for money to the consumer.

In his essay '**Crime and Ornament**', the Viennese architect-designer Adolf Loos made a similar observation: 'The result of omitting **decoration** is a reduction in working hours and an increase in wages. ... If I pay as much for a plain box as for one with ornamentation, the difference in labour time belongs to the worker.' Certainly, it was these social imperatives that lay at the very heart of the Modernists' adoption of 'Less is more' and their advancement of it as an ideological article of faith.

The American architect, design theorist and futurologist Richard Buckminster Fuller took the notion of 'Less is more' one step further through his concept of 'ephemeralization', which meant 'doing more with less'. He saw this as a means of achieving not only greater **sustainability**, but also a better quality of life for all. Fuller's famous geodesic dome design is perhaps the ultimate expression of this approach, for it employs minimal materials to the maximal effect – or in other words, getting the most with the least.

The German **industrial design**er Dieter Rams likewise spent the whole of his career advancing the philosophy of 'Less but better', which in many ways can be understood as a thoughtful evolution of the original idea of 'Less is more' in that it gives an important nod to the notion of quality. Today, as increasing **digitalization** enables ever-growing **convergence of functionality** within products, so more **utility** is being packed into less physicality. In terms of contemporary design, this means that 'Less is more' is being achieved in a more profound sense. And that is a good thing, especially in relation to our enduring need to deploy resources more efficiently and more responsibly, and to reduce waste wherever possible. ∎

Reducing mass for greater efficiency

IDEA № 53

LIGHTNESS

Lightness has always been a critical theme in modern design practice, for it is related to both material and structural efficiency – or doing more with less. The idea of lightness is also related to other key concepts in design, such as **portability**, **miniaturization** and **essentialism**.

Early Cassina publicity photography (c.1957) demonstrating the lightness of Gio Ponti's Superleggera chair.

Among the earliest historic examples of lightness in design are the many different types of tent-like living structures used by nomadic tribes, including yurts and tepees, which employ wooden poles and animal skins to create wind- and waterproof shelters that can be easily dismantled, transported and then reassembled. Even today, modern high-tech tents are an excellent example of how, with a minimum amount of material and a bit of design ingenuity, highly portable and resilient temporary living spaces can be created. It is, however, Richard Buckminster Fuller's geodesic dome (see page 110), patented in 1951, that is actually the most efficient lightweight building structure – its geodesic polyhedron geometry provides better rigidity and stress distribution than any other shape.

Reducing mass in order to increase lightness also enabled the conquering of manned flight. The first properly recorded incidence of this was a tethered hot-air balloon designed by Joseph-Michel and Jacques-Étienne Montgolfier, which was demonstrated in Paris in 1783. This remarkable feat of design engineering was accomplished through the use of a super-lightweight balloon-shaped sackcloth envelope made airtight with layers of paper glued to its underside and then reinforced with a corded net on its outside. Because this construction was so light, when it was inflated with heated air it was able to lift skywards, rather like today's helium-filled Hybrid Air Vehicles' Airlander 10 – currently the largest aircraft capable of flight.

Early experimental gliders also relied on lightweight structures made of wood struts and canvas that had good strength-to-weight ratios. Orville and Wilbur Wright's famous Flyer 1, which made the first-ever controlled and sustained flight of a powered aircraft near Kill Devil Hills, North Carolina, in 1903, also used an airframe constructed of these lightweight materials. One of the main reasons the Wright brothers were able to achieve their remarkable feat, however, was due to a lightweight alloy (92 per cent aluminium and 8 per cent copper) used in the casting of their aircraft's engine block, which helped reduce its overall mass considerably. Today, the aircraft industry continues to rely on the use of lightweight alloys and other composite materials. For example, the airframes of Boeing's 787 and Airbus's A350 both employ carbon-fibre-reinforced plastic composite – a material that is lighter and stronger than metal – because the heavier a plane is, the more energy it needs to propel it through the air, making it more costly to operate.

In the world of chair design, the concept of material and structural lightness has been a guiding force for over 150 years, an early exemplar of this being Michael Thonet's Model No. 14 café chair (1859), which comprises just six structural elements and weighs only 3 kg (6½ lb). A remarkable tour de force of reductivist design, the Model No. 14 was stripped of all ornamentation, so only the elements essential for its function were left. Since then, other landmark seating designs have been celebrated for their physical lightness, most notably: Gio Ponti's Superleggera chair (1957) for Cassina, which is a modern reworking of an Italian fisherman's chair, and weighs in at a single-finger-lifting 1.7 kg (3¾ lb); De Pas, D'Urbino and Lomazzi's air-filled Blow chair (1967), made of electronically welded PVC and filled with air; Alberto Meda's Light Light chair (1987) for Alias, one of the very first chairs to be made of carbon-fibre composite; Marcel Wanders's Knotted chair (1996) for Droog, which cleverly utilizes woven aramide carbon rope dipped in epoxy; and more recently Piero Lissoni's Piuma chair (2016) for Kartell, which is the world's first industrial design to be injection-moulded in a carbon-fibre-reinforced thermoplastic. These innovative chairs demonstrate how new materials have helped to substantially lighten the load in design again and again, and will undoubtedly continue to do so because, in most cases in design, greater lightness equals greater efficiency. ∎

'Reducing mass in order to increase lightness also enabled the eventual conquering of manned flight.'

The Airlander 10 aircraft (first UK flight 2016) built by Hybrid Air Vehicles – originally created for the US Army's Long Endurance Multi-intelligence Vehicle (LEMV) programme, and currently the world's largest aircraft.

Sculpting design from the study of airflows

AERODYNAMICS

Aerodynamics is a branch of physics that relates to the study of air and liquid motion, and the forces that act upon an object when it travels through such media.

Model of the Zeppelin LZ120 'Bodensee' being tested in Wind Tunnel II at Göttingen (1920) – this early wind tunnel was the brainchild of the 'father of modern aerodynamics', Ludwig Prandtl.

As a modern scientific principle, aerodynamics did not emerge until the late seventeenth century, thanks to research undertaken by various physicists, including Sir Isaac Newton, who famously explained 'air resistance' in relation to his laws of motion – published in *Philosophiae Naturalis Principia Mathematica* in 1687. Importantly, Newton noted that the resisting force that acts on the motion of a body was proportional to the square of the body's velocity.

These natural laws had, of course, been observed far earlier, with both Aristotle and Archimedes laying down the theoretical foundations for aerodynamics during the second and third centuries BC. During the Renaissance, Leonardo da Vinci produced designs for experimental flying machines, which revealed an understanding that swept-back forms were, in theory, more likely to fly because they offered less wind resistance.

It was, however, in the early twentieth century that the science of aerodynamics came into its own with the design of the earliest powered aircraft – notably the original Flyer 1, successfully flown by Orville and Wilbur Wright in 1903. The design of this famous aircraft had been informed by airflow studies using a simple air tunnel. The following year, the German physicist Ludwig Prandtl defined the boundary layer – the stratum of gas or liquid that adjoins the surface of an object and that possesses different viscosity properties – which contributed to a better understanding of drag

forces. This in turn led to wing theory, as expounded by the British engineer Frederick W. Lanchester in 1907, which helped explain the concept of lift.

In 1919, the Hungarian engineer Paul Jaray designed a wind tunnel for Zeppelin and consequently introduced the teardrop shape into airship design. Jaray also helped pioneer the usage of aerodynamic forms in automotive design, filing a patent for streamlined car bodies in 1922. His revolutionary design had an air-sweeping dynamic form and incorporated various innovative features, including a wrap-around windscreen, integrated headlights and flush door-handles – all intended to reduce drag and thereby increase speed and performance. Jaray's design was

later put into serial production as the Tatra 77 in 1934 – made in Czechoslovakia, it was marketed as 'The Car of the Future' and was the first truly aerodynamically designed model to be manufactured, though in relatively low numbers. Jaray's design informed the development of other later, more mainstream, cars, including Ferdinand Porsche's Volkswagen Beetle (1936).

In America during the 1930s, **industrial design** consultants Henry Dreyfuss and Raymond Loewy designed streamlined trains that were aerodynamically contoured, notably the 20th Century Limited locomotive (1938) and the S1 locomotive (1937) respectively. Loewy also redesigned the Greyhound bus into a much more aerodynamic

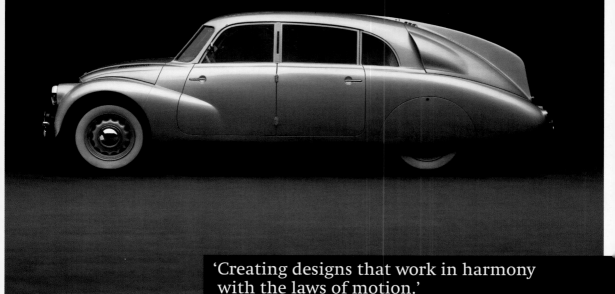

T87 car (1940) designed by Hans Ledwinka and Erich Übelacker and built by Czechoslovakian automotive manufacturer Tatra – this model was an evolution of Paul Jaray's earlier teardrop-shaped T77 automobile.

'Creating designs that work in harmony with the laws of motion.'

model in 1935–37, which eventually evolved into the Scenicrusier in 1954. However, while employing aerodynamic forms in transportation design – cars, trains, planes and even bicycles – was entirely logical for scientifically proven reasons of enhanced performance, the **streamlining** of consumer products, such as electric irons, toasters, refrigerators and ovens, was purely for stylistic purposes.

Today, thanks to the advent of sophisticated **CAD/CAM** software, aerodynamics informs the design of transportation more than ever – the less drag a design has, the more energy efficient it will be, and the better it will perform. Whether it is a Formula One car, a superyacht or a high-tech racing

bike, all use the science of aerodynamics to create shapes that allow air to flow around them as easily as possible. Ultimately, the application of aerodynamics is about creating designs that work in harmony with the laws of motion. ∎

ASH 30 two-seater open class sailplane (first flight 2011) designed by Martin Heide and manufactured by Alexander Schleicher in Poppenhausen,

Germany – a state-of-the-art glider that achieves the maximum possible aerodynamic performance standard.

Subaru 360 city car (1958) – this was Subaru's first production model and over 392,000 units were sold (1958–71), a success that can be attributed to the wholesale acceptance of quality control.

Instigating systems to maintain a level of quality throughout the creation and production of a design

IDEA № 55
QUALITY CONTROL

Quality control as an idea in design and manufacturing is incredibly important. For while **standardization** enables designs to be successfully replicated in mass volume, to maintain standardization over the course of production it is essential to have a system of quality control in place to ensure that the established standards are consistently met.

China's first emperor, Qin Shi Huang, was the first to introduce an exacting quality-control system for the **mass production** of weapons, as well as for weights and measures. Indeed, Qin's vice-like grip on quality control was the reason he was able to produce a very early example of **mass customization** – the extraordinary Terracotta Army that accompanied him into the afterlife. The quality-control systems ushered in during Qin's reign became responsible for the extraordinary manufacturing quality associated with Chinese design for centuries to come.

Early forms of quality control involved time-consuming post-manu-facture inspection, with designs being either accepted or rejected depending on whether they met the established quality specifications or not. It was, however, not until the early 1920s that the concept of statistical process control (SPC) was developed at Bell Laboratories by Walter A. Shewhart. This used statistical tools to reduce the chance of producing sub-standard articles and involved the constant monitoring of production processes using sampling methods. SPC also instigated a culture of continuous improvement and the devising of experiments that led to the develop-ment of better manufacturing processes, all of which helped to eliminate as much risk as possible within the production process, and resulted in better-quality manufacturing.

In 1951, Armand V. Feigenbaum wrote a book entitled *Total Quality Control*. This took the whole idea of quality-control management one step further by employing a much more holistic approach to what became known by the acronym TQC, defining it as, 'An effective system for coordinating the quality maintenance and quality improvement efforts of the various groups in an organization so as to enable production at the most economical levels which allow for full customer satisfaction'.[35]

It was, however, the Romanian-born American management consultant and engineer Joseph M. Juran – author of the *Quality Control Handbook* (1951) – who had the greatest impact on the world of design, for he became a sort of guru to Japanese manufacturers. Following his advice, they instigated rigorous quality-control systems in the 1950s that helped transform Japanese design-and-manufacturing culture to such an extent that 'made in Japan' no longer meant shoddy manufacture but instead became associated with cutting-edge, technologically advanced design.

Today, all large-scale manufacturers use quality-control systems, with the Six Sigma system (devised by the engineers Bill Smith and Mikel J. Harry while working at Motorola in 1986) being among the most popular. However, the use of such systems does have its detractors, who claim that over-reliance on them can lead to a corporate culture that feels **innovation** is 'covered', and ironically, therefore, is less likely to innovate. ∎

The Six Sigma logo, with 'sigma' being the eighteenth letter of the modern Greek alphabet and in the field of statistics representing standard deviation.

The external shell that contains, protects and promotes products

Ecolean Air Aseptic packaging (2009) – this lightweight packaging is made of a highly eco-efficient yet flexible and tough material comprising up to 35 per cent calcium carbonate.

IDEA № 56
PACKAGING

Packaging is such an intrinsic part of contemporary life that it is hard to imagine the world without it, yet throughout most of history it did not exist. Indeed, the idea of packaging design was driven by the rise of consumerism in the mid- to late nineteenth century.

As more products – from alcohol to cosmetics – became available to buy in shops, new forms of packaging were designed not only to contain them and protect them, but also to distinguish them from other similar products.

Packaging can be defined as the materials used to contain, protect, handle, deliver and preserve goods on their journey from manufacturer to end-user. There are three classes of packaging in total: 'primary', which means point-of-sale packaging, such as a box containing breakfast cereal; 'secondary' or 'grouped', referring to the boxes that contain a number of individual primary products, such as a cardboard container protecting cereal boxes in transit or storage; and 'tertiary' or 'transport' packaging used for the bulk transport of secondary packaging – pallets, shrink-wrapping and so forth.

The main materials used in packaging are paper, cardboard, plastic, glass, steel and aluminium. Although packaging has been used since the founding of the earliest commercial ventures – for example, seed packets, ceramic cream pots and medicine bottles – it was during the Depression in the 1930s that packaging design came to play an increasingly important role in how a product was marketed. Then as now, packaging not only helped a manufacturer differentiate its products from those of its competitors at relatively little cost, it could also be used to attract consumers and create a recognizable brand.

In 1929, Dr Ruben Rausing, having previously studied economics in the United States, established the first specialist packaging company in Scandinavia, based on his belief that 'A package should save more than it costs'. In 1943, one of the firm's engineers, Erik Wallenberg, began the development of a revolutionary new type of packaging design that took the form of a paper tetrahedron – determined to be the most space-efficient shape for a milk carton. That same year, the firm was renamed Tetra Pak in tribute to this invention, and subsequently developed innovative techniques for not only coating paper with waterproof plastics, but also for sealing seams below the contained liquid level. Rausing demonstrated the resultant Tetra Pak model in 1946, and after this milestone his company became a world leader in packaging design and manufacture.

The advent of inexpensive plastics, new types of polymeric films and cheaper colour printing during the latter half of the twentieth century greatly diversified the range of packaging that could be designed. This led to a large amount of material wastage, as manufacturers saw packaging as a low-cost way of adding perceived value to a product. By the 1990s, however, with rising environmental concerns, the design of packaging increasingly came under the spotlight. Since then, the overuse of packaging has been seen ever more widely as unacceptably wasteful. In response to these concerns, Tetra Pak is making concerted efforts to ensure that more FSC-compliant Tetra Pak cartons are being manufactured, and that **recycling** levels are increased. Likewise, another Swedish company, Ecolean, has developed a new form of lightweight aseptic and recyclable packaging that is made from a composite plastic and calcium-carbonate material. This new generation of pouch-type packages weighs approximately 50 to 60 per cent less than conventional liquid cartons or bottles, and is therefore much more eco-efficient in terms of material usage and the energy needed for transportation. Given that in today's globalized world products are often made in the hundreds of thousands, or even millions – with consumable products far beyond that – any reduction in their packaging can make quite a sizeable difference to their overall environmental impact and **sustainability**.

But over and above its function to protect a product up to its point of use, a packaging design can also be used to emotionally connect users with its manufacturer's brand values, often on

BELOW: The Swedish engineer Erik Wallenberg shown c.1944 with the tetrahedron packaging design he invented for Tetra Pak.

BELOW RIGHT: 100ml Tetra Classic carton (1952) by Tetra Pak – a revolutionary tetrahedral packaging design that is still in use today.

an almost subliminal level. For instance, Apple uses cleanly designed, high-quality packaging as a means of enhancing the brand identity of its products, while keeping them as safe as possible in transit. Increasingly, packaging design is about creating surprise, instilling a satisfying usage ritual, or adding a touch of personalization and localization. Given these different considerations, packaging design today is all about thinking creatively outside the box. ∎

Tailoring personalized solutions

CUSTOMIZATION + MASS CUSTOMIZATION

The polar opposite of design **universality** is 'customization', which is all about tailoring or adapting a product to a specific individual's needs or desires. Put simply, it is the personalization of an object. The ability of a mass-produced product to facilitate user customization is a growing trend in contemporary design, as new technologies – from data mining to **3D printing** – are enabling ever-more astute mass customization of mass-manufactured things.

Rod & Custom *magazine cover (September 1963) featuring the 'Mysterion', a custom-built hotrod by Ed 'Big Daddy' Roth, which was powered by two Ford V-8 engines.*

Today, 'named' Coca-Cola cans and Nike running shoes customized by purchasers online are leading this new phenomenon in design, which is ultimately about creating better **connections** between people, the products they use and the companies that make them.

'Why have ordinary, when you can have special?' probably sums up best the reasoning behind why, over the ages, people have sought to have designs customized to their own requirements. In centuries gone by, skilled master craftsmen relied on the patronage of wealthy clients, who would commission from them bespoke designs. These designs would be personalized according to the buyer's individual needs or desires, such as a dinner service emblazoned with a family crest or a suit of armour carefully tailored to the client's vital statistics.

During the early years of the automotive industry, customization was a widespread practice among former horse-drawn coachbuilders. Such enterprises evolved their business to create bespoke car bodies that could

then be used on standardized chassis. Indeed, the celebrated automotive designer Harley Earl started his career in his father's coach works in Los Angeles (later absorbed into the Don Lee Coach & Body Works) designing custom car bodies for Hollywood's glitterati, including the legendary producer-director Cecil B. DeMille and the infamous actor Rosco 'Fatty' Arbuckle.

During the late 1920s and early 1930s, the customization of cars developed into a completely new automotive phenomenon: the 'hot rod' – whereby old classic American cars were 'souped up' to enhance their performance, initially so that bootleggers could outrun law-enforcement officers during Prohibition. In the late 1930s, these 'speedster' vehicles – as they were then known – began to be raced on Los Angeles' dry lakebeds. After World War II, the hot rod phenomenon grew exponentially as military airports were repurposed into drag strips; as a consequence, these modified cars began to be given flamboyant makeover paint jobs.

The postwar era saw a massive surge in the customization of motorcycles,

too. Many American soldiers had enjoyed riding European models during their years abroad, so on their return home they took advantage of the ready availability of cheap military-decommissioned motorbikes and began customizing them, both in terms of performance and **aesthetics**. In the 1960s, the increasing 'artisanal' customization of motorbikes saw the birth of an entirely new design genre: the chopper, which was so memorably immortalized in the 1969 film *Easy Rider*, starring Peter Fonda. And, of course, today, the customization of both cars and bikes has become the daily fodder of innumerable reality television series.

The origin of mass customization, which involves standardized designs that can be personally tailored through either changing their choice of options or arrangement of components, can similarly be traced back to the automotive industry. Yet mass customization has long been a feature of furniture design, too, with designers coming up with modular products that can be flexibly mixed-and-matched to provide a degree of customization.

'Why have ordinary, when you can have special?'

Classic examples of this include the glass-fronted sectional bookcases manufactured by Globe-Wernicke in the early 1900s, and the colourful Tomado shelving system (1958) designed by Adriaan Dekker, which became an almost ubiquitous feature of Dutch interiors in the late 1950s. Since then, there have been numerous examples of the exploitation of mass customization in the furniture industry, especially in the office contract market, where functional flexibility is most often sought.

But the most significant driver of mass customization over the last 30 years has been **digitalization**, which has ushered in an unprecedented level of **convergence of functionality** within consumer electronics. Take Apple's iPhone, for example, which is a universal mass-produced product that can be subject to mass customization, depending on which apps its users choose to download, what screen wallpaper they opt for, and what ringtones and sound settings they select. Ultimately, when something is specially tailored to *my* individual needs it works better for *me*, and it is that type of targeted design solution that we all seek because it is so personalized. ■

The use-it-today, sling-it-tomorrow designs of our throwaway society

IDEA № 58
DISPOSABILITY

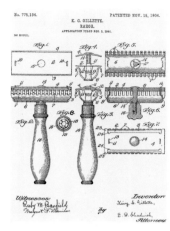

Patent for a wet razor with disposable blades (filed 1901) invented by King Camp Gillette.

The idea of disposability in design is, of course, inextricably linked to consumption, but as a concept it also sits along the fault line of two long-established, but at times seemingly disparate, moral values that have long been associated with good housekeeping practice – thrift and hygiene.

Although the Industrial Revolution accelerated consumption by making goods cheaper and more plentiful to buy, the idea of disposability did not really gain much traction until the American businessman King Camp Gillette made a fortune with his invention of a razor that came with thin and inexpensive disposable blades. At a stroke, men no longer needed to resharpen their straight razors using leather strops. Instead, when one of Gillette's slot-in blades was dulled, they could easily and efficiently replace it with a brand new one. Indeed, Gillette's clever invention heralded an entirely new business model, and soon the notion of disposability became synonymous with profitability and, ultimately, modernity.

It was, however, during the Depression-laden 1930s that disposability, in the guise of **planned obsolescence**, became widely regarded as an economic panacea during turbulent financial times. As Earnest Elmo Calkins, widely regarded as the 'father of modern advertising' in America, explained, 'Obsoletism is another device for stimulating consumption. ... Clothes go out of **style** and are replaced long before they are worn out. That principle extends to other products. ... People are persuaded to

abandon the old and buy the new to be up-to-date, to have the right and correct thing. Does there seem to be a sad waste in the process? Not at all. Wearing things out does not increase prosperity but buying things does.'[36]

Ultimately, the American economy became dependent on this kind of throwaway approach to consumption, which culminated in many manufacturers purposely and strategically shortening their products' physical and stylistic lifespans so as to precipitate their disposability. With the outbreak of World War II, however, the ascendency of disposability in design was abruptly curtailed because of widespread rationing, which saw a make-do-and-mend approach come to the fore by necessity. However, once prosperity returned after the war, so did disposability as a manufacturing strategy, with the early 1960s marking the highpoint of use-it-today, sling-it-tomorrow designs. Indeed, **Pop** design was all about the celebration of the ephemeral and the disposable, as evinced with the advent of, for example, paper mini dresses and blow-up plastic chairs.

Yet despite the publication of Vance Packard's *The Waste Makers* in 1960 – a seminal critique of consumerism that castigated manufacturers and the

advertising industry for their encouragement of mindless consumption based on the disposability model – disposability was a phenomenon that was not going away, thanks to its financial profitability. One of the leading pioneers of disposable design was the French manufacturer BIC, which introduced its plastic 'Biro' ballpoint pen in 1950, its first disposable lighter in 1973 and its first throwaway razor in 1975.

Today, although the environmental impact of disposability is better understood, it remains a problem. While there are certain kinds of product that by their very nature need to be as disposable as possible because of hygiene concerns, such as one-time-use syringes and the like, there are also far too many other products being mass-produced that are far too disposable for **sustainability**. ∎

LEFT: BIC disposable lighters (1972–73) – since their introduction, BIC has sold more than 30 billion disposable lighters in over 160 countries.

BELOW: BOMAG refuse compacting vehicle being operated on a landfill site in Dorset, England, 2013.

'Sheathing a product in a skin that strengthens its eye appeal.'

Vespa GS125 motor scooter (1955)
by Corradino D'Ascanio for
Piaggio – an exemplar of
postwar Italian styling and the
'Linea Italiana'.

Wrapping function in visually seductive form

IDEA № 59
STYLING

As a key idea in design, 'styling' is all about the look of a product, rather than how it actually works. Often styling is used to fashionably update a product's appearance to make it more appealing to consumers without actually enhancing its functionality – this is especially true in the design of household appliances and consumer electronics.

Design and styling are often regarded as separate disciplines, and certainly there are designers who specialize in the nuts-and-bolts engineering side of design, while others are more concerned with the surface treatment and appearance of an object. Yet styling is an important aspect in the overall design of an object because it helps to enhance it aesthetically, which can ultimately play a key role in whether someone is willing to buy it or not. In the past, styling was either used to hide the mechanical underpinning of a design, such as with the housing of a typewriter or sewing machine, or was used to enhance it visually, as with the body of a streamlined automobile.

Ultimately, styling is all about sheathing a product in a skin that strengthens its eye appeal. The legendary **industrial design** consultant Raymond Loewy viewed styling as a way of allowing a design to express itself, while also helping to, as he put it, 'streamline the sales curve'. Perhaps Loewy's best explanation of why styling mattered, at least to his potential clients, was the motto printed on his business card: 'Between two products equal in price, function, and quality, the better looking will outsell the other.' This was, and still is, an irrefutable fact of design.

During the 1930s the terms 'industrial designer' and 'industrial stylist' were virtually interchangeable because styling was such an important part of design throughout that eco-nomically difficult decade. Styling played an especially crucial role in automotive design, with companies such as General Motors instigating annual styling programmes to boost sales interest. Indeed, GM's later Motorama auto shows, which ran from 1949 to 1961, were fabled razzmatazz showcases of automotive styling at its most audaciously inventive.

During the postwar period and into the 1950s, Italian designers also utilized styling as a means of establishing a serious foothold in the international design scene. The so-called *Linea Italiana* (Italian Line) – a form of visually seductive **streamlining** achieved by wrapping a product in a sensuous flowing skin – was the easiest and most cost-effective way Italian designers could compensate for any technical deficiencies. This focus on styling enabled Italian manufacturers to export their goods all around the world, and ultimately led to *il miracolo economico* (the economic miracle) that saw Italy transform itself into the design powerhouse it is today.

It is no surprise then that it was the Italian design maestro Vico Magistretti who perhaps best defined the key differences between design and styling when he noted: 'Design does not need drawing, but styling does. What I mean by this is that an object of design could be described ... by spoken or written words, because what materializes through the process is a precise function, and, in particular, a special use of materials which, as a matter of principle, leaves all aesthetic questions out of consideration because the object is to achieve a precise practical aim. That does not of course mean that a precise image cannot be produced that will reflect and express "aesthetic" qualities proper to the new meth-odology used in the conception of the object. Styling, on the other hand, has to be expressed by the most exact drawings, not because it disregards function but simply because it wraps that function in a cloak of essentially expressed qualities that are called "**style**" and that are decisive in making the quality of the object recognizable.'[37]

Ultimately it is the expressive nature of styling that helps give a design **character**, and it is that sense of personality that people connect with, both consciously and subconsciously. ∎

Raymond Loewy on the cover of Time *magazine (31 October 1949) – accompanied by the immortal byline 'He streamlines the sales curve', and surrounded by a selection of vehicles and products he had styled for a host of different manufacturers.*

Shaping a design to make it more efficient in motion or more visually alluring

CSSR Sifang CHR380A EMU
locomotive (2010) designed and
engineered by CRRC Sifang in
collaboration with PriestmanGoode
– this state-of-the-art supremely
streamlined bullet train operates
at a cruise speed of 350 km/h
(217 mph) and a maximum of
380 km/h (236 mph) in
commercial service.

IDEA № 60
STREAMLINING

The concept of streamlining evolved out of research into **aerodynamics** and involves the use of swept-back, drag-reducing contoured forms that are often teardrop in shape.

Originally, streamlining was used to optimize the aerodynamic perform-ance of cars, trains and aeroplanes. By the 1930s, however, it was also being used for **styling** purposes in order to give furniture, lighting, electronic appliances and other household products the allure of sleek modernity. The Wall Street Crash of 1929, the ensuing Great Depression and the instigation of the price-fixing National Industrial Recovery Act of 1933 had made market conditions extremely tough for manufacturers in America, who were vying with one another for ever-dwindling sales. Rather than investing in the costly ground-up development of innovative new products, these struggling manu-facturers sought instead to superficially update their existing product ranges through styling, which was much more cost-effective, at least in the short term. With this aim they hired a new cohort of talented professional **indust-rial design** consultants – including, most notably, Henry Dreyfuss, Norman Bel Geddes, Raymond Loewy and Walter Dorwin Teague – to restyle their products using streamlined forms, which had futuristic connotations of speed and progress.

Borrowing a modelling technique originally developed for the automotive industry, these designers and their assistants would fashion streamlined clay models in their studios, which would then be translated into sleek, modern-looking casings for all sorts of products and appliances. These design-ers were essentially skinning existing products with new and alluring streamlined forms for stylistic and commercial ends rather than for any real functional advantage. That said, occasionally the use of streamlined forms would help to improve manu-facturers' bottom lines by facilitating the use of cheaper plastics over more expensive metals, or optimizing efficiency within a metal-stamping process – the implementation of stream-lined forms tended to help visually and physically unify designs by smoothing out their contours, and unified forms are generally easier to mould in plastic or stamp out in metal. They can often also be more hygienic, as smooth single surfaces are easier to clean.

More than anything else, though, it was the seductive eye-appeal resulting from streamlining that helped sell products – so much so that Loewy's streamlined Coldspot refrigerator of 1934 for Sears became the first domestic appliance to be promoted on its looks rather than on its per-formance. Later, in 1949, Loewy became the first industrial designer to be featured on a cover of *Time* magazine, where his portrait was accompanied by the memorable byline, 'He streamlines the sales curve', which pretty much summed up the way streamlining was able to inexpensively provide added value and stimulate sales.

But even before this, the stream-lining craze had its detractors, with Edgar Kaufmann Jr, the influential Director of the Industrial Design Department at New York's Museum of Modern Art, stating as early as 1944, 'Streamlining is not **good design**. Its theme is the magic of speed, expressed by teardrop shapes, fairings, and a curious ornament of parallel lines – sometimes called speed whiskers. The continued misuse of these devices has spoiled them for most designers.' And as the 1950s dawned, streamlining had been consigned to design history as just another short-lived **style** that epitomized the zeitgeist of its times. ∎

Spacelander bicycle (1946) by Benjamin Bowden for Bomard Industries – designed for the 'Britain Can Make It' exhibition (1946), this streamlined design incorporated an energy-storing dynamo to make pedalling uphill easier.

Designs conceived as seasonal fashion items

IDEA № 61
FASHION-LED DESIGN

High shoes (2006) by Karim Rashid for Melissa – made of high-quality injection-moulded PVC.

Design has always been both a dedicated follower of fashion and a setter of fashionable trends. The evolution of decorative **style**s, from Gothic and Renaissance to Baroque and Rococo, verifies this. Yet the idea of fashion-led design is still a relatively recent concept.

During the *fin de siècle* period, when the Art Nouveau style was at the zenith of its popularity, the worlds of fashion and design were often very close bedfellows, with, for example, Liberty & Co. in London retailing fashionable clothing alongside on-trend furniture and homewares that channelled the same aesthetic spirit. But while the cyclic following of seasonal fashion trends had long been a feature of clothing design, it was not until the late 1920s that it fully occurred to manufacturers of other kinds of products that they could be subjected to a system of seasonal updating, too. The upside for manufacturers was that this kind of fashion-driven initiative would accelerate the stylistic obsolescence of existing products and thereby boost sales of new ones.

General Motors was the first company to introduce to the automotive market a seasonal makeover programme when it established its legendary Art and Color Section in 1927. Crucially, its director Harley Earl introduced female designers into this **styling** department in the 1940s and 1950s to work on the creation of on-trend cars featuring modish interiors that would appeal to women – in America it had been recently found that women 'cast the final vote' in three out of four car purchases. Soon known as GM's 'Damsels of Design', these pioneering women designers were presumably chosen by Earl

because they were more in tune with all-important fashion trends than their male counterparts.

In the 1960s, the boundaries between art, design, music and fashion began to blur, and Pierre Cardin became the first high-profile couturier to dabble in product design through his creation of a studio dedicated to the design of futuristic furniture and lighting, which he described as *sculptures utilitaires* (functional sculptures). Another fashion designer who has been very much aligned to the world of design throughout his career is Issey Miyake, who has collaborated with various well-known **industrial designer**s on a startling array of synergetic projects – ranging from exhibition installations to catwalk presentations. He has long been a champion of avant-garde product design that has a fashion crossover: the Cabbage chair (2008), for example, designed by Oki Sato of the innovative Japanese design studio Nendo, made clever reuse of the paper used to make Miyake's famous pleated fabrics.

In 2004, Tom Dixon, the then creative director of Habitat, spearheaded the development of the company's VIP (Very Important Products) Collection to mark its fortieth anniversary. The idea was that 22 celebrities would be asked to design a piece for the collection. This resulted in, among other things, a shoehorn by the stiletto-meister Manolo Blahnik, a

velvet-covered safe by the multifaceted jeweller Solange Azagury-Partridge, and a series of toy monsters by the exuberant baron of French couture, Christian Lacroix.

It was, however, the Italian furniture manufacturer Kartell that really grasped the potential of fashion-led design. In 2005 it began inviting various fashion designers to collaborate on its 'Mademoiselle à la Mode' project, with Philippe Starck's Mademoiselle chair (2004) being given a fashion makeover with covers designed by, among others, Rosita Missoni, Moschino and Ermenegildo Zegna. There has been a fashion/design crossover going the other way, too, with the Brazilian shoe brand Melissa inviting established designers such as the Campana brothers and Zaha Hadid to create shoes for them. And then, completing the fashion-led design circle, Kartell has recently moved into fashion with the launch of its own shoe collections, showing just how merged the two worlds have become. ■

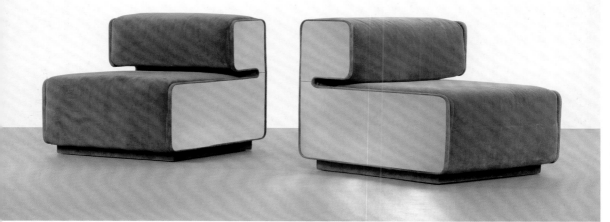

ABOVE: Lounge chairs with
mirrored side panels (c.1970)
manufactured by Pierre Cardin.

RIGHT: Cesendello pendant lamp
(c.1906) by Mariano Fortuny for
Venetia Studium.

Building in calculated failure or stylistic ephemerality

IDEA № 62

PLANNED OBSOLESCENCE

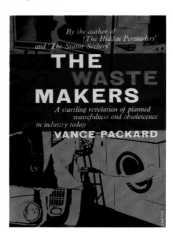

Cover of Vance Packard's The Waste Makers (1960) – this bestselling book exposed the widespread practice of planned obsolescence among manufacturers.

Planned obsolescence is a strategy used by manufacturers to shorten the lifespan of products so that they become obsolete faster and need to be replaced sooner. Today, this practice is largely seen as morally repugnant, yet in some quarters it is still considered crucial to economic growth.

Planned obsolescence in design is the antithesis of **sustainability** and can be seen as a symptom of a broken consumerist culture, where financial greed triumphs over ethical concerns and common sense. The most insidious form of planned obsolescence is when manufacturers cynically incorporate parts into products that are calculated to fail in such a way after a certain period of time that it is cheaper to replace the entire product rather than repair the failed component. Another way of accelerating the life cycle of a product is through its **styling**, which can render its **aesthetics** much less desirable when newer, more fashionably styled models come onto the market – typical examples being found in the car industry and the mobile phone market. This type of **style**-driven obsolescence was first introduced by General Motors, when it set up its Art and Color Section in 1927 in order to instigate a system of annual stylistic changes so as to minimize the aesthetic longevity of its cars. Headed by Harley Earl, it was later renamed the Style Section in 1937.

The consequential sales up-tick enjoyed by GM caught the attention of various design commentators, including the American journalist Christine Frederick, who argued that society as a whole would benefit economically if people bought more goods, and that the best way of ensuring this happened was to accelerate the life cycle of products through what she termed 'creative waste' – meaning planned obsolescence. With no thought for its potential environmental impact, planned or built-in obsolescence was generally seen as a necessary economy booster during the 1930s – more product purchases meant more jobs, which equalled a booming economy, at least in theory.

The term 'planned obsolescence' was actually coined by Bernard London, a Russian-American real-estate broker, who penned a pamphlet in 1932 entitled *Ending the Depression Through Planned Obsolescence*. In it he argued for the government to assign 'a lease of life' to products that 'would be sold and used within the term of their existence'; after that allotted time had expired they 'would become legally dead' and be destroyed if there was widespread unemployment so that 'new products would constantly … take the place of the obsolete, and the wheels of industry would be kept going and employment regularized and assured for the masses'.

This almost messianic belief in the economic benefits of a never-ending supply of latest, must-have things fuelled the American Dream throughout the postwar period and into the 1950s. In North America, home-makers were offered an endless supply of fashionably designed goods via ad campaigns that promised to make their lives easier and happier.

In 1960, however, the first major exposé of this abhorrent manufacturing strategy was published by Vance Packard. Entitled *The Waste Makers*, it described the practice of planned obsolescence as 'the systematic attempt of business to make us wasteful, debt-ridden, permanently discontented individuals'. Half a century later, nothing much has changed, despite global environmental concerns and the growing realization that sustainability can only be achieved by reducing waste.

And yet, an increasing awareness of this cynical practice is reflected in the popularity of design icons – the antithesis of buy-it-today-sling-it-tomorrow goods (see page 122). But perhaps even more encouraging is the phenomenon of Repair Cafés – a concept launched by Martine Postma in Amsterdam in 2009 – with their resident 'fixperts' on hand to help mend all kinds of things that would otherwise end up in landfill. ∎

Rocket-shaped tail fin of a 1959 Cadillac – these extravagant elements appeared for only one year and marked the zenith of stylistic planned obsolescence in automotive design.

Allowing technology to shape products

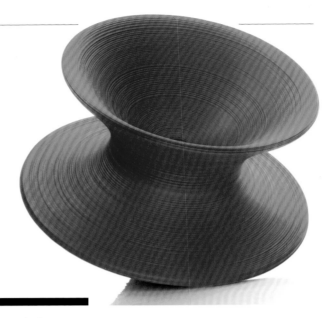

IDEA № 63
PROCESS-LED DESIGN

Although the phrase 'process-led design' is regularly used by designers and manufacturers to describe a manufacturing- and technology-driven approach to problem-solving, it is rarely heard outside the world of professional **industrial design** practice.

Spun chair (2010) by Thomas Heatherwick for Magis – the form of this rocking chair and the striations on its body are a direct outcome of the rotational moulding process used in its manufacture.

That is because most people do not think too much about the technological processes used to make things, from metal stamping, spinning and casting, to glass blowing, casting and etching, to wood carving, lathing and laminating, to all the innumerable kinds of plastic moulding – to name just a few. All man-made things are not only the result of design forethought (conception and planning) but also making (doing), which involves the harnessing of different production processes in order to turn ideas and raw materials into physical products.

A process-led approach to design invariably begins with the material: How best to turn iron into a cooking pot? Casting. Or strips of willow into a picnic basket? Weaving. Or a thermoplastic into a drinks bottle? Blow moulding. All manufacturing processes have their own technical parameters, so when a designer adopts a process-led approach to problem-solving, they study these factors in order to come up with a design solution that best exploits them.

One of humanity's greatest inventions, the incandescent light bulb, is a shining exemplar of an early 'modern' process-led design. Its iconic form is ultimately the way it is because its design was wholly informed by the then cutting-edge technology used to manufacture it – with the glass bulb providing the necessary vacuum-filled chamber for the delicate filament that sat at its core. Likewise, from the mid-1920s onwards, the Hungarian-born architect-designer Marcel Breuer created a range of tubular metal furniture that was wholly informed by the groundbreaking manufacturing process that had been pioneered by the Mannesmann brothers in Germany in the 1890s, which enabled the production of seamless steel tubing. This new material quite literally reshaped the formal vocabulary of furniture design during the interwar period.

Throughout the 1930s, other designers also began exploiting the design potential of new manufacturing techniques, with the American designer Russel Wright creating an extensive range of homewares made of spun aluminium, and the Norwegian sculptor Jean Heiberg devising a revolutionary ergonomic housing for L. M. Ericsson's DBH 1001 telephone (1931) that was guided by the formal potential of moulded Bakelite. Meanwhile, Alvar and Aino Aalto devised techniques for moulding and laminating wood that they then used to create furniture, the like of which had never been seen before. During the postwar period, Charles and Ray Eames similarly created furniture that was entirely process-driven, from their Moulded Plywood Seating series (1945–46) to their landmark Plastic Shell Group of chairs (1948–50) – indeed they personally helped develop the technological processes that enabled these designs to be manufactured.

More recently, other process-led seating designs have come prominently to the fore, including: Konstantin Grcic's MYTO chair (2007), the form of which was only made possible by the high flow-rate of a new polybutylene-terephthalate polymer developed by

BASF; and Thomas Heatherwick's Extrusion bench (2009) and Spun chair (2010), the playful designs of which are wholly informed by the form-giving potential of aluminium extrusion and plastic rotational-moulding techniques.

Today, an advanced type of process-led design is evolving that relates to **parametricism**, whereby a design is process-grown using generative software. This type of digitally determined and artificially evolved design is still only in its technological infancy but is already bearing interesting design fruit, from Mathias Bengtsson's Growth table (the form of which was devised using generative software) to a 3D-printed robot recently developed at the

University of Oslo that speculates on the idea of robots being able to self-generatively design themselves so that they can 'evolve, manufacture and assemble themselves without human input'.[38] ∎

ABOVE LEFT: Preliminary sketch of Tŷ Nant water bottle (1999) by Ross Lovegrove, showing water-flow patterns that helped determine the vessel's form.

ABOVE: Tŷ Nant water bottle (1999–2001) by Ross Lovegrove for Tŷ Nant – using blow-moulded PET, the design exploits the material's plasticity, while conveying the preciousness and fluidity of its contents.

Designs inspired by nature's forms and systems

IDEA № 64
ORGANIC DESIGN

'Organic design' refers to objects and buildings that exhibit the characteristics of a biological entity or organism, or that are based on biological forms or systems. As a holistic and human-centric approach to problem-solving, it has long motivated designers to seek better solutions inspired by 'designs' found in the natural world.

Frank Lloyd Wright was one of the great pioneers of organic design. His **Gesamtkunstwerk** buildings were holistically conceived as unified compositions that were intended to be harmoniously in tune with their natural surroundings. During the 1930s the Finnish architect-designer Alvar Aalto similarly developed a language of organic form that would come to redefine Modernism during the interwar period.

Fundamentally, organic design was and still is about propagating better functional, intellectual and emotional **connections** between object and user through a more mindful, structurally appropriate, visually seductive, human-centric approach. Its tenets were outlined in the catalogue accompanying MoMA's 1941 'Organic Design in Home Furnishings' competition, which stated that this new approach was about 'a harmonious organization of the parts within the whole, according to structure, material and purpose. With this definition there can be no vain ornamentation or superfluity, but the part of beauty is none the less great – in ideal choice of materials, in visual refinement, and in the rational elegance of things intended for use.' During the postwar era, organic design became increasingly associated with the concept of **good design**. It was not confined to products either. It also found

architectural expression – most notably in Eero Saarinen's extraordinary TWA Terminal (1956–62) at New York's John F. Kennedy Airport.

The success of organic design during the postwar years prompted the rise of biomorphism, which rather than attempting to capture the abstract essence of natural forms, distorted them for purely decorative purposes. Indeed, during this period, kitsch kidney-shaped coffee tables and boomerang sofas became somewhat of a 1950s interior-design cliché. Despite this short-lived stylistic appropriation, the precepts of organic design continued over subsequent decades to guide a particular approach to design problem-solving, especially with regard to the increasing use of **ergonomics**.

During the 1990s, a new form of organic design emerged, initially exemplified by the work of Ross Lovegrove, which married state-of-the-art manufacturing technologies and high-performance materials with careful studies of natural forms. This led to, for example, the shapes made by falling water informing the design of a water bottle, or the lightweight yet strong structure of bone inspiring the back of a chair. Futuristic-looking yet possessing a strong primal resonance, these designs are described by Lovegrove as 'supernatural', and they inspired other designers to explore a more organic language of design.

As **CAD/CAM** software became increasingly sophisticated, it became possible for designers to model ever more complex forms, which were often inspired by nature. This trend became even more emphatic with the introduction of generative software programs in the mid-2000s, such as those associated with **parametricism**. At the same time, **3D printing** techniques became not only better but also more affordable, which meant that the complex forms generated with such software could be produced using additive manufacturing systems. This has led to the creation of various 'biotech' **design art** pieces, most notably Joris Laarman's Bone Chair (2006) and Arm Chair (2007), and Mathias Bengtsson's Cellular chair (2011) and Growth table (2014), which reveal a strong sculptural organicism that is both beautiful and complex, much like nature itself.

Today, the widespread use of **biomimicry** in design practice can be seen as the logical evolution of organic design, for it takes nature as its model, measure and mentor. More than anything, organic design is about cultivating better connections. It is based on the knowledge that people are psychologically predisposed to biological forms, and that the visual and tactile seduction of such forms can provoke an inbuilt emotional response, often on a subliminal level. ∎

Capisco office chair (1984) by Peter Opsvik for Håg – also known as 'The Saddle Chair', this design was based on the dynamic sitting posture used when riding a horse. Designed from an ergonomic standpoint, it provides continuous padded support and automatically adjusts position in response to the body's movements.

Taking the measure of man, and designing for people

IDEA № 65
ERGONOMICS

Ergonomics is the scientific and systematic study of human characteristics and their relationship to products, systems and environments. Based on human measurement studies and psychological data, ergonomics enables designers to create solutions that work in harmony with their users.

Because of this, ergonomics is an extremely useful tool for designers hoping to create products that are safer to use, better-performing and ultimately more healthful – which is really what the development of **good design** is all about.

The origin of ergonomics goes back to the nineteenth century, with the study of anthropometrics – the systematic collection and correlation of human body measurements. However, this kind of data was not applied widely to design until after World War II. During the wartime, a large amount of research had been undertaken by the US military into anthropometrics – or 'human factors'. The resulting data gave postwar designers a new understanding of how to create designs that would work better because they were based on a more in-depth knowledge of the physical needs of the user.

Rather than being based on an average measurement of the human body, ergonomics is instead based on a range of average measurements. As Henry Dreyfuss, one of the great pioneers of human factors in the postwar period, explained: 'we must consider the variations from small to large in men and women. After all, people come in assorted rather than average sizes.' His book *Designing for People* (1955), was hugely influential, and anthropometrics were subsequently used to inform the ergonomic development of all kinds of products, from large hand-operated machinery and tractors to telephones and office chairs.

During the 1960s and 1970s, the use of ergonomics in design increased dramatically, evolving from anthropometrics to also encompass anatomical, physiological and psychological factors in conjunction with a greater understanding of human behaviours and capabilities. By quantifying the potential users' needs from a scientific viewpoint, ergonomics enables designers to create design solutions that are safer and more user-friendly, being easier to understand and use. In the workplace, for instance, the use of ergonomics in the design of office equipment and office furniture leads to greater working efficiency and productivity. A product designed from an ergonomic standpoint is also often more comfortable to use than a similar product that has not.

Whether at work, travelling or at home, products that have been informed by ergonomics help to minimize the risk of accidents and injuries. Ergonomics are, therefore, an important consideration for designers when creating products that need to meet health and **safety** standards.

Since the introduction of **CAD** systems, ergonomic data has been increasingly implemented in many different types of design – the reason for this is that when you design a product based on ergonomic considerations, it generally performs better and therefore sells better, too. As the Chartered Institute of Ergonomics and Human Factors observes, 'Ergonomics is about "fit": the fit between people, the things they do, the objects they use and the environments they work, travel and play in. If good fit is achieved, the stresses on people are reduced. They are more comfortable, they can do things more quickly and easily, and they make fewer mistakes.' ■

So easy to use, you don't need any instructions

IDEA № 66

FUNCTIONAL INTUITIVENESS

Functional intuitiveness is the holy grail for most **industrial design**ers – the aim being to make a product that virtually anyone can operate without any form of explanation.

This is achieved by designing a user interface that is so efficient and easily understandable that it enables a product to be used intuitively.

Certainly, two other big design ideas help industrial designers achieve this kind of operational Zen – **clarity of layout** and **essentialism**. Both of these are all about de-cluttering a design visually and physically, for the truth of the matter is that the simpler the product, the easier it is to operate.

Dieter Rams at Braun understood this better than most. The electronic products that he and his team designed featured a remarkable clarity of layout that allowed them to be operated easily by anyone picking them up. For instance, any of the numerous alarm

clocks that Dietrich Lubs designed for Braun can be used with infinite ease, for he employed the simplest and most logical colour system of red, green and yellow to highlight the key on and off buttons and the time-changing dial at the back.

Today, functional intuitiveness is crucial to the success of a product, which is why, over the last couple of decades or so, designers have gone to increasing lengths to design into their solutions a high degree of operational clarity – whether it is an electric oven or a robotic vacuum cleaner. Most people today have neither the time nor inclination to read thick manuals, and have instead come to expect instant 'plug-and-play' accessibility.

It is, however, products with digital interfaces – such as mobile phones, tablets, desktop computers, car dashboard displays, satellite-navigation systems and the like – where the idea of functional intuitiveness really comes into its own and can make a product a pleasure to use, rather than something that is frustrating and time-consuming to operate. In our increasingly digitally complex 24/7 lives, easy-to-understand functionality is one of the best ways for designers to forge those all-important emotional **connections** between products and their users. Jony Ive and his team at Apple are among the most skilled practitioners of this form-follows-intuitive-function approach to design, which is all about creating the

Detail of the BNC012 alarm clock – this is an updated version of an earlier clock designed by Dieter Lubs for Braun in 1987.

most elegant and easily comprehensible connections between man and machine.

The ultimate goal of designing a high degree of functional intuitiveness into a product is that its operation becomes a thoughtless act, in the truest sense of the phrase. And the best way of achieving this is to base a design's operation on close observation and real-world testing. Ultimately, functional intuitiveness is all about coming up with a design solution – which could be a product, a service or a space – that is so user-friendly that the users interacting with it do not even have to think about it. Increasingly, so-called smart products are featuring a

'The simpler the product, the easier it is to operate.'

predictive element, and with the rapid onset of machine-learning technology, this will only accelerate, which means that functional intuitiveness will be achieved ever more efficaciously in the designs of tomorrow. ■

670 lounge chair and 671 ottoman (1956) by Charles and Ray Eames for Herman Miller – a modern interpretation of an English club chair that was intended to have the 'warm receptive look of a well-used first baseman's mitt'.

BELOW: Exploded drawing of the Eameses' 670 lounge chair and 671 ottoman by Charles Kratka (with lettering by Sister Corita Kent) showing components and connections.

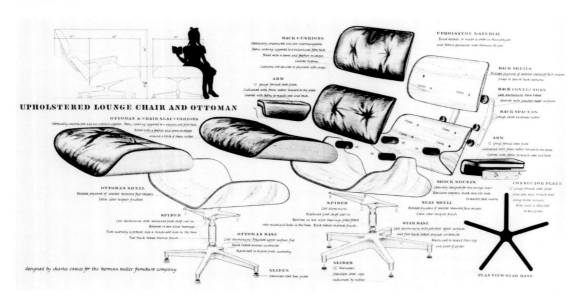

Designing from a holistic standpoint

ESU 400-N (1950) by Charles and
Ray Eames for Herman Miller –
a variant configuration from
a highly integrated modular
storage system that relied on
good constructional connections.

IDEA № 67
CONNECTIONS

The idea of connections in design is a powerfully persuasive one, which was first mooted by Charles and Ray Eames in the late 1940s with the development of their plywood chairs. In a film they made in 1961 to explain the concept behind their ECS storage system, Charles declared, 'The details are not the details. They make the product. The connections, the connections, the connections.'

The Eameses evolved and enlarged their idea of connections, with Charles later noting, 'Eventually everything connects – people, ideas, objects. The quality of the connections is the key to quality per se.' As America's most high-profile design couple during the latter half of the twentieth century, a retrospective exhibition of the Eameses' work, entitled 'Connections: The Work of Charles and Ray Eames', was held at the Frederick S. Wight Art Gallery at UCLA in 1976/77, which tellingly reveals just how key the concept was to an understanding of their work, as well as to its critical and commercial success.

Fundamentally, the Eameses' idea of connections was about looking at the process of design in a completely interconnected and holistic way so as to take on board the various levels of connections that need to be addressed when designing a solution to a particular problem – from structural and material connections to economic and emotional connections. The exhibition's accompanying catalogue included an essay by the well-known design thinker and communications consultant Ralph Caplan, who summed up the concept thus: 'the art of solving problems by making connections. Connections between what? Between such disparate materials as wood and steel, between such seemingly alien disciplines as physics and painting, between clowns and mathematical concepts, between people – architects and mathematicians and poets and philosophers and corporate executives.'

Two years later Caplan wrote another publication focusing on this idea for the furniture manufacturer Herman Miller entitled *Notes on Connection: Some Incomplete Thoughts with Room for Improvements*, one of a series of four 'notebooks' primarily intended for in-house consumption among the company's employees. That same year Caplan also chaired a conference programme entitled 'Making Connections' at the International Design Conference in Aspen, which was where Charles Eames gave his last public presentation. For Eames, the idea of connections was intrinsic to design and architecture, and was as close as he ever got to 'a unified field theory of design', as Caplan put it, yet as this august critic noted, he probably never thought of it in those terms.

The incredible growth and expansion of **digitalization** over the last three decades has made the creation of connections within design easier than ever, for it has allowed an unprecedented level of global cultural cross-pollination between not only disciplines, but also design practitioners and design thinkers across the world. The Eamesian idea of connections has also undoubtedly inspired the growing phenomenon of **haptic** feedback systems being integrated into various product designs, from cars, computers and smartphones to gaming consoles and robotic vacuum cleaners, which is largely about forging sensorial connections between object and user. ∎

Designing to minimize the risk of danger and injury

IDEA № 68
SAFETY

The concept of safety in design first came to prominence in the mid-1960s thanks to the American attorney and activist Ralph Nader's best-selling book *Unsafe at Any Speed: the Designed-In Dangers of the American Automobile* (1965), which uncovered the US car industry's cynical disregard for the wellbeing of its customers.

In his damning publication, Nader specifically revealed the fatal flaws that were inherent in the design of the Chevrolet Corvair (1960) – a rear-mounted, air-cooled engine car manufactured by General Motors that tended to roll when cornering sharply because it lacked a front anti-roll bar that would have helped stabilize it. This serious omission was due to cost-cutting measures; if the device had been fitted, it would have protected the car's passengers from this deadly shortcoming. But what was even more concerning was that GM was aware of the defect, yet continued to produce and sell the Corvair – thereby putting corporate profit above consumer safety. In fact, Nader was able to reveal that at this time GM was spending around $700 per car on **styling**, yet only a derisory 23 cents on safety features.

As a result of Nader's findings, the United States Congress subsequently passed 25 different pieces of consumer legislation, which heralded the beginning of the product-liability industry, as well as a greater awareness of design safety issues among both designers and consumers. Importantly, the threat of being made accountable through fines or possible imprisonment for any injuries caused by an unsafe product made manufacturers focus much more on safety.

Safety is a fundamental human requirement, and companies that have a good track record in this area – such as Volvo, who throughout its history

has been a pioneer of numerous safety **innovation**s, from the three-point seat belt (1959) to collision avoidance technology (2006) – tend to reap economic advantages as a result because they are seen to care more about the buyers of their cars. This ultimately breeds customer loyalty as well as prestige. One of the greatest developments in the ongoing improvement of car safety has been the crash test dummy – with the world's first dummy, known as Sierra Sam, having been designed in 1949 by Samuel W. Alderson to test aircraft ejection seats. Since then, dummies have become increasingly sophisticated in their deliverance of data feedback, which in turn has helped designers and engineers develop ever-safer cars, whether in the form of more shock-absorbent children's car seats or more rigid side-impact protection systems.

Often the design of safer products is based as much on well-informed material choices as on **ergonomics**. For example, over the last 25 years in Britain there have been strict regulations concerning the flammability of materials used for upholstered furniture and bedding, which has led to countless lives being saved. But over and above the development of inherently safer products, 'safety in design' also covers the development of all kinds of equipment specifically devised for enhancing protection, from fire extinguishers and smoke alarms to specialist welding helmets and hazmat

(hazardous material) suits. Often these types of designs have to meet stringent government safety standards, which have been devised by relevant industry experts prior to undergoing a process of testing and certification. Likewise, other types of product designs, such as toys or domestic appliances, have to comply with rafts of different government safety legislation, which helps to make them safer to use.

And yet there are still far too many products available for sale that are not safe, or are just plain dangerous. These might be counterfeit aircraft parts or fake medical equipment, or a doll or toy car cheaply made in some far-flung country that does not have a developed culture of safety standards for manufactured goods. As consumers, the best way of avoiding dangerous things is to buy only products of high design and manufacturing quality from reputable companies. Enhancing your safety in terms of the products you use really is that simple because ultimately **good design** is life-enhancing. Poor design can be life-changing, too – but not in a good way. ■

'Dummies have become increasingly sophisticated.'

ABOVE: A crash test dummy carelessly using a mobile phone while driving with a crash test dummy passenger, 2009.

RIGHT: Zero 1 impact-reducing football helmet (2016) by VICIS – this innovative flexible helmet has a multilayered construction that includes a bendable outer shell and was designed to tackle the problem of concussion in American football.

Repurposing existing objects for new design ends

OBJET TROUVÉ (THE FOUND OBJECT)

Throughout history, humans have found things and repurposed them – the perfectly formed stone that was made into a mallet head, or the porcupine quills that were used to make needles, or the deer's antler made into a pickaxe. Indeed, the whole notion of the hunter-gatherer implies not only the finding of food, but also the sourcing of things that can be turned into useful tools.

The specifically modern notion of the objet trouvé, or 'found object', emerged in 1912 with Pablo Picasso pasting a photograph of a chair onto a canvas. A couple of years later, the Dada artist Marcel Duchamp took this idea of objet trouvé – meaning an existing object consciously repurposed into a work of fine art – and transformed it into a definable art form with his 'ready-mades'. His first artwork of this kind was *Bottle Rack* (1914), which was then famously followed up with *Fountain* (1917), a urinal that was signed 'R. Mutt'.

Despite the enormous impact Duchamp's work had on the international art world, the concept of readymades did not transfer across to the world of design for several decades. Design is primarily a practical, problem-solving discipline, strongly linked to industry and commerce, so for most of the twentieth century, **rationalism** dominated its direction. The readymade was viewed as far too radical and conceptual for serious design consideration.

During World War II and its immediate aftermath, however, rationing necessitated making use of any materials that were readily available, and this led designers to start incorporating wartime surplus 'found

objects' into their work. One of the first was a chair designed by the American designer William H. Miller Jr around 1944, which incorporated wartime netting and a Vinylite inner tube.

It was, however, the Mezzadro (Sharecropper) and Sella stools – incorporating a tractor seat and a racing bicycle seat respectively, and designed by Achille and Pier Giacomo Castiglioni for an exhibition entitled 'Colours and Forms in Today's Home', held in Como in 1957 – that became the first designs to be celebrated as Modern readymade products. As the design historian Silvana Annicchiarico notes of these two landmark designs, 'The designers' compositional principle is clearly provocative; it assembles morphemes in a new semantic context in which irony is combined with the object's overall rationale.'[39] Yet tellingly, even though widely lauded designs such as these were only eventually put into production by Zanotta in 1971, it was the Castiglioni brothers' later Toio floor lamp (1962), which cleverly utilized a 'found' car headlamp, that actually made it into production first, with the progressive lighting manufacturer Flos.

The idea of repurposing found objects into new designs was later

Toio (Toy) floor light (1962) by Achille and Pier Giacomo Castiglioni for Flos – this design comprises a playful assemblage of found objects, including an imported US car headlight.

exploited by Alessandro Mendini through a series of so-called redesigns, which included the Proust armchair (1978) – a 'found' replica antique chair that Mendini decorated with Signac-inspired painted dots. As Mendini explained, 'Besides the idea of obtaining a piece of design based on [an] unusual ... design process, I also wanted to ... make a culturally grounded object based on a false one ... a piece of kitsch, a fake-antique.'[40]

Crucially, Mendini's redesigns were the progenitors of a new kind of **design art** based on the assemblage of found objects, which emerged in the early 1980s. Ron Arad's Rover chair (1981), comprising an existing car seat on a frame of repurposed scaffolding, was an early outcome of this new spirit in design. It was, however, Tom Dixon and Mark Brazier-Jones who would later coin the term 'Creative Salvage' (for the title of an exhibition) in 1983 to describe a new kind of Neo-Punk designer-making that involved roughly welding together found objects, such as frying pans, manhole covers and antique railings, into poetic, one-off design art pieces. This repurposing of objets trouvés has since been closely identified with the New Dutch Design movement and avant-garde designers such as Martino Gamper. As a well-established approach to design, it has also spawned the related idea of **design hacking**. ■

Mezzadro stool (1962) by Achille and Pier Giacomo Castiglioni for Zanotta – the name of this ready-made design means 'sharecropper' and alludes to its incorporation of a 'found' tractor seat.

Investing personality in design

IDEA № 70
CHARACTER

Incorporating 'character' used to be one of the most subversive ideas in design. For much of the twentieth century, Modernism ruled the design roost, and its central aim was design **universality** derived from a reductivist aesthetic **purity**.

Bubu container stools (1991) by Philippe Starck for XO – this cutely named design epitomizes its creator's whimsical humour and his ability to imbue objects with identifiable character.

Indeed, the expunging of individualistic character from objects and buildings became a defining trait of the **Modern Movement**, for the plainer and less sense of personality a design had, the more likely it would be to appeal universally, or so the argument went.

The consequence of this **form follows function** approach was a certain emotional sterility even among the acknowledged Modernist icons of design, created by the likes of Marcel Breuer and Le Corbusier. And while the work of Modern Movement pioneers such as these does have an identifiable 'signature' character, it is not easily engaged with on an emotional level, at least in comparison to, say, a contemporaneous design by Alvar Aalto. Certainly, in lesser hands the results of this one-size-fits-all design mindset amounted to an all too often vanilla-like blandness and aesthetic triteness. The problem was that while most people are happy to use serviceable, rationally begat utilitarian things in their everyday lives, they often find it easier to connect emotionally with objects that have been designed to delight the senses, or express their creator's individuality, or transmit ideas. This is because the personality or thoughts of a designer shine through such designs, and that is what people respond to – both consciously and subconsciously. It is part of the human condition to be attracted to things that give sensorial pleasure, or that are thought-provoking or humorous.

Interestingly, two of the most successful seating designs to fall within

the pantheon of **good design** possess a palpable sense of character. Charles and Ray Eames' LCW chair (1945) has an alluring anthropomorphism, with its poised frame and moulded-plywood seat elements, while the joyful character of Arne Jacobsen's 3017 chair (1955) is derived from the smile-like line of its seat's front edge. Likewise, George Nelson's Ball clock (1949) conveys a playful spirit, while still having been rationally conceived. But these good-humoured mid-century icons are largely the exception to the Modernist rule.

In Scandinavia, however, designers during the postwar era and into the 1960s and 1970s were less in thrall to the Modernist concept of universality, and mostly created work that had a strong sense of character derived from the use of forms inspired by the natural world and/or craft-derived techniques. Indeed, within Nordic design, the importance of 'form-giving' reveals an approach to design that understands the emotional resonance of eye-pleasing, tactile shapes, and is less interested in purely functional concerns per se. The result is that Scandinavian designs from this period often have a more emotionally engaging character, whether it is a Hans Wegner chair or a Timo Sarpaneva vase. And it is for this reason that these types of design enjoy such longevity of appeal.

It was, though, only with the rise of **Pop** design and **Anti-Design** in the 1960s that the idea of infusing consumer products with character really came back into play, as the various furniture

pieces produced by Gufram and Poltronova demonstrated to dramatic effect. This trend became more emphatic as the influence of **semiotics** began infiltrating design teaching during the 1970s and ultimately led to the emergence of the outlandish cartoonish designs of Post-Modernism in the late 1970s and 1980s.

It was, however, Philippe Starck who best grasped the commercial potential of character in design. He did this by constructing personalities for his designs, giving them human-sounding names such as Lilla Hunter and Dr Glob, or childish nicknames such as Bubu and Aha. This sense of personality was also reflected in the expressive forms of his designs. Indeed, the friendly character of Starck's furniture expressed a new globalized, non-verbal language of design that transcended national and cultural boundaries.

Another designer who has exploited the emotional connectivity of character is Stefano Giovannoni, who has designed a host of personality-infused homewares. More recently, Studio Job has created characterful **design art** pieces that likewise express the idea of form follows fun. ∎

Anna G corkscrew (1994) by Alessandro Mendini for Alessi – this figurative design, which gives a friendly personality to an everyday household item, became an instant hit, selling 20,000 units in its first year.

The drive for ever smaller design solutions

IDEA № 71

MINIATURIZATION

Miniaturization has been an idea-motivated trend in design throughout the modern era because as technology has evolved, so has the capacity for doing more with less.

The real breakthrough in product miniaturization came about with the advent of the world's first transistor, which was famously developed at Bell Labs in 1947. By 1952, transistors were being incorporated into the design of hearing aids, thereby considerably reducing their bulk. Then, thanks to an early licensing transistor-technology agreement between Western Electric and Tokyo Tsushin Kogyo (later Sony) in 1953, which was subsequently approved by the Japanese government in 1954, miniaturization went on to become a defining feature of postwar Japanese design as the Tokyo-based company developed increasingly compact consumer electronics. Included among these products was Sony's TR-55 (1955), which was not only Japan's first transistor radio, but also a remarkable feat of miniaturization, measuring just 8.9 x 14 x 3.8 cm (3.5 x 5.5 x 1.5 inches). It was, however, the company's later and far more compact TR-63 (1957) that heralded the era of miniaturized pocket-sized electronics.

In 1965, Gordon Moore, the founder of Intel, famously predicted that the number of transistors would double per integrated circuit every year – this was later revised to 18 months and is now known as Moore's Law. The upshot is that the exponential increase of transistors per microchip has meant that electronic products have, over the years, become ever more compact and powerful. Indeed, the unrelenting drive for increasing miniaturization means we now have fly-sized airborne surveillance bots and tiny implantable medical devices that incorporate nanotechnologies. This ultra-miniaturization will undoubtedly become an increasingly common aspect of contemporary **industrial design**.

The process of miniaturization, however, often involves a lot more than just the incorporation of faster and smaller processors and the scaling down of components. For example, when a product incorporates a number of different technologies, it is often found that reducing the scale of one element in the design will adversely affect the performance tolerances of another. Nevertheless, where there is intelligent engineering, there is a way. Consequently, design engineers working in collaboration with manufacturers who are willing to make the necessary investment in time and money are increasingly able to develop smaller yet smarter products.

The convergence of technologies has also helped the miniaturization of products, too – or, in some cases, their complete physical 'ephemeralization', as Richard Buckminster Fuller would have put it. Take, for example, a smartphone and all the analogue-age products it now has imbedded into its functionality, from an alarm clock and compass to flashlight and music player, all of which have been effectively miniaturized into bits and bytes thanks to the process of **digitalization**.

Ultimately, the drive for ever-greater miniaturization is leading us into a brave new world of molecular-scale design – with nanomotors, nanopumps and nanorobotics already being developed to power infinitesimal micromachines with a mind-boggling range of potential applications, from in vitro drug delivery to toxic clean-up operations. What this will all mean for design practice only time will tell, but one thing is for sure: designers will become captivated by the extraordinary problem-solving possibilities thrown up by these profound advances in micro-miniaturization. ∎

The promise of trustworthiness and authenticity

IDEA № 72

BRANDING

Branding is the means by which a company distinguishes its products from those of its competitors, and is used as a way of communicating its corporate values and beliefs. At its most basic, a brand is the promise of authenticity and trustworthiness based on an already established track record.

It is used by manufacturers as a means to add value to a design, for people are generally prepared to pay more for a branded product thanks to its promise of better performance – which may or may not actually be true.

The word 'branding' originally referred to the practice of searing the hides of livestock with hot irons for purposes of identification. Today, of course, branding is more often used to refer to the creation and management of a company's identity or corporate personality. Generally, the building of a firm's identity falls within the remit of visual communication design – logos, **packaging**, marketing materials, websites, social media platforms, and so on. However, the way in which it chooses to design its physical products can help establish a powerful brand, too.

Indeed, most design-led manufacturing companies – from Apple and Sony to Kartell and Alessi to Muji and IKEA – have an identifiable and distinguishing language of design, known as house **style**, that is as much a part of their brand identity as their logo. More often than not, design and brand are largely indivisible, and in many cases, although a product might come 'branded' with a logo, if you removed that logo you would still be able to identify the product – whether it was an Apple laptop or a Ducati motorbike. This is because the individual design approach or **design management** strategies a company adopts often result in its products having a shared familial style or look, even if their range of

products has actually been designed by a number of different designers.

Within most companies a set of brand guidelines has been carefully and strategically established that not only cover, the design of marketing materials and the like, but the development of physical products, too. One of the best ways of creating a strong brand identity is by using an evolutionary approach to design so that each generation of a product is a technological improvement and a more honed design than the one that went before. This way, the core brand identity of the product is not lost but rather enhanced. A good example of this is the Porsche 911, which has been in production for over 55 years, yet its design DNA is traceable throughout its steady, incremental evolution over that time.

In today's interconnected world, branding in design has become increasingly important to the commercial global success of products. Indeed, brand messages act as a transcultural language that can be understood on a non-verbal level – in a sea of similar products, people tend to choose those that are made by companies whose values they know and can identify with. But no matter how much advertising and marketing money is thrown at building a brand, ultimately its core values depend on the design of its products. As any serious large-scale manufacturer will tell you, a brand is only as good as its last product, for it can take years to build a brand, but only one serious product recall to damage it irreparably. ∎

TOP: Cans of Coca-Cola from the 'Share a Coke' marketing campaign (2013) – the traditional Coke logo is replaced with different names in order to personalize bottles and cans.

ABOVE: Coca-Cola advertising image (1950s) used on a vintage Coke-vending machine.

RIGHT: Apple logo (1977) by Rob Janoff for Apple – shown here adorning the entrance of the Apple store on 5th Avenue, New York.

Futuristic visions for a better tomorrow's world

THE WORLD OF TOMORROW

Designers have long dreamt of what 'the world of tomorrow' might look like. Indeed, it is one of the most tantalizing concepts in the world of design, for it allows designers to think outside the box of their contemporary reality and make futuristic projections that may or may not come true.

Città Nuova (New City) urban planning proposal (1914) by Antonio Sant'Elia – this remarkably progessive scheme reveals just how forward-looking the Italian Futurists were.

Some of the earliest modern design expressions of this entrancement with the future came from the Italian Futurists – a consciously avant-garde cultural movement founded in Milan in 1909, which lauded technological progress for its own sake. Antonio Sant'Elia's utopian proto-Brutalist Città Nuova (New City) of 1914, and Fortunato Depero's Cubist-like textile and clothing designs, for example, reflected the Futurists' rejection of **historicism** and nature in favour of a forward-looking language of design that accorded with the burgeoning Machine Age.

A decade on, this desire fully coalesced in the design of Arne Jacobsen and Flemming Lassen's competition-winning House of the Future (1929), which featured a compact circular plan, a rooftop helipad and even roll-down windows – which at the time must have seemed like a science-fiction take on modern living, yet today looks almost commonplace.

This was followed up by a glut of futuristic design predictions that were showcased at the New York World's Fair of 1939, which was the first international exposition to be entirely focused on the future, presumably in response to the Depression – for what better way was there to shrug off the woes of the day than to speculate on a brighter, better-designed tomorrow. Taking as its central theme 'Building the World of Tomorrow', this exhibition included such futuristic attractions as Westinghouse Electric Corporation's audience-electrifying Elektro robot and Norman Bel Geddes' Futurama, a show-stopping mechanical diorama in the General Motors pavilion – a projection of what America's highway system would look like in 1960 that turned out to be surprisingly accurate in its predictions.

During World War II, the Bohn Aluminum and Brass Corporation ran a series of advertisements that featured futuristic depictions of what the longed-for peacetime might look like – from streamlined locomotives and tractors to state-of-the-future refrigerators and merry-go-rounds – once new wartime alloys became available for non-military purposes. Although these visionary designs never came to pass, General Motors subsequently took up the lead in design futures forecasting in the postwar era with its annual Motorama extravaganzas, held from 1949 to 1961. These legendary automobile shows offered up a surfeit of futuristic concept cars, including Harley Earl's extraordinary Firebird XP-21 (1953), a Space Age 'rolling rocket' prototypical design, and his sublime Centurion XP-301 (1956), which was

'Nothing dates as fast as speculative views of the future.'

decades ahead of its time, featuring as it did a rear-view camera linked to a dashboard screen.

It was, however, from the mid-1960s through to the early 1970s when Space Age dreams really came to maturity as a new generation of designers, inspired by the first Moon landing (1969), made utopian projections of future living environments. The German company Bayer famously commissioned Joe Colombo and Verner Panton to create its futuristic *Visiona I* (1969) and *Visiona II* (1970) installations respectively at the Cologne Furniture Fair, which typified the era's general optimism about the future. Colombo opted for an integrated micro-living pod, whereas Panton created a riotously colourful 'Phantasy' landscape that provided visitors with an unforgettable sensory experience. Likewise, the landmark exhibition 'Italy: The New Domestic Landscape' held in 1972 at MoMA in New York featured various future-speculating designs, such as Joe Colombo's Total Furnishing Unit and Ettore Sottsass's Microenvironment.

The oil crisis in 1973, however, ended these utopian visions very quickly, as environmental concerns set in and optimism about the future ebbed away. Suddenly the Space Age looked strangely dated and much less alluring. Indeed, the irony is that nothing dates as fast as speculative views of the future. However, over the succeeding decades there has been a handful of visionary designers, from Luigi Colani in the 1970s to Ross Lovegrove in the 2000s, who have dared to lay out their personal predictions of the future and thereby provide us with thought-provoking glimpses of what design might one day become. And as history has often shown, what seems like science fiction in one era may eventually become a technologically driven design reality in another. ■

Keeping it simple in order to signpost functionality

TP1 portable radio and record player (1959) by Dieter Rams for Braun exemplifies Rams' dictum 'Less but better'.

CLARITY OF LAYOUT

The concept of 'clarity of layout' is most often used with regard to graphic design, but it also applies to many different types of three-dimensional design. It means creating a sense of order within the design of a thing so that its potential users can understand its operation effortlessly.

Within product design, clarity of layout is associated mainly with the exterior appearance and functionality of the types of product that require an operational interface, such as electrical appliances, business machines, white goods and consumer electronics. One of the first companies to become internationally celebrated for the clarity of its products' layouts was the Italian typewriter manufacturer Olivetti. Its Compasso d'Oro-winning Lettera 22 typewriter, designed by Marcello Nizzoli in 1950, is hailed as a classic exemplar of good layout clarity. Ultimately, this can be put down to the fact that, apart from being a talented **industrial design**er, Nizzoli was also a gifted graphic designer – so much so that he was also tasked with designing posters and print advertisements for the Ivrea-based firm. In fact, the skills needed for the laying out of graphic artwork were directly transferable to the layout of machines, and especially their controls.

Another company specializing in consumer electronics that became world-renowned for the clarity of layout of its product designs during the late 1950s was Braun. This was in large part due to Dieter Rams who, in 1956, designed his first product for the company, the SK4 radio and record player, before going on to become its design director – a legendary tenure that lasted from 1961 to 1995. During this period the company's product lines accorded with Rams's 10 principles of **good design**, one of which is that 'Good design makes a product understandable: it clarifies the product's structure. Better still, it can make the product clearly express its function by making use of the user's intuition. At best, it is self-explanatory.'

When a product features an intelligently conceived layout it not only makes its operation easier to understand, it also often gives the design a certain visual **rightness**. Whether it is an aircraft cockpit full of instrumentation, a car's dashboard or the keypad of an ATM, if a layout is well considered, it will have a sense of visual clarity that enables the user to more readily access the design's functionality. Take any Dyson appliance or Apple product, for example, and you will probably be able to figure out how to use it within a very short period of time, without having to read any operating instructions. Both of these companies pride themselves on painstakingly designing into their products a high level of layout clarity in order to ensure the easiest and most intuitive operation possible.

Clarity of layout is also an important aspect of both interior design and exhibition design. This is most often achieved by looking at how users will interact with a particular space and the different objects or features contained within it, and then designing in what is ostensibly a logical interface, whereby the space is delineated into specific functional areas that can be navigated efficiently by anyone entering into it. Ultimately, clarity of layout means eliminating any extraneous elements so that the appearance of a design is both clean and logical in order that its function is more easily understandable and its operation more intuitive. ∎

'Clarity of layout means eliminating any extraneous elements.'

Lettera 22 typewriter (1950) by Marcello Nizzoli for Olivetti is a design masterpiece and an early and influential paragon of clarity of layout.

Products with integrity that are designed in accordance with modern ideals

Cover of the catalogue Good Design: An Exhibition of Home Furnishings Selected by the Museum of Modern Art, New York, for the the Merchandise Mart Chicago, *written by the exhibition's curator Edgar Kaufmann Jr (1950).*

IDEA № 75

GOOD DESIGN

The idea of 'good design' presupposes that there exists such a thing as 'bad design', which clearly is the case, given the amount of meaningless and wasteful tat that is produced each and every year.

But over and above this, a lot of designs are also created that are just plain mediocre, whereas the notion of good design implies a higher level of quality, based on functional excellence, aesthetic refinement and, if possible, a degree of affordability. Throughout the decades, various **design reform**ing organizations and institutions have championed the cause of good design, which was perhaps best summed up by the British designer Gordon Russell, who noted: 'good design is not precious, arty or highfalutin. ... It is true that new **styles** not infrequently start in **luxury** markets ... but **mass production** so spreads the cost that there is no reason why well-designed things should not be available for everyone to buy. The idea that only wealthy people like well-designed things is as false as that they are the only people to get pleasure from looking at flowers, listening to music, or reading Shaw. Equally false is the notion that because a thing is low in price it cannot be of good quality.'

Indeed, for most of the early to mid-twentieth century the concept of good design was explicitly bound to the notion of 'good **taste**', thanks to its promotion by various high-profile institutions and government bodies, including the Museum of Modern Art in New York. In 1950, the museum's Director of **Industrial Design**, Edgar Kaufmann Jr, established the annual exhibition 'Good Design: An Exhibition of Home Furnishings' (which ran until 1955) in collaboration with the Merchandise Mart in Chicago. This event in many ways helped to codify the notion of good design, for only well-made designs characterized by clean lines, practical function, material truthfulness and the restrained use of colour made the grade for inclusion.

During the postwar period, Scandinavian design became so synonymous with the concept of good design that the terms became almost interchangeable. Meanwhile, in Germany, manufacturers and designers alike put their faith in the transformative power of good design, or as they called it *Gute Form*, to rebuild their war-shattered nation. One of the leading proponents of *Gute Form* in Germany was Dieter Rams, who headed up Braun's influential design department from 1961 and helped guide the company's development of a truly impressive portfolio of electronic products that came to epitomize the core values of good design. Indeed, Rams would later write, 'Good design means as little design as possible. ... Design is the effort to make products in such a way that they are useful to people. ... The work of designers can contribute more concretely and effectively toward a more humane existence in the future.'[41] Ultimately, that is what makes the argument for good design still so compelling – and necessary. ■

'Good design means as little design as possible.' – *Dieter Rams*

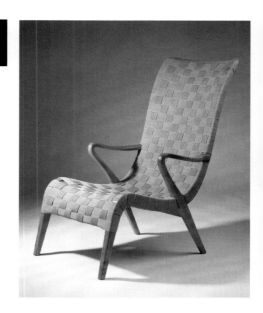

BELOW: CTM (Coffee Table Metal) (1946) by Charles and Ray Eames for Herman Miller – the Eameses range of plywood furniture exemplifies the key characteristics of good design: clean lines, practical function, material truthfulness and the restrained use of colour.

RIGHT: Armchair (c.1937) by Axel Larsson for Svenska Möbelfabrikerna – this Swedish design's ergonomic contours reflect the human-centric nature of good design, as it was pioneered in the Nordic region in the 1920s and 1930s.

Design in balance
with Earth's ecology

IDEA № 76

SUSTAINABILITY

Sustainability in design – also known as environmental design, eco-design or **green design** – is primarily concerned with reducing the amount of materials, waste and energy wherever possible throughout the whole of a product's life cycle. It is inextricably linked to ethical consumerism and the goal of achieving human-ecosystem equilibrium.

The concept of sustainable design was initially pioneered in the 1920s by the American architect and systems theorist Richard Buckminster Fuller, who termed it 'design science'. It was also Fuller who, later in the 1950s, coined the term 'Spaceship Earth', which led people to think of the planet in a more holistic way. With the goal of providing 'the most with the least', Fuller's design science was a problem-solving approach that entailed, as the Buckminster Fuller Institute observes, 'a rigorous, systematic study of the deliberate ordering of the components in our Universe. Fuller believed that this study needs to be comprehensive in order to gain a global perspective when pursuing solutions to problems humanity is facing.'

To achieve this goal, sustainable design must take into consideration holistically a product's entire life cycle, from cradle to grave – the extraction of the raw materials used in its manufacture and the ecological impact of their processing; the energy consumed in the manufacturing process, together with any negative byproducts; the energy required for and the impact of the distribution system; the length of the product's service life; component recovery and the efficiency of re-cyclability; and the ultimate effects of its disposal on the environment through, for example, landfill or incineration, or its reusability, as posited by the idea of **upcycling**.

Although **recycling** can reduce energy consumption, it does not minimize it and can be seen to encourage a throwaway culture, as if there were no upper limit to levels of consumption. Rather than increasing society's capacity to absorb waste, the highest priority must be to reduce the flow of energy and materials through the economy by producing longer-lasting products. **Product durability** is the key to achieving sustainable design – by doubling the life of a product, its environmental impact can be halved.

Products essentially fall into two categories: those that need to be made more durable, and those that need to be made more efficiently disposable – for instance, furniture or light bulbs would fall into the former category, while consumer electronic products such as mobile phones, which are rendered technologically obsolete relatively quickly, fall into the latter category. Beyond the pressing need for more sustainable design solutions, **packaging** is another area of design where much more needs to be done to reduce waste. An excellent example of how this can be achieved is Yves Béhar's award-winning Clever Little Bag concept (2010) for PUMA. This design led to a 65 per cent reduction of paper usage in its packaging, demonstrating how intelligent design thinking can enhance sustainability.

During the early 2000s through to the economic crisis of 2008 there was an enormous focus on green solutions within the design community. However, today one is more likely to find designers in the thrall of technology than concerned with the **morality** of what humanity is doing to the Earth's ecology. Yet in many ways this is because, for most design practices and manufacturers, designing greener has become a given, which means it is not talked about so much. As Marcus Fairs, the founder and editor-in-chief of the influential online architecture and design magazine *Dezeen*, has noted, 'Green became normal'. ∎

Clever Little Bag (2010) by Yves Béhar / Fuseproject for Puma – a more sustainable answer to the traditional shoebox, comprising a reusable and recyclable polyester bag with a die-cut cardboard inset, which uses 65 per cent less material.

Model of the Dymaxion house (c.1929) alongside its inventor, Richard Buckminster Fuller. Suspended from a central mast, this hexagonal five-room dwelling employed minimal materials to maximum effect.

Radio-in-a-Bag (1981) by Daniel Weil for Parenthesis/Apex International Company – a Post-Modern design that subverted the notion of what a radio could look like.

Contesting design of the counterculture

IDEA № 77
ANTI-DESIGN

Anti-Design first emerged in the late 1950s and early 1960s as a counterargument to the prevailing notion of **good design**, which was itself guided by the **Modern Movement**'s dogmatic belief that form should always follow function.

Lassù chair (1974) designed and then burnt symbolically by Alessandro Mendini − the photograph of this legendary performance was taken for the cover of Casabella *magazine, N.391, 1974.*

The main aim of Anti-Design was to demonstrate that Modernism did not possess all the answers when it came to design, as its adherents liked to think, but that in actuality the Modern Movement's doctrinal grip on design practice had become a stultifying force that was inhibiting creative **innovation**. In many ways Anti-Design was the design world's equivalent of Dadaism or Surrealism, a reactionary movement that rejected **rationalism** per se, and sought more imaginative forms of expression.

Initially, Anti-Design sentiments fuelled the rise of the playful **Pop** design movement, with colourful and sculptural designs often taking the form of out-of-context and oversized homages to past **styles** or popular culture that intentionally poked fun at the Modern Movement's pretensions of 'good **taste**'. The lighthearted Anti-Design of Pop design, however, was quickly overtaken by the emergence of various Radical Design groups in Italy, who formulated a more intellectualized and politicized form of Anti-Design. These counter-design groups ultimately gave rise to the short-lived Global Tools collective in 1973, which functioned as a kind of hands-on laboratory for Anti-Design ideas.

Global Tools famously ran design workshops for underprivileged children in the slum areas of Naples, which were social experiments in DIY design creativity. Through this initiative, and others like it, the collective demonstrated that the act of design was not just the preserve of professional practitioners, but that, given the right tools, anyone could be a designer − a powerful proposition, at least within design circles at the time. A similarly provocative Anti-Design statement was provided by Alessandro Mendini in 1974, who undertook an ideal-chair-burning act outside the offices of *Casabella*, where he was editor-in-chief, in order to show that a more meaningful, symbolic-laden form of design could be born phoenix-like from the flames of Modernism's destruction.

The Anti-Design movement in Italy eventually coalesced around Studio Alchimia, founded by Alessandro Guerriero in 1976, and was later internationally popularized by the Memphis design group led by Ettore Sottsass in the early 1980s. With its desire for, as Charles Jencks put it, 'messy vitality over obvious **unity**', Anti-Design eventually evolved into a major international style: Post-Modernism. Around the same time as this was happening, a new brash, raw and youthful expression of Anti-Design was emerging in Britain in the form of the anarchic punk-inspired Creative Salvage move-ment spearheaded by designer-welder Tom Dixon (see page 145).

For designers who chose to work outside the industrial mainstream, or who found it difficult to find a foothold within the world of corporate design practice, Anti-Design offered an alternative design pathway that was both expressive and individualistic. The idea of Anti-Design ultimately changed the course of design, for it helped to generate a more creatively open design landscape, which allowed experimental explorations of form, function and materials to flourish, especially from the 1990s onwards.

Today, Anti-Design continues with the work of designers who use it as a platform for social commentary as well as a conduit for personal **creative expression**, from the 'poor-material' assemblages of the Campana brothers in Brazil, to the craft-meets-tech work of the New Dutch Design movement. ■

Design inspired by popular mass culture

IDEA № 78
POP

With the ascendency of Modern design during the interwar years of the twentieth century, and then the tireless government promotion of **good design** in the postwar period in the United States and Great Britain, by the early 1960s a new generation of young designers and architects was casting about for an alternative design idea that offered a fresh approach. What they came up with was Pop.

Prior to this, the Independent Group, a radical collective of youthful creatives that had been founded in 1952 at the Institute of Contemporary Art (ICA) in London, had already begun a much-needed questioning of the **Modern Movement**'s dominance of art, architecture and design. Independent Group members – including the artists Richard Hamilton and Eduardo Paolozzi, the architects Alison and Peter Smithson, and the cultural critic Reyner Banham – admonished Modernism for being too elitist and called for a more relevant language of art and design to emerge: one that was inspired by, and at the same time celebrated, popular mass culture, such as television shows and movies, advertising and **packaging**, science fiction and pop music. This was the genesis of the Pop art movement, which in turn led to Pop making significant inroads into the world of design.

Richard Hamilton penned the best-ever definition of Pop in a letter to the Smithsons in 1957, in which he defined this new **style** as:

Popular (designed for a mass audience),
Transient (short-term solution),
Expendable (easily forgotten),
Low Cost,
Mass Produced,
Young (aimed at youth),
Witty,
Sexy,
Gimmicky,
Glamorous,
Big Business.

In fact, design was in many ways a much better vehicle for this new movement than fine art, which was never able to shake off its associations with high culture, despite the efforts of artists such as Andy Warhol and Roy Lichtenstein. During the late 1960s and early 1970s, Italy became the epicentre of Pop design, with numerous Radical designers and **Anti-Design** groups creating work that was not only formally inventive and intellectually challenging, but also mocked what was widely regarded as the dogmatism of good design.

Driven by fashion, Pop design was all about style over substance, and ultimately it was only able to thrive in a booming economy. When the recession of the early 1970s kicked in, Pop's throwaway ethos was no longer viable and was eventually supplanted by a form of Neo-**Rationalism**. This was itself swept away by Post-Modernism in the 1980s, which can be considered to some extent a form of Neo-Pop. Today, the playful and irreverent spirit of Pop lives on and can be detected in the characteristic designs of various **industrial design**ers, including most notably, Stefano Giovannoni and Karim Rashid. ∎

Videosphere portable television (1970) by Japan Victor Company (JVC) – based on an astronaut's helmet, this design typifies the Pop obsession with the Space Age future.

'Pop design was all about style over substance.'

C&B catalogue photograph (1969 – photographed by Klaus Zaugg) featuring Gaetano Pesce's Up series. The chairs were vacuum packed into PVC envelopes and then sprang to life when opened, thereby creating Pop design happenings for the home.

LEFT: *Sheraton chairs (1978/1986) by Robert Venturi for Knoll International − these cartoonized seating designs playfully mocked the perceived high culture of past decorative styles.*

ABOVE: *Carlton room divider/ bookcase (1981) by Ettore Sottsas for Memphis − one of the most quintessentially Post-Modern furniture designs of all time.*

More equals more

Vase on Orange Sphere (2017) by Lee Broom for Wedgwood – this limited edition Post-Modern design references the company's famous Panther vase of 1770.

IDEA № 79
LESS IS A BORE

Robert Venturi came up with the dictum 'Less is a bore' as a rebuttal to the phrase **Less is more**, which had been famously popularized by Ludwig Mies van der Rohe. As an idea, it implied that the sterility of Bauhaus-**style** Modernism and the staidness of postwar **good design** had had their day, and that, in fact, more might just be more.

As a status-quo-challenging idea, it helped Post-Modernism contest the **Modern Movement**'s long-held stranglehold on the philosophical foundations of design, and opened up the tantalizing possibility of designing, in the first instance, for delight.

Indeed, 'Less is more' was *the* ideological catchphrase of the Modern Movement, and its reductivist philosophy was perfectly summed up in Mies van der Rohe's *mots justes*. For adherents of Modernism, it had a satisfyingly emphatic quality, which gave the impression that no one could possibly argue with the idea, so it became an article of faith for the designers and architects associated with International Modernism. But by the late 1960s, Le Corbusier's utopian planning visions, which had inspired the building of 'modern' urban social housing on an unprecedented scale, were beginning to be viewed in certain quarters as a dystopian nightmare – with Corbusier-inspired, high-rise and, frankly, alienating housing projects becoming hotbeds of poverty, crime and racial segregation.

In 1972, the highly publicized demolition of the failed Pruitt–Igoe post-war housing project designed by Minoru Yamasaki in 1951 marked a seismic turning point in design history, for not only did it symbolize the demise of the American urban dream, it also tolled the death knell of Modernism's long-held moral superiority. As the architecture critic, Charles Jencks later gleefully penned in reference to this event, 'Modern architecture died in St Louis, Missouri on July 15, 1972 at 3.32pm (or thereabouts).'

Venturi's subsequent quip, 'Less is bore', was born of similar sentiments. It not only cleverly encapsulated one of the most fundamental shortcomings of Modernism, but at a stroke also captured the tongue-in-cheek humour of Post-Modernism. This irreverent rallying cry became a live-by slogan for Post-Modernists because it not only referenced the emerging discipline of **semiotics**, but also gave a nod to a growing ennui with good design and product **universality**. In addition, it highlighted the inherent emotional barrenness of so many designs created within the Modernist idiom.

It was this problematic meaninglessness of Modernism that led to the successive backlash of the **Anti-Design** of **Pop**, Italian Radical Design, and ultimately Post-Modernism. Ever the polemicist, Venturi gave three-dimensional form to his catchy 'Less is a bore' idea by creating a series of cartoon-like cutout chairs that parodied a number of historic **styles**; these were not only the very antithesis of Modernist 'good taste', but also an utter rejection of Mies's 'Less is more' entreaty. Crucially, by encapsulating the ethos of Post-Modernism in a very succinct way, 'Less is a bore' caught the imaginations of a new generation of youthful designers looking for a fresh approach to design, and this eventually led to today's more pragmatic outlook, which could be summed up as 'Less is more, more or less'. ■

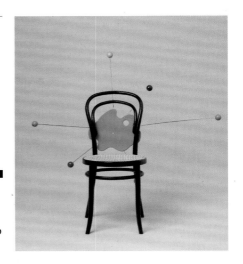

Appropriating a design and repurposing it into something else

IDEA № 80
DESIGN HACKING

In days gone by, design hacking was quite common – if something got broken, people invariably used their ingenuity to fix it. These historic 'hacks' are now referred to as 'make-dos' and are highly prized by specialist collectors.

What is so interesting is that these antique make-do-and-mend survivors often have a rather quirky deconstructed aspect, which is not that dissimilar from the mutant-like aesthetic expressed by so many of today's contemporary design hacks.

One of the most important and celebrated design hackers is the Italian architect and design provocateur Alessandro Mendini. In the mid- to late 1970s he produced a remarkable series of designs that took pre-existing iconic chairs and embellished them – or should we say, hacked them – with various kinds of **decoration**. The resultant 'redesigns', as Mendini called them, were created for Studio Alchimia; they irreverently poked fun at the pretensions of the **Modern Movement** and questioned its blind ideological adherence to **rationalism** – for instance, Joe Colombo's Universale chair (1965– 67) was given a faux-marble makeover, while Michael Thonet's Model No. 14 chair (1859) was adorned with a bright blue blobular nucleus from which coloured ball 'atoms' erupted in order 'to illustrate the impossibility of designing something new in respect to what has already been designed'.[42]

Later, Mendini, along with Franco Raggi, Daniela Puppa and Paola Navone, created a group of 'hacked' everyday objects, including various small household appliances and a pair of court shoes that had been decoratively 'pimped' for an exhibition entitled 'The Banal Object' at the Venice Biennale in 1980. These redesigned pieces, thanks to their applied decoration, functioned more as **design art** than as the functional things they had started out as.

The next generation of designers in the mid- to late 1980s also began appropriating and repurposing **found object**s into innovative design hacks, but in an altogether more subtle and minimalistic way. For example, Jasper Morrison's Flower Pot table (1984) for Cappellini was simply constructed from a size-graduated stack of terracotta garden pots, while Marcel Wanders' Set Up Shade lamps (1988) for Droog took the form of a tower of standard fabric lampshades. These two designs were among the first examples of this new Late Modern do-it-yourself direction in design.

It was, however, Martino Gamper's '100 Chairs in 100 Days' travelling exhibition (from 2007) of 100 mutant chairs that really put the idea of design hacking on the map, at least among the design cognoscenti. Gamper's clever redesigns deconstructed some well-known existing chairs and then, using various techniques, synthesized the parts of two or more into new hybrid seating designs. By making new chairs out of old, sometimes even discarded ones, Gamper revealed the endlessly creative potential of design hacking in a very immediate and easily understood way. As he notes, 'My intention was to investigate the potential of creating useful new chairs by blending together the stylistic and structural elements of found ones. The process produced something like a three-dimensional sketchbook, a collection of possibilities ... the creative potential of random individual elements spontaneously thrown together. The process of personal action that leads towards making rather than hesitating.'[43]

Crucially, this idea of design hacking jibed perfectly with the emerging millennial zeitgeist, with its predilection for reuse, **creative expression**, **customization** and authenticity. The internet also helped fuel the phenomenon, as it gave its participants an easy way to share their ideas and find inspiration. Even IKEA's ubiquitous Billy bookcase (1979) became ripe for design hacking, as numerous internet postings proudly attest. Today, there are vast numbers of websites dedicated to design hacking, which is essentially a democratic trend within design that encourages both designers and non-designers alike to creatively repurpose the ordinary into the extraordinary. ∎

Philippe Fantastique chair (2007) by Martino Gamper – from his exhibition '100 Chairs in 100 Days' for which he made a new chair a day for a hundred days by collaging together bits of chairs that he had found discarded on the street or in friends' homes.

OPPOSITE: Redesign of a proto-modern masterpiece, Thonet No. 14 chair (1975) by Alessandro Mendini.

BELOW: DELAKTIG 'platform for living' (2018) by Tom Dixon for IKEA – comes with numerous add-ons so people can 'hack' it to suit 'different looks, activities and lifestyles' – i.e. IKEA's very own hack platform.

'If something got broken, people invariably used their ingenuity to fix it.'

Putting the user upfront and centre when it comes to design planning

Cover of Victor Papanek's Design for the Real World: Making to Measure *(first published in English in 1972) – a seminal publication that promoted a more ethical and human-centred approach to design.*

IDEA № 81

HUMAN-CENTRED DESIGN

Human-centred design is a creative approach to problem-solving that starts with the needs of the user, and ultimately ends with design solutions tailored specifically to those requirements. It is all about designing from an empathetic perspective so that user-related concerns can inform the design of a product, environment or service throughout its development.

In simple terms, this putting-the-user-first methodology helps to ensure that the eventual design outcomes work as well as they possibly can for the people they were originally intended for.

Apart from the numerous advantages afforded to users from designers taking a human-centred approach to problem-solving, there are also many benefits that can be gained by manufacturers, including improved user uptake, increased customer loyalty and minimized environmental impact. These help to enhance a company's reputation, which consequently leads to better brand recognition. In fact, to design from any other perspective does not really make much sense, because ultimately most design endeavour is about finding solutions to human-related problems, needs and concerns.

All too often, however, design is not human-centred, but, instead, profit-focused. Sadly, this has been a problem in design for a very long time, as designers and manufacturers have focused more on short-term gain than on the overall longer-term picture. The irony is that when a designer or manufacturer does the right thing by pursuing human-centred design, it can often lead to the development of world-beating products that reap much larger profits in the long run.

Although the origins of human-centred design can be traced back to the development of more ergonomic prosthetics and better-functioning disability aids during the postwar period, it did not properly coalesce into a definable approach to design until the early 1970s. The social politics of that period had a strongly inclusive remit, which in turn prompted the development of more human-centric solutions, whether it was designs intended for children, or the disabled, or the elderly. With the later thawing of the Cold War, international relations between countries began improving and this in turn eventually led to a greater sense of global community, which resulted in some designers turning their attention towards making people's lives better in the developing world.

This more ethical direction in design was underpinned ideologically with the publication of Victor Papanek's *Design for the Real World*, which was first published in Swedish in 1970, and then in English the following year. Beginning with the memorable line, 'There are professions more harmful than **industrial design**, but only a very few of them', this seminal publication went on to explain how poorly designed automobiles were so criminally unsafe that they had 'put murder on a mass-production basis' – thus chiming with Ralph Nader's earlier profit-before-**safety** assessments of the American car industry (see page 142). Papanek's book also highlighted how the industrial design profession was supportive of 'the worst excess of a profit-seeking system',[44] and admonished the emerging and wasteful phenomenon of gift culture, whereby huge amounts of time, energy and materials are used in the design and manufacture of completely non-essential and often gimmicky items, from kitchen gadgets to pet

'Most design endeavour is about finding solutions to human-related problems.'

SNOO Smart Sleeper bassinet (2016) by Fuseproject for Happiest Baby – an app-linked cot that is claimed to be 'the world's safest baby bed' having been developed in conjunction with the eminent paediatrician Dr Harvey Karp.

clothing. Nader argued that design instead should be more socially and morally responsive, as well as 'revolutionary and radical', and that it needed to be in harmony with 'nature's principle' of doing the most with the least.[45]

Today, human-centred design is practised by most large-scale multi-disciplinary design consultancies – from IDEO and Teague to Smart and Fuseproject – and has become a doctrine of faith among certain global technology companies. Yet, sadly, these are just shining exemplars of best design practice, and all too often designers are still creating products that do not benefit users in any meaningful way. For example, over the last few decades the rise of gift culture has continued unabated, and the problem with such wasteful products is that while their novelty value is invariably short-lived, their net environmental impact is not. How much more sense would it make to put all these precious resources into the development of longer-lived, human-centric designs that actually make life better? ∎

Design for everyone, regardless of age and ability

IDEA № 82
INCLUSIVE DESIGN

The idea of inclusive design was born out of what used to be known as 'design for disability'. It is a virtuous approach to the design of products and services that attempts to be transgenerational while providing design solutions aimed at the widest range of users.

Although historically some designs had been specifically conceived for people with physical impairments, such as wooden peg legs and Victorian invalid carriages, it was not until after World War II that the discipline of design for disability properly emerged. The leading American **industrial design** consultant Henry Dreyfuss, who was at the forefront of human factors research, was one of the great pioneers in this field. Around 1950, in collaboration with the Army Prosthetics Research Laboratory and the Sierra Engineering Company, he designed an amputee hook for wounded veterans that was far more ergonomically resolved and functionally responsive than any previous models. In fact, this innovative prosthetic provided its users with so much life-enhancing dexterity that they were even able to handle small objects, such as coins and matches.

During the 1950s and 1960s, most designs for disability were developed from a medical perspective and had a strong utilitarian aspect; it was not until the late 1960s, when social responsibility in design became a hot topic – thanks in part to Victor Papanek's *Design for the Real World*, first published in 1971 – that design for disability began to be rethought from a more psycho-physiological perspective. The Swedish design group Ergonomi Design Gruppen was one of the great pioneers of this new user-friendly approach, and its various enabling

designs – such as its widely publicized plastic-handled bread knife and cutting board (1973), and melamine-handled Eat and Drink cutlery (1981) for RSFU Rehab – heralded a new aesthetic consciousness within this previously unglamorous field of design activity. But even so, these were still designs specifically created for the disabled and not intended to be used by the able-bodied.

A sea change came in the late 1980s, however, when the founder of the Copco cookware company, Sam Farber, read an article penned by Mary Reader for the *Journal of the Institute of Home Economics* that called for the development of a new breed of transgenerational kitchen tools. He got the idea completely because his wife was an arthritis sufferer and he had already noticed how difficult it was for her to use most kitchen tools. Farber subsequently commissioned the socially motivated New York **design consultancy** Smart Design to develop a range of inclusively designed kitchen tools that everyone could use, regardless of physical ability. The resulting Good Grips range incorporated ergonomic handles made of a soft elastomer that moulded comfortably to the contours of anybody's hand, thereby providing a significantly better level of handling stability. These remarkable tools were not just better for the disabled, but worked better for all users. Since its launch in 1990, this successful range has expanded to include hundreds of

Good Grips Pro Jar Opener with Base Pad (2013) by Smart Design for OXO – from the inclusively designed Good Grips Range.

different tools, and is now hailed as an outstanding exemplar of **good design**. But even more importantly, with these products, Smart Design had shown how design for disability could be completely rethought – instead of focusing on designing for a narrow sector of society, one could design inclusively for the widest catchment of users.

As a people-centred strategy, inclusive design starts with the premise that design can positively impact people's lives and then attempts to create solutions that work for everyone. As Dr Dan Formosa of Smart Design explains, 'We don't care about average people, we look at extremes' because that is what helps establish the parameters for an inclusive design approach, which, in turn, is ultimately guided by 'the idea that design should be about people, not things'. ∎

Scooter for Life prototype (2017) by PriestmanGoode executed as a special commission for the 'New Old' exhibition at the Design Museum, London, and intended to provide users with greater mobile independence.

The standout appeal
of a design classic

IDEA № 83
THE ICONIC DESIGN

Within the world of design history, the idea of 'the iconic design', or the 'design classic', is often admonished for being on the one hand too exclusive, yet on the other, too popularist. Indeed, the whole idea is seen in some academic circles as being rather 'old school' and passé – a bit regressively absolutist in our increasingly relativistic age.

ABOVE: Concorde (first flight 1969) by Aérospatiale/BAC – one of the most iconic aircraft of all time, with its sleek profile, ogival delta wing planform and droop nose being instantly recognizable.

BELOW: Model 1227 task light (1934–38) by George Carwardine for Herbert Terry & Sons (later Anglepoise) – this archetypal Anglepoise light is an icon of British design thanks as much to its unique silhouette as to its impressive functionality.

Yet as a concept, the iconic design has had a profound influence on both professional design practitioners' and the general public's understanding of what constitutes **good design**.

But more than this, iconic designs act as shining exemplars to designers following in their aftermath, motivating them to find an *even* better way of doing things that will enjoy a similar critical and commercial success. So what exactly makes a design iconic? One of the best ways to gauge whether a product really can be considered iconic is if it can be readily recognized just from its silhouette. For instance, there are many Scandinavian design classics that are instantly identifiable because of their strong graphic outlines – Hans Wegner's Valet chair, Verner Panton's Heart Cone chair, Eero Aarnio's Globe chair, Poul Henningsen's PH and Artichoke lights, Arne Jacobsen's AJ cutlery and AJ table light, and Henning Koppel's Model No. 978 silver pitcher, to name but a few. All of Charles and Ray Eames's famous seating designs are completely recognizable, too, thanks to their simple yet bold lines.

Most iconic designs have a timeless appeal, yet are also very much of their own period. Take, for example, Hans Wegner's Peacock chair (1947), which epitomizes mid-century Danish Modernism, but also transcends it across the decades. Another key element of an iconic design is its enduring functionality, which means that most designs deemed to be classics tend to fall into the category of furniture, lighting, homewares and so on, rather than, say, consumer electronics.

That said, it is entirely possible for product designs such as Apple's first iMac computer or Dyson's DC01 vacuum cleaner to be called 'iconic', for that is exactly what they are: historic totems of design **innovation**, which might have now been functionally surpassed but are still paradigms of pioneering design excellence. The same goes for classic cars, which are avidly collected for their nostalgic associations and beautiful lines – so redolent of simpler, less technically complicated ages – but which offer nothing like the performance of today's cars.

The idea of iconic designs can really be traced back to the postwar era, when Knoll International in America swung a licensing deal with Ludwig Mies van der Rohe and from 1953 began re-editioning his famous Barcelona chair (1929) alongside some of his other furniture designs. In 1960, the Italian furniture entrepreneur Dino Gavina established his eponymous furniture company and began manufacturing a number of Marcel Breuer's seating designs under licence, too. Likewise, Le Corbusier signed a licensing agreement with Cassina in 1964, and the following

PH Artichoke pendant light (1957–58) by Poul Henningsen for Louis Poulsen – like so many other acknowledged design icons, this light is very much of its time, yet paradoxically also timeless.

year his first re-editioned models – LC1, LC2, LC3 and LC4 – went into production. It was, however, in the 1970s when the idea of design classics really caught on, with these Bauhaus re-editions becoming a bit of a status symbol within the interior design of corporate headquarters. They were also favoured by many architects and designers, thanks to their association with the **Modern Movement**, and consequently became intrinsic elements of many progressive mid- to late 1970s interiors. Certainly, these Bauhaus classics were the absolute antithesis of **Pop** design, possessing as they did a

timeless elegance rather than a use-it-today-sling-it-tomorrow ephemerality.

The concept of the design icon, however, took something of a drubbing in the late 1970s with Alessandro Mendini's mocking redesigns of seating design classics, and also in the early to mid-1980s with the rise of Post-Modernism. Yet by the late 1980s, a new generation of collectors and specialist dealers was beginning to re-discover the classic designs of the mid-century era. A number of seminal books were published in the early 1990s that reassessed the classic designs of this period, and by the early 2000s the idea

of the iconic design was firmly established among the general public.

Today, these designs are being increasingly re-editioned, as demand has now far outstripped the supply of original period examples. The reason iconic designs have such an enduring appeal is that they embody in their own highly recognizable outlines our shared notion of design excellence, and this icon-like identity gives them a strong sense of **character** that speaks across the generations. ■

Machines programmed to work and to think for themselves

IDEA № 84

ROBOTICS

We are on the cusp of a brave new world 'peopled' by intelligent robots with rapidly evolving cognitive abilities. In addition, a new industrial revolution is emerging, made possible by increasingly sophisticated manufacturing robots that will have far-reaching consequences for us all.

The idea of robots – meaning machines that can automatically carry out a series of predetermined actions – stretches back to various historic accounts of mechanical automata originating from, among other places, Ancient China, Renaissance Italy and eighteenth-century France. The term 'robot' was, however, first coined by the Czech painter Josef Čapek, whose brother, the sci-fi author Karel Čapek, used it in 1920 in a play entitled *R.U.R.* (short for 'Rossum's Universal Robots'). As Domin, one of the play's characters, explained, 'Robots are not people. Mechanically they are more perfect than we are, they have an enormously developed intelligence, but they have no soul.'[46] This was a prescient assessment, given that no proper robot had yet been built.

Although personal and domestic robots – from robovacs to window-cleaning robots – are increasingly becoming a present-day design reality over the decades the concept of robots has always been firmly linked to futuristic visions. So it is not surprising that the world's very first electronically controlled robot, Elektro the Moto-Man, was debuted at the 1939 New York World's Fair – the theme of which was **the world of tomorrow**. Made by Westinghouse Electric Corporation, this 120-kg (265-lb), 2-metre (7-ft)-tall Goliathan was a veritable showstopper, thanks to his seeming ability to count on his fingers and smoke a cigarette, all of which was made possible through an innovative pre-programmed electronic sound/voice-activated system. The following year, Elektro was given a companion, a robot dog called Sparko, which could walk, sit and wag its tail. While this double act wowed audiences at the fair, they were pretty primitive in terms of their technology and functional capabilities.

Elektro did, however, spark imaginations as to what a robotic future could look like, as did the novels of the American sci-fi writer Isaac Asimov. He had the foresight to formulate his Three Laws of Robotics – which coined the term 'robotics' – in a short story in 1942 entitled 'Runaround'. Asimov's often-quoted laws are:

1. A robot may not injure a human being or, through inaction, allow a human being to come to harm;

2. A robot must obey orders given it by human beings except where such orders would conflict with the First Law;

3. A robot must protect its own existence as long as such protection does not conflict with the First or Second Law.

These common-sense directives established the idea of a moral framework for robotics and continue to have enormous relevance to current as well as future applications of 'intelligent' robot technology, especially in regard to lethal autonomous weaponry.

The next big step for robotics was the world's first industrial robot, Unimate 1900 (1961). This machine was developed from an earlier mechanical arm design, patented by George Devol in 1954. It was, however, Joseph Engelberger – known as 'the Father of Robotics' – that took this idea and refined it. The resultant Unimate was first installed on the assembly line of General Motors' die-casting plant in Trenton, New Jersey, and as the very first mass-produced robot arm, it heralded a new age of robotic factory automation.

Significant technical advances were subsequently made in the field of humanoid robotics with the piano-playing Wabot-2 robot developed at Waseda University, Japan, from 1980 to 1984. This robot represented a breakthrough in that its 16-bit microcomputer mimicked the human nervous system and showcased the potential of robotics with its 20-times-a-second key-tapping fingers. Since then, there have been numerous robotic advances from the WHL-11 (1985) – the first autonomous walking robot – to the remarkable stable of robots currently being developed by Boston Dynamics. Combining biology with technology, these mutant-like machines, such as the Atlas robot that can carry heavy loads over difficult terrain, have formidable capabilities.

Intelligent robots are an emerging species that will either threaten our survival or be of huge benefit to us, and this choice between a good or a bad outcome will ultimately be determined by the establishment of design ethics needed to govern their creation. ■

Chihira Junko, a humanoid robot developed by Toshiba, being demonstrated at a shopping mall in Tokyo (2015). This lifelike android has been designed to be able to give visitor guidance in Japanese, English and Chinese.

RIGHT: Elektro, the very first electronically controlled robot, which was debuted at the 1939 New York World's Fair.

FAR RIGHT: Asimo, a humanoid robot developed by Honda, balancing on one leg during a demonstration (2015). Incorporating intelligent, real-time, flexible-walking technology, it is able to carry on walking while changing directions.

Design innovation inspired by the wonders of nature

IDEA № 85

BIOMIMICRY

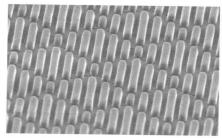

Sharklet micro patterning (2015) by Sharklet Technologies Inc. – inspired by the form and function of real sharkskin and now being incorporated into various medical devices and consumer products to inhibit bacterial growth.

Biomimicry is a scientific discipline related to design practice that takes nature as its model, measure and mentor. In many ways, it must be considered the ultimate evolutionary approach to design, for it seeks solutions that are inspired directly by the wonders of the natural world.

The ancestry of biomimicry (also known as biomimetics) can be traced back to a number of historical sources – from Leonardo da Vinci's design of a flying machine based on the structure of a bat's wing, to the British architect Joseph Paxton's Crystal Palace for the 'Great Exhibition of the Works of Industry of All Nations' (1851), the construction of which was inspired by the gigantic pads of an Amazonian water lily. During the 1850s, the British **industrial design**er Christopher Dresser began making analytical studies of the 'divine' structures found in the botanical world that helped to establish a new field of design study: Art Botany – which was the ideological precursor of biomimicry. Some years later, during the *belle époque*, the idea of designs inspired by the divine **rightness** of nature saw the emergence of the Art Nouveau **style**, with its sinuous lines echoing forms found in the biological world.

This early flowering of bio-inspired design was later followed by a new interpretation of Modernism known as **organic design**, which sought to imitate biological forms or systems, and was typified by flowing lines and soft, amorphous shapes that captured the abstract essence of nature. Later, the sculptural work of the Finnish designers Tapio Wirkkala and Timo Sarpaneva during the 1960s and 1970s, while still closely adhering to the organic design idiom, was based more on the literal forms found in the natural world – leaves, tree bark, birds, mushrooms and icicles.

The first known use of the term 'biomimcry' was in the title of a PhD biochemistry dissertation written by Connie Lange Merrill at Rice University in 1982, yet it did not relate in any way to design. In fact, the term was not widely used in the design community until the publication in 1997 of the American biologist Janine Benyus's influential book *Biomimicry: Innovation Inspired by Nature*. The premise of this book was that if you are trying to solve a design problem, you should first look to nature because there you will find inspiration in the genius of natural organisms.

Very often organisms have evolved the way they have in order to be super-efficient at what they are meant to do – fly through the air, swim through water, and so on. When faced with any design conundrum it is worth looking at what nature has come up with through the evolutionary honing process of natural selection. For example, in 2009, engineers at MIT created a fast, ultra-broadband radio chip modelled on the structure of the cochlea of a human ear, which was far more energy efficient than traditional chips. And in 2010, Professor Frank Fish of West Chester University developed a wind turbine design that mimicked the scallop-edged flippers of a humpback whale, which reduced drag by 32 per cent. More recently, Sharklet Technologies, a Florida-based biotech company, has designed an adhesive film that mimics the diamond patterning of the denticles on sharkskin. In nature, this distinctive topography repels barnacles, algae and the like from sticking to a shark's body, while on the newly developed plastic film it has been found to discourage bacteria build-up, and as a consequence is now being used for wound dressings and other medical applications. What these very different examples of bio-informed design clearly demonstrate is how nature is often way ahead of the curve when it comes to finding the best, most effective solutions to particular problems.

Dr Jeffrey Karp, a leading pioneer of biomimicry in the realm of medical design, notes, 'I strongly believe that evolution is truly the best problem-solver; we can learn so much from nature.' And this bio-inspirationalist should know, having already developed a waterproof surgical adhesive bandage

based on the hill-and-valley contours found on geckos' padded feet, which enable these crea-tures to stick to almost anything, including glass. Karp is also currently developing a new kind of surgical staple based on the quills of porcupines, known as the Porcupine Tie. The hope is that this design will create smaller punctures in the skin, thereby reducing the risk of infection. In addition, Karp is researching a new kind of surgical glue based on the sticky secretions of marine worms, which it is hoped will be strong enough to bind moving tissues inside the human body's major organs.

Ingenious bio-simulating designs such as these demonstrate how innovative breakthroughs can be directly inspired by natural organisms, which have themselves been honed by evolutionary systems often over millennia. And the more we discover about the astonishing design logic of nature, the more we should be able to develop better and more sustainable design solutions to overcome some of the world's biggest problems. ∎

Making technology easier to interact with

INTERFACE / INTERACTION DESIGN

An attendee experiences VIVE HTC Steam VR during the annual Mobile World Congress (Barcelona, 2016) one of the most important events for mobile technologies, all of which need good interface design capabilities.

Interface design is all about creating easy-to-understand human–product interactions, so that people can use things effortlessly. As a discipline it originally evolved out of early human factors research, and later studies into **ergonomics**. These sought to provide detailed scientific data on how people interact with products, systems or services so that better **human-centred design** solutions could be devised.

By their very nature, some types of designs have always required a greater level of user interaction than others. For instance, the operation of a car requires far more human input than, say, a bicycle or a dishwasher. This means that the design of its human–product interface is immensely more complex and, as a result, needs to be more thoughtfully researched and developed. Successful interface design generally relies on **clarity of layout** in order to facilitate a degree of **functional intuitiveness**.

When someone talks about interface design, they are generally referring to a human–machine interface because machines tend to be the types of product that require the greatest amount of interactive participation. One of the greatest pioneers of interface design was the German **industrial design**er Dieter Rams who, during his tenure from 1961 to 1995 as head of design at the German electronics company Braun, developed a language of design based on his belief in 'Less but better'. This helped him create machines that had such innate visual and functional **simplicity** that they were effortless to use. His influence on the development of later digital user interfaces (UI) is now widely acknowledged, and his belief

that 'Design should not dominate things. Not dominate people. It should help people' has become almost a mantra for today's UI designers.

In the mid-1980s, Bill Moggridge and Bill Verplank of IDEO coined the term 'interaction design' to describe a new type of interface design that involved the use of graphic user interfaces (GUI) within the realm of product design – whereby graphical icons and pointing devices were used to control computerized systems. Apple was one of the trailblazers in this field with its Lisa and Macintosh computers, released in 1983 and 1984 respectively, heralding a new level of digital interface design, thanks to their use of, among other things, skeuomorphic icons that playfully referenced real-life objects, such as a trashcan, a bomb, a wristwatch, and so forth.

Often abbreviated to IxD, interaction design relates specifically to human–computer interfaces and is concerned with how to provide them with enhanced usability. There are some rule-of-thumb guidelines that govern the development of successful interaction-design systems, namely: efficiency, learnability and memorability. When interactive design achieves these goals, users are easily able to learn how to use a computerized system without too many

errors, so that they can execute the tasks they want to perform; it also helps them remember how to perform those tasks again the next time, all of which provides a positive user experience. The best type of interactive design is when the functionality of a system has such a natural logic that the user does not even notice the delivery system, but is able just to get on with the job in hand.

Within the rapid **digitalization** of design, which is witnessing the rising emergence of connected **IoT** products, the need for better interactive design is becoming ever more critical. Indeed, when it comes to interactive design, it really is a case of the simpler, the better – for increasingly, we just want straightforward usability in order to navigate ever more complex digital advances. ∎

'Design should not dominate things' – *Dieter Rams*

GUI (graphical user interface) icons (c.1983–84) by Susan Kare for Apple – including the 'Happy Mac' icon, which so succinctly summed up the more user-friendly aspect of the Apple Mac.

Designing for sustainability /
Marketing designs on false eco-credentials

IDEA Nº 87

GREEN DESIGN / GREENWASH

The term 'green design' is analogous with other often bandied-about phrases – eco-design, ecological design and sustainable design – all of which are based on the same idea: designing products, transportation, living and working environments and services from an ecologically efficient standpoint in order to minimize their harmful environmental impact.

Caper stacking chair (2012) by Jeff Weber for Herman Miller – this 'hard-working, earth-friendly chair' was designed from an environmental perspective and has Level 3 certification for sustainability from BIFMA (the Business and Institutional Furniture Manufacturers Association).

This means looking at the complete life cycle of a product, from the sourcing of raw materials, to manufacture, use and eventual disposal, and attempting to minimize as much waste all along the way as possible.

In recent times, however, the phrase 'green design' has largely fallen out of favour because during the 1990s it was used falsely by many manufacturers as a way of marketing products that were in no way environmentally friendly. This commercially driven phenomenon is usually referred to as 'greenwashing', and has had a major impact on the perception of green issues in design. Greenwash basically takes the idea of green design and effectively appropriates it for reasons to do with profitability. As one commentator noted regarding a supposedly eco-friendly shampoo being launched by a major global brand, the greenest thing about it was the colour of its bottle, yet consumers are often cynically hoodwinked into buying things based on fictitious eco-credentials. This, sadly, has led to the concept of **sustainability** in design being somewhat undermined, at least among many average consumers.

The term 'greenwash' was first coined in 1986 by the New York-based eco-activist and biological researcher Jay Westerveld in an essay outlining how hotels were using 'Save the Environment' notices to promote the reuse of towels by guests; in actuality the hotels were doing little to reduce their overall carbon footprints. Their energy consumption, in fact, remained more or less the same, whether their guests were reusing their towels or not. Westerveld opined that this type of 'green campaign' was actually marketing hype intended to increase profits of hoteliers, rather than being of any real benefit to the environment.

Since then, although there is now a far greater awareness of how mis-leading green claims are used by companies to sell products, greenwash continues to be a relatively widespread practice among manufacturers, both large and small. Indeed, as consumers become increasingly environmentally aware, companies are going to greater lengths to present themselves as champions of environmental sustainability. And while some of the more ethically based ones will actually take the necessary steps and invest in the research and development of more sustainable design solutions, others will just make up exaggerated – or even false – 'green' claims. One of the most flagrant examples of greenwash to date was Volkswagen's installation of 'defeat' software, which had been developed by Bosch, in order to reduce the emissions readings of some of its diesel-engine cars.

Unfortunately, the over-egging or at times falsification of truth, about how green a design actually is has had the

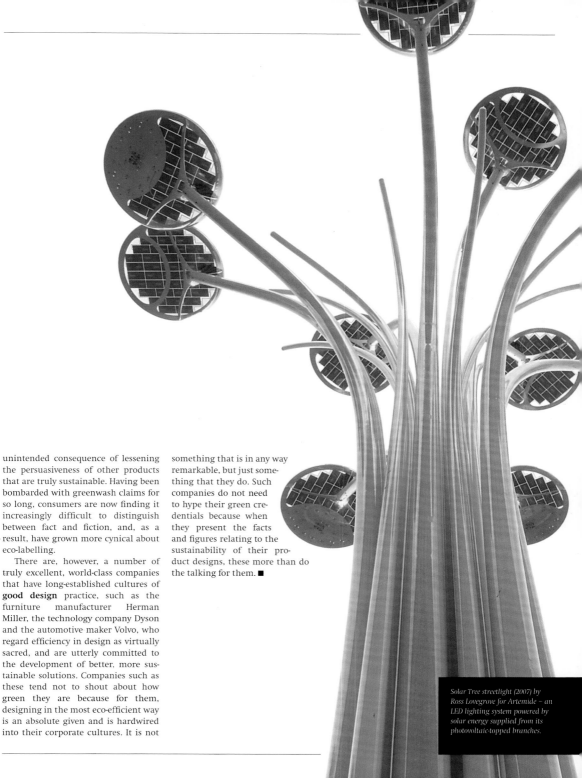

unintended consequence of lessening the persuasiveness of other products that are truly sustainable. Having been bombarded with greenwash claims for so long, consumers are now finding it increasingly difficult to distinguish between fact and fiction, and, as a result, have grown more cynical about eco-labelling.

There are, however, a number of truly excellent, world-class companies that have long-established cultures of **good design** practice, such as the furniture manufacturer Herman Miller, the technology company Dyson and the automotive maker Volvo, who regard efficiency in design as virtually sacred, and are utterly committed to the development of better, more sustainable solutions. Companies such as these tend not to shout about how green they are because for them, designing in the most eco-efficient way is an absolute given and is hardwired into their corporate cultures. It is not

something that is in any way remarkable, but just something that they do. Such companies do not need to hype their green credentials because when they present the facts and figures relating to the sustainability of their product designs, these more than do the talking for them. ■

Solar Tree streetlight (2007) by Ross Lovegrove for Artemide – an LED lighting system powered by solar energy supplied from its photovoltaic-topped branches.

LEFT: The various components
of the Axyl stacking chair,
showing how they can be easily
separated for re-recycling.

The reincarnation of things in a world of environmental limitation

RECYCLING + UPCYCLING

In the UK alone, over 20 million tonnes of municipal solid waste is produced each year. The vast majority of this is landfilled, 6 per cent is incinerated and only a tiny percentage is actually recycled.

Landfill sites, however, are beginning to dry up. This is not so much due to a lack of space as it is to the environmental problems they create – contamination of ground water, for instance – and the fact that no one wants a landfill site near them. As a result, across the industrialized world, there is pressure to reduce waste, to recycle, and to incinerate the rest.

Although recycling is viewed by politicians, local authorities, manufacturers and most environmentalists as intrinsically 'green' and has come to symbolize good environmental practice, it does have an effect on the environment. As waste products are collected, sorted, cleaned and separated into their constituent materials, energy is consumed and pollution is caused, both as a byproduct of this energy consumption and, more directly, by materials reclamation processes. The subsequent manufacture and distribution of the products made from recycled materials also has an impact on the environment. Furthermore, recycling can be seen to encourage a throwaway culture by failing to restrict levels of consumption. Rather than tackling waste management, therefore, **sustainability** requires a focus on the production of longer-lasting products, to reduce the flow of energy and materials through the economy.

With designers and manufacturers increasingly confronted with the need to make decisions based on the total environmental impact of their products from 'cradle to grave' – in other words, from extraction of raw materials to eventual disposal – it has become necessary to think in terms of both **product durability** and recycling. The value of recycling varies according to materials, but in general its benefits are that it conserves natural resources and reduces energy consumption.

A landmark book published in 2002, however, provided a better and more holistic solution to the way designers and manufacturing companies think about the life cycles of the products they create. Written by the American architect William McDonough and the German chemist Michael Braungart, *Cradle to Cradle: Remaking the Way We Make Things* exposed the astonishing fact that, on average, a product contains only 5 per cent of the raw materials used to make and distribute it, so constitutes only the 'tip of a material iceberg' of wastage.[47] It also advanced the idea that rather than conceiving of a product's life cycle in terms of cradle to grave, products could instead be designed from the outset to 'provide nourishment for something new' after the expiry of their useful lives. In simple terms, rather than being 'downcycled' into something materially inferior, as is traditional with recycling, they could instead become part of a closed-loop system based on the concept of 'upcycling'. The idea of 'cradle to cradle' (C2C) inspired designers to think more meaningfully about the complete life cycle of products, and accordingly design things that are more likely to feature an element of recyclability or, even better, upcyclability.

Since 2006, the US Institute of Scrap Recycling Industries (ISRI) has also run its annual Design for Recycling® Award as a way of encouraging companies to take on board its Design for Recycling® Principles. These include, but are by no means limited to: manufacturing products that can be safely and economically recycled using existing recycling technology and methods; all durable consumer items must, where possible, have recyclability designed into them; for any products that by necessity have hazardous constituents, cooperative arrangements should be established between manufacturers and recyclers to ensure their safe recycling; and the provision of technical and economic assistance to manufacturers, especially smaller ones, who need to alter the design or manufacture of products to make them more appropriate for recycling.

Ultimately, however, the most sustainable approach to design is not recycling or even up-cycling but rather enhancing product durability, wherever that is functionally most appropriate. Because by doubling the useful life of a product, its environmental impact can be halved. ∎

Getting the most with the least

ESSENTIALISM

REX Model 11002 vegetable peeler (1947) by Alfred Neweczerzal for Zena – a celebrated icon of Swiss design that is a fine example of essentialism.

The Chinese writer Lin Yutang once noted, 'The wisdom of life consists in the elimination of non-essentials.' And that is fundamentally what the idea of essentialism in design is all about – simplifying a design down to its most reduced state, where it comprises only the elements that are absolutely necessary to perform its intended function.

Essentialism is a 'fat-free' approach to design that not only eliminates any decorative elements, but also reduces to an optimal minimum the amount of materials and energy needed to realize a design. The notion of essentialism derives from the **Modern Movement**'s idea of '**less is more**', and is an approach to design that is closely linked to **green design** (meaning sustainable design), in that it is driven by the desire to reduce waste wherever possible. The ideological roots of essentialism can be traced back to the architect-designer, systems theorist, inventor and futurologist Richard Buckminster Fuller and his Dymaxion (dynamic + maximum efficiency) concept, which was based on 'the potential of innovative design to create technology that does "more with less" and thereby improves human lives'.

Essentialism is also closely related to **rationalism** and **functionalism**, both of which are similarly guided by the aim of maximizing material, formal and functional efficiency. However, the key difference is that essentialism tends to be far more human-centric. Essentialism can be interpreted through either a geometric or an organic language of design, with Dieter Rams and Charles Eames having created designs that fall into these two categories respectively.

Interestingly, both tools and vernacular designs often embody essentialism, with their forms having been functionally evolved over time. Today, Jasper Morrison and Naoto Fukasawa are well known for their pioneering essentialist designs, which are often based on vernacular archetypes. Together they curated an influential travelling exhibition in 2007 entitled 'Super Normal: Sensations of the Ordinary', which showcased many anonymous designs, from the Swiss-designed REX vegetable peeler to a standard plastic bucket, all of which could best be described as essentialist. The exhibition helped to bring the idea of essentialism in design to a wider audience. The Muji chain has also helped promote essentialist design by successfully retailing products of this type across their vast network of retail shops. This is not so surprising, given that Fukasawa has long been involved in product development and design there.

The British designer Ross Lovegrove is also well known for his organic approach to essentialism, the results of which are often derived from using generative design-engineering software algorithms that cleverly calculate the way of getting the maximum functionality from the minimum amount of material. As Lovegrove explains, 'my work ... relates to nature, in an evolutionary sense, as I'm concerned with reduction. I exercise what is called "organic essentialism" which means using nothing more – nothing less than is needed.'

Unlike Minimalism, which is fundamentally a **style** based on aesthetic **purity**, essentialism is a highly valid twenty-first-century approach to design, for it not only addresses issues to do with **sustainability**, it also considers design problem-solving holistically and attempts to find optimized human-centric solutions. This is patently logical because there is no real value in getting the most with the least in terms of manufacturing efficiency if, in the end, a design does not fulfil its intended function properly. ∎

'Essentialism is a "fat-free" approach to design.'

ABOVE: Saucepans (2014) by Jasper Morrison for Muji – a range of double-layer stainless steel saucepans with an aluminium core, which exemplify Morrison's essentialist approach to problem-solving.

LEFT: Supernatural chair (2005) by Ross Lovegrove for Moroso – the perfect example of Lovegrove's pioneering design language of 'organic essentialism'.

Design as art, or art as design

IDEA № 90

DESIGN ART

While design and art can at times be close bedfellows, there is a defining difference: functional **utility**. That said, the boundaries between the two disciplines are often quite blurred, especially when artists create practical designs, and designers create unique or limited-edition pieces that are akin to fine art – or in other words, design art.

Bocca sofa (1970) by Studio 65 for Gufram – an iconic Pop Art design piece that referenced Salvador Dalí's earlier surrealistic 'Mae West Lips Sofa' of 1937.

The Surrealists produced some of the earliest examples of design art, with Salvador Dalí famously creating a sofa based on the form of Mae West's lips in 1937, and Cecil Beaton designing a child's chair that took the form of a drum. It was, however, the emergence of **Pop** art in the 1960s that saw the increasing crossover of art and design with artists such as Allen Jones creating fine-art pieces that took the form of furniture, such as his provocative *Hatstand*, *Table* and *Chair*, featuring mannequins dressed in erotic lingerie. As he noted, 'By giving my sculpture a functional connotation it acted as a distancing device that further dislocated the expectation of what a sculpture could be.' The work of the French sculptors François-Xavier and Claude Lalanne similarly eroded the distinctions between art and design, with the former's *Rhinocrétaire* bar (1966) and *Hippopotamus* bathtub (1968–69) having an overtly Surrealistic flavour yet providing some degree of function, too.

Around the same time, a number of avant-garde designers experimenting with form and function began creating furniture and lighting that more often than not fell into the category of quasi-functional sculpture. Often these Pop art design pieces, such as those manufactured by Gufram, would be sold by specialist galleries alongside fine art. The Italian design entrepreneur Dino Gavina was also instrumental in the wider dissemination of design art with his influential Ultramobile collection, launched in 1971, which included limited-edition designs by various well-known artists and sculptors such as Man Ray, Sebastian Matta, Meret Oppenheim and Marion Baruch.

During the 1980s and early 1990s, the concept of design art evolved further with the creation of art furniture by the sculptors Donald Judd and Richard Artschwager, while at the same time the designer Gaetano Pesce began creating design art pieces using interesting materials and techniques that were sold as limited editions, most notably his Pratt chair of 1983.

In the late 1990s and early 2000s, a new form of design art began to emerge that catered to an elite of super-rich fine-art collectors, who bought one-off or limited-edition, highly experimental designs by a handful of superstar designers, including Ron Arad, Marc Newson, Zaha Hadid, and Fernando and Humberto Campana. This new phenomenon was initially spearheaded by the leading auction houses, with the term 'design art' being generally credited to Phillips de Pury & Co., who organized the first design-art auction in 2001. At around the same time, various high-end art galleries began to expand their business activities into design art, most notably the Gagosian Gallery. This made sense, for it was contemporary art collectors who were predominantly buying into design art.

Spotting an opportunity, in 2005 the organizers of the famous Art Basel international art fairs branched out into the world of design by setting up annual design-focused sister shows in Miami and Basel. There, exhibiting specialist galleries from around the world showcase the very latest design-art offerings, which like so much contemporary fine art today is often prized as much for its investment potential as for its originality and artistry.

Rhinocrétaire II (Grand) *by*
François-Xavier Lalanne
(2002/2007) – a re-edition piece
based on an earlier design
from 1966.

'Design art offers an arena for greater creative expression.'

For a small coterie of designers working within industry for established manufacturers, design art offers an arena for greater **creative expression** and unfettered experimental freedom. Here they can create designs that push the very boundaries of form and materials, unconstrained by the limitations of the industrial process. Exclusive and often very expensive, the substantial income that can be generated by designs such as these helps their creators underwrite blue-sky research, and also day-to-day studio operations. Over and above this, however, design art pieces can raise the profile of designers in the media – which helps shift their more mainstream, industrially produced designs, much like haute couture helps sell ready-to-wear collections in the world of fashion. ■

A visual lightness of design being

IDEA № 91
TRANSPARENCY

One of the key features of Modern design has been the desire for **lightness**, both physical and visual. Over the decades, the related concept of transparency has expressed itself time and again through the use of glass, acrylic and PVC. These see-through materials give products a lightness of spirit, which is inherently forward-looking.

The strong dematerialist tendency associated with the **Modern Movement** in the early twentieth century was most memorably expressed in a series of film stills published in the July 1926 issue of the *Bauhaus* magazine. These stills tracked the five-year evolutionary progress of chairs designed by Marcel Breuer through six images, with the last one projecting into the future and showing a woman sitting on 'resilient air columns'. This invisible conceptual design was the logical conclusion of the Modernists' desire to do more with less, and the use of transparent materials became utterly symbolic of this aspiration.

In the early twentieth century, architect-designers exploited extensively what was then considered a state-of-the-art modern industrial material – reinforced plate glass – in not only their buildings but also their furniture designs. These stridently Modern buildings and furnishings linked the idea of transparency with the notion of progress. Glass, however, has two inherent problems: its weight and breakability. These drawbacks were nevertheless overcome by Otto Röhm and Otto Haas's development and commercialization of a new wonder material, known as Plexiglas, in the late 1920s. First used in the German auto industry, this state-of-the-art acrylic thermoplastic soon found other design applications, with both Jacques André

and Gilbert Rohde utilizing it for the seat sections of chairs they designed in 1936 and 1938 respectively.

It was, however, the 1960s that would see acrylic being used more expressively in design, thanks to a plethora of futuristic fluorescent PMMA (polymethyl methacrylate) lighting designs emanating mainly from Italy, which exploited the material's otherworldly optical properties – whereby the material glows brightest along its so-called 'live edges'. Another transparent polymer that similarly came of age in the **Pop** era was PVC (polyvinyl chloride), which was famously utilized in the design and manufacture of various inflatable furniture pieces.

Transparency re-emerged in the late 1980s and 1990s in the design of all kinds of different products. The first of this new breed of transparent designs was the Basic thermos flask designed by Ross Lovegrove and Julian Brown for Alfi in 1988, which introduced the influential idea of skinning products with bubble-like techno-polymer housings. Another design to feature a very early transparent element was James Dyson's revolutionary DC01 vacuum cleaner (1993) with its dust-collecting bin made of clear and impact-resistant acrylic. It was, however, Jony Ive and the Apple design team's iMac, with its gumdrop-shaped PMMA housing available in numerous attractive

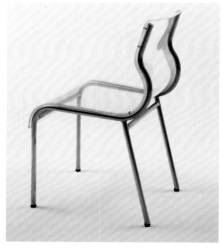

TOP: Louis Ghost chair (2002) by Philippe Starck for Kartell – one of the bestselling chairs of the early 2000s, this design combines an historic archetypal form with state-of-the-art injection-moulded transparent PMMA.

ABOVE: Side chair (1938) by Gilbert Rohde for Röhm & Haas – this remarkably progressive chair was designed to showcase the manufacturer's newly developed acrylic thermoplastic, Plexiglas, at the 1939 New York World's Fair.

Basic thermal carafe (1988–90) by Ross Lovegrove and Julian Brown for Alfi – with its polycarbonate bubble-like body, this product heralded a major new trend for transparency in design.

'Transparent "smart" films will inevitably replace computer screens.'

colours, that kicked off this new obsession with transparency in design when it was launched in 1998.

Today, this phenomenon is still very much in evidence, as a trip to any Muji store will attest, with its shelves and shelves of transparent and translucent minimalist homewares. As for the future, transparent 'smart' films will inevitably replace computer screens as products become ever more de-materialized, and will ultimately be incorporated into the design of a completely new generation of consumer electronics that feature augmented reality data-overlaying. ∎

Growth | Chair Bronze (2012) by Mathias Bengtsson – a limited-edition design art piece that was created using a generative software program.

Transforming design through bits and bytes

IDEA № 92

DIGITALIZATION

Throughout history there have been periods of great technological change, but it could be argued that the greatest change of all has come about in the last 50 years, due to digitalization.

Very few areas of life have remained untouched by this technology, and it has certainly completely transformed not only professional design practice, but also the types of product that are now being designed.

Within **industrial design** practice, digitalization has spawned the introduction of increasingly sophisticated **CAD/CAM** software programs that have speeded up the whole design process, from initial concept to final product. Today, most drafting and modelling is executed on screen, while prototyping is more often than not carried out with the aid of digital-data-fed 3D printers. The digitalization of design through CAD/CAM and **3D printing**, among other things, has not only helped to accelerate design **innovation**, it has also significantly reduced research and development costs, which in turn has reduced the relative price of certain goods, such as furniture and consumer electronics. In fact, digitalization has democratized design considerably, not only in terms of affordability to users, but also in terms of practice.

What we would have thought of as highly sophisticated digital design tools only a few years back are now freely available as **open-source design** downloads, while even the most advanced proprietary software packages have become much more affordable than they once were. This means that CAD is now used in the vast majority of professional design practices throughout the world, while in the 1960s and 1970s it was found only in the big and well-funded in-house design departments of mega-corporations

such as Xerox, Boeing, General Motors and Siemens.

Mathias Bengtsson, a **design art** specialist and one of the most progressive and digitally competent designers working today, recently noted, 'Software is not like it used to be ... you don't buy Photoshop and use it now, but you use open-source software, like Houdini. You can do everything with it, and you can adjust it to fit your needs.' This phenomenon of tailoring design software to suit bespoke needs will undoubtedly become much more commonplace in the years to come.

In addition to fundamentally changing the working tools of the designer, digitalization has also had an enormous impact on the dissemination of design ideas. Through the power of the internet, designs are now launched in front of a global audience, and information on not only designed products, but also on design history and design issues, is now far more readily accessible. This has led to a greater awareness of design among the general public, who are now able to make more informed choices when it comes to buying designed products.

Digitalization has also had a transformative effect on the types of products now being developed. As the **convergence of functionality** becomes a greater feature of ever-smarter digital-centric designs, including mobile phones, laptops and the like, so a growing number of formerly 'dumb' household products have now also become 'smart'. The recent appearance of app-connected **IoT** products is likewise a direct outcome of the rapid

acceleration of digitalization over the last five to ten years.

Today, thanks to digitalization, we are also witnessing the advent of smart factories reliant on cyber-physical systems and cloud computing, among other things. This new development in manufacturing, referred to as 'Industry 4.0' (the Fourth Industrial Revolution), promises to be as disruptive in terms of design as any previous technological revolution. But, just as in the past, we can be sure of one thing – designers will use their problem-solving abilities to come up with innovative solutions that fully exploit the benefits of this new and evolving technology. ∎

Smart wind turbines (2017) by Siemens – these adjust to the wind's direction to optimize energy generation.

Computer programs that help turn design ideas into manufactured products

IDEA № 93
CAD/CAM

Sketchpad software (1963) being demonstrated by its inventor, Ivan Sutherland, which introduced 3D computer modelling, visual simulation and compute-aided design.

CAD/CAM is the acronym for computer-aided design and computer-aided manufacture. While it could be argued that this is a technology rather than a concept per se, the ideas behind its development were responsible for seismic changes in design practice as well as the evolution of computing.

Since the widespread introduction of CAD/CAM programs in the early 1990s, the landscape of design practice has changed immeasurably. Not only did the advent of this type of software enable the creation of previously impossible forms, which age-old drafting and modelling skills could never have allowed, it also led to the rapid acceleration of design **innovation**. The reason for this is that these programs dramatically shortened both prototyping and modelling times, which made it much faster and less costly to take a design from concept stage to final pre-production stage, and then into full-blown industrial production.

The origins of CAD software can be traced back to the first commercial numerical-control programming system, known as Pronto, which was developed by Dr Patrick Hanratty at the Massachusetts Institute of Technology (MIT) in 1957. This was followed up in 1963 by Sketchpad, developed by Ivan Sutherland as part of his PhD dissertation at MIT, which crucially established the basic principles behind computer-aided drafting and was the first computer program to boast a GUI (graphic user interface). Importantly, Sutherland's Sketchpad ingeniously introduced a light-pen, which presaged the later development of the first computer mouse. Despite its limited distribution within the confines of the university's labs, this program – which functioned as a 2D digital drawing board – nevertheless demonstrated the technical feasibility of CAD as an idea.

As the preface to a 2003 facsimile edition of Sutherland's thesis states, 'Sketchpad is one of the most influential computer programs ever written by an individual ... its influence has been via the ideas that it introduced rather than in its execution.'[48] One of those key ideas was to make computing more accessible not only to artists and draftsmen, but also to various types of design practitioner. It is, however, the French engineer Pierre Bézier who is credited with the subsequent invention of the first 3D CAD/CAM program, UNISURF, which was developed between 1966 and 1968 for the car manufacturer Renault.

During the 1970s and early 1980s, early CAD programs such as these were still relatively primitive and were rarely found outside the aerospace and automotive industries. This was primarily to do with cost as well as memory and related processing power – you basically needed mainframe computers to run them. However, over time, as hardware became increasingly more powerful and less expensive, CAD became much more commonplace within design studios, especially after the widespread introduction of desktop computing in the early 1990s.

Currently, CAD programs help designers and manufacturers to model, adapt and develop design concepts, and are used mainly for 2D drafting, 3D solid and surface modelling, and for working out virtually the assembly of components. They can also be used in conjunction with laser scanning and CMM (coordinate measuring machines) for the reverse engineering of existing real components.

By contrast, the main applications of CAM software are laser cutting, milling, turning and **3D printing**. Providing useful three-dimensional visualization and the means of taking a design idea from the virtual to the physical, CAD/CAM has become a transformative tool that helps designers arrive at optimized design-engineering solutions. Today, CAD/CAM is an essential tool for professional design practitioners and design-led companies, and already, new kinds of generative CAD software, including those related to **parametricism**, are coming on stream that promise to be even better at design problem-solving than anything that has gone before. ■

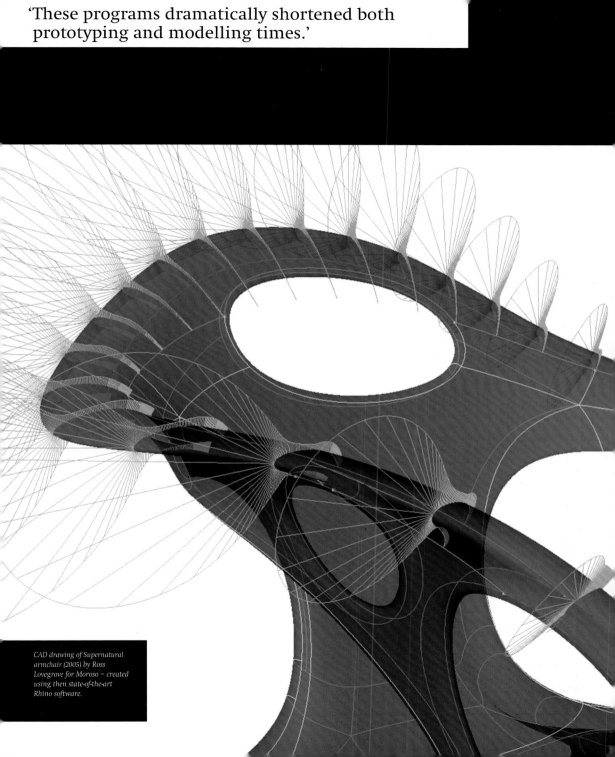

'These programs dramatically shortened both prototyping and modelling times.'

CAD drawing of Supernatural armchair (2005) by Ross Lovegrove for Moroso – created using then state-of-the-art Rhino software.

Fewer products but with more multifunctionality

IDEA № 94

CONVERGENCE OF FUNCTIONALITY

Functional convergence is mainly about combining the functionality of multiple individual products into a single entity – or in other words, doing more with less.

Among the earliest examples of the convergence of functionality can be found in farm machinery – most notably, the first successful combine harvester, which was patented by Hiram Moore in 1835 and was capable of mowing, threshing and winnowing, and the first reaper-binder designed by John Appleby (c.1867), which was subsequently manufactured in 1878 by what later became the Deering Harvester Company.

Another early example of functional convergence can be found in the iconic Swiss Army knife made by Victorinox. First manufactured by the firm in 1891, the earliest model was a simple soldier's penknife that featured just four tools. However, six years later an officer's knife was introduced that boasted an additional cutting blade and a corkscrew. Over the succeeding decades more tools have been added to the classic Swiss Army knife, which to this day is a great example of how design thinking can be used to create a compact product with a high degree of multifunctionality.

It was, however, the invention of the transistor at Bell Laboratories in December 1947 that first sparked the idea of greater functional convergence in

designed products through the application of advanced electronics. This tiny yet groundbreaking semi-conducting triode enabled the development of wireless radios, which were more compact than their valve-laden predecessors. As radios got increasingly smaller in line with advances in transistor technology, so it gradually became possible to integrate a radio function into a gramophone, thereby heralding the advent of combi audio systems. Eventually this led to the development of so-called hi-fi systems and, later, boom boxes that went even further by integrating a cassette player, a CD player and a radio into a single portable unit.

It was, however, the widespread introduction of personal desktop computers in the late 1980s and early 1990s that heralded a new digital age of functional convergence. Although far less powerful than today's machines and relying on relatively primitive software, these early computers were still able to pack into a relatively compact space various functions – namely, word processing, spreadsheet accounting, design and drafting tools, and a certain level of media play, including very simple video games. But

as computers got more powerful, their capacity for multifunctionality increased exponentially. The subsequent emergence of mobile telephony and the internet in the mid- to late 1990s massively accelerated the convergence of functionality, and rapidly rendered various types of stand-alone products virtually obsolete, as analogue physicality was replaced with digital functionality.

Over the next two decades, as **digitalization** continued apace – especially after the introduction of apps – each generation of smartphone was able to integrate more functionality, so much so that today's devices function as mini-computers, encompassing a previously unthinkable multitude of functions. In many ways this convergence of functionality is part and parcel of both **miniaturization** and digitalization, for the more compact a product or functionality can be made, the more likely it is that it can be integrated with others.

The steady pace of progress within the realms of artificial intelligence, biotechnology and nanotechnology will undoubtedly ensure that functional convergence in designed products continues at an increasing rate, with

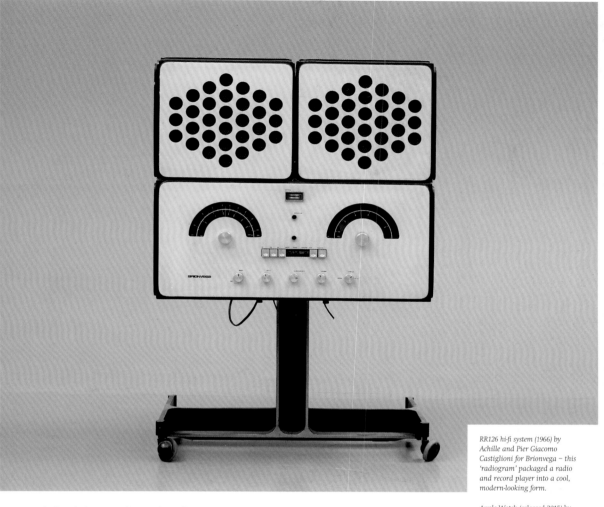

RR126 hi-fi system (1966) by Achille and Pier Giacomo Castiglioni for Brionvega – this 'radiogram' packaged a radio and record player into a cool, modern-looking form.

Apple Watch (released 2015) by Jonathan Ive and the Apple Design Team – this displays extraordinary functional convergence thanks to its host of applications, including telephone, calendar, music player and weather station.

designs being created on such a micro scale that their implantation into our bodies will undoubtedly become commonplace. In fact, today's early experiments within this area are only just the beginning of what must surely become a new and growing convergence between man and machine. ∎

The additive manufacturing of three-dimensional designs

IDEA № 95
3D PRINTING

Although a relatively youthful technology, 3D printing – or additive manufacturing – has already had a massive impact on design practice since its invention in the early 1980s.

It has heralded a new era of rapid prototyping that has speeded up the time it takes to transform a design idea into a marketable product, and has also helped to democratize the design process, taking it out of the professional realm and into classrooms and teenage bedrooms around the world. It has also enabled the realization of new design practices, from **open-source design** to **mass customization**, which are transforming the very nature of design and manufacturing.

The origins of 3D printing go back to a paper published by Hideo Kodama of the Nagoya Municipal Industrial Research Institute in 1981, which put forward the concept of a rapid prototyping system that built up models from cross-sectional layers of cured photopolymers. Two years later, American engineer Chuck Hull also hit upon the idea for 3D printing when he was using an ultraviolet light to harden a polymeric tabletop coating. But unlike Kodama, Hull decided to put theory into practice. He subsequently developed a solid imaging system, known as stereolithography, that involved a vat filled with a liquid photo-curable polymer, which was hardened into the required shape with beams of ultraviolet light. Using **CAD/CAM** software, this process allowed the design to be 'grown' out of the liquid plastic, thin layer by thin layer. In his related patent application, Hull explained his invention thus: 'A system for generating three-dimensional objects by creating a cross-sectional pattern of the object to be formed at a selected surface of a fluid medium capable of altering its physical state in response to appropriate synergistic stimulation ... whereby a three-dimensional object is formed and drawn from a substantially planar surface of the fluid medium.' This additive manufacturing process, which turned the liquid, acrylic-based polymer into solid plastic using a UV laser beam, was developed by Hull's company, 3D Systems, and became the first-ever rapid-prototyping technology to be successfully commercialized.

Initially, stereolithographic apparatus (SLA) machines – as 3D printers were then known – were not only very expensive to buy, but also to operate, because of the copious amounts of energy they consumed. As a result, only large manufacturing companies, well-funded teaching institutions, and top-flight design studios and agencies could afford to use them. However, in 1992 the DTM Corporation of Austin, Texas, introduced a new kind of 3D printing known as selective laser sintering (SLS), which employed polymeric powders rather than liquid plastics. This new technology used the energy from laser beams to melt and fuse plastic powders in order to grow prototypical models based on CAD/CAM data inputs. Importantly, the SLS process could also be used with different media, notably foundry sands and metal sintering powders, which meant that it had a wider range of applications.

Another form of 3D printing also debuted in 1992 – fused deposition modelling (FDM). Three years before, its inventor, S. Scott Crump, had been making a toy frog for his daughter using a glue-gun, which he had loaded with a mixture of polyethylene and candle wax, when he hit upon the idea of a new additive-manufacturing technology based on a thermoplastic extrusion technique. Essentially a melted polymeric material was used to build up the required design, layer by layer, which then solidified on cooling. Crump's company, Stratasys, subsequently commercialized the technology with the launch of its first 3D printer, known as the 3D Modeler. Considerably less high-tech than other 3D printing techniques on offer, by 2003, FDM had become the bestselling rapid-prototyping technology.

During the early 2000s, 3D printing technologies became increasingly sophisticated and economically democratized, and as a result went from being a niche technology to a mainstream technology in design practice. Today, design professionals and non-professionals alike are using 3D printing to turn their design visions into realities, because if you can think it, you can in all likelihood print it. ∎

LEFT: Urban Cabin (2016) by DUS Architects – detail of 3D printer hotend and structural elements of a small urban dwelling that is entirely 3D-printed in recyclable bio-plastic.

BELOW: Aluminum Gradient chair (2014) by Joris Laarman – designed using generative CAD software and then directly 3D-printed (laser sintering) in aluminium.

ECOnnect Post-Disaster Shelter for Haiti (2013) by Pieter Stoutjesdijk – this open-source design intended for humanitarian aid can be cut entirely using CNC (computer numerical control) technology, and fits together like a giant 3D puzzle.

OPPOSITE: Liberator handgun (2013) by Defense Distributed – the world's first open-source 3D printable firearm to be made available over the internet.

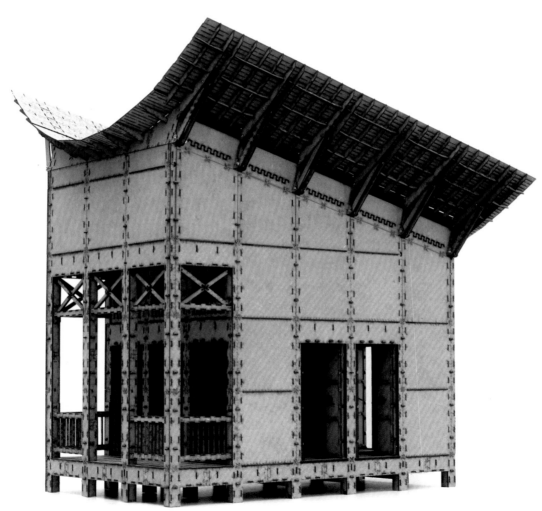

Disseminating design democratically through digital means

IDEA № 96
OPEN-SOURCE DESIGN

The concept of open-source design is all about freely sharing problem-solving ideas, and can be seen to have evolved from the principles of openness and cooperation that have long been a feature of the academic world, especially within the sciences. Open-source design also has a strong anti-establishment, anti-corporate aspect, and accords with the knowledge-sharing culture that has been fuelled by the internet over the last two decades.

Open-source design first emerged in public-domain computer software in the mid-1980s. But it was the release of Linux as a freely available, anyone-can-use-it modifiable source code in 1991 that really constituted the most significant milestone in not only the history of software development, but also the idea of democratically available open-source design.

Around the same time, the rollout of the World Wide Web, or Web 1.0, heralded a new era of international cooperation in the design world, which in turn helped globalize the practice of design with, for instance, Japanese designers working for Italian companies, British designers working for German companies, and so forth. It is no small coincidence that this was the era when global superstar designers came to the fore because design had ostensibly now become a globalized activity. Indeed, more than anything else that had ever gone before, the internet helped break down long-established national barriers in design practice because it provided designers with an instant window onto the international design world, and a means of forging synergetic alliances remotely.

During the early 2000s, the concept of open-source became well established with regard to software development,

and the internet was increasingly providing the communicative platform through which design ideas could be digitally transmitted with ease from one design community or studio to another. At the same time, the development of increasingly sophisticated **CAD/CAM** software had also largely helped the **digitalization** of design practice. However, another piece of the design-and-manufacturing jigsaw puzzle was needed in order to fully realize the potential of open-source design. This key final element eventually came to pass in the 2010s with the advent of a new generation of 3D printers, which were far more affordable and accessible than their large and costly precursors. These new machines readily allowed design ideas created in one place to be translated into physical realities in another. But over and above this, these new lower-cost printers signified that **3D printing** as a design-transforming technology had now finally been completely democratized.

As with any new and emerging technology-driven idea, the concept of open-source design has since raised many ethical questions. Especially when, in May 2013, Defense Distributed controversially shared online the first open-source design for a fully workable, 3D-printable single-shot handgun known as the Liberator. This was followed up

two months later with the first open-source, 3D-printable .22 calibre rifle (the Grizzly), designed by a Canadian digital gunsmith known simply as 'Matthew', who had named it in tribute to the 'Canadian built Sherman Tanks of WWII'.

However, it is not the concept of open-source per se that is the problem, but what people choose to do with it. Thankfully, more ethical uses for this new and emerging area of design are materializing, such as the ECOnnect emergency shelter system designed by the Dutch architect Pieter Stoutjesdijk, which comprises CNC (computer numerical control)-milled components made of a wholly sustainable material that snap-fit together like Lego bricks. Crucially, open-source design means that in the future there is much more likelihood of **innovation** in design. Just as open-source software is evolved through the creation of functionally adapted plug-ins, so all manner of open-source designed objects will be subjected to the same type of experimental tweaks in the future. In due course, this process of repeated design honing will inevitably help to accelerate the functional evolution of products at an ever-increasing rate. ∎

Diatom chair (2013–15) by Ross Lovegrove for Moroso – employing automotive pressing technology, this 100 per cent aluminium design utilized parametric software to create a rationalized pattern of strengthening 'micro points' to reduce material.

Murena bench (2015) by Oleg Soroko – this Moscow-based architect-designer uses parametric software to create furniture pieces with complex fluid forms made from plywood slices that are joined together.

'Forms that are highly complex yet also extremely rational.'

Designing with computer algorithms

IDEA № 97

PARAMETRICISM

Parametric design is a process-based approach to problem-solving that employs algorithmic calculations to work out optimum responses to predetermined design goals. While parametric design is not a new concept, having been used by, among others, the architect Antoni Gaudí, it has found a new technological expression with the advent of computers.

Heydar Aliyev Centre (2013) in Baku, Azerbaijan – designed by Zaha Hadid and Patrick Schumacher (Zaha Hadid Architects) – its complex form was created using parametric software.

Today when people refer to parametric design, they usually mean designs modelled by computer programs, which essentially are expressions of the parameters and rules that make up the algorithm driving the software being used.

Parametric design, especially in the design of buildings, can be used to manipulate and inform the creation of structures with highly complex geometries, many of which would have been impossible to make without immense computer processing power. Parametric modelling systems divide into two distinct categories: form-finding propagation-based systems using dataflow modelling based on a set of constraints, and constraint systems that employ sets of continuous parameters. Parametric-design-based generative computer algorithms now offer designers, engineers and architects a more effective way of scientifically determining the most efficient solution to their design goals. For instance, they can be used to create buildings that use structural materials in the most efficient way possible,

thereby reducing their overall ecological footprint.

A new global language of architecture, known as parametricism, has already begun to emerge thanks to the advent of computational parametric design. This new international architectural **style** represents a paradigm shift away from the one-size-fits-all **standardization** of Modernism to the **mass customization** of Late Modernism. As a new and powerful modelling tool, parametric design will also increasingly determine how tomorrow's products are developed and manufactured. A number of **industrial design**ers, most notably Ross Lovegrove and Joris Laarman, are already exploring the potential of parametricism to create designs that are computationally determined in order to find the most efficient constructions, whether for a chair or a footbridge. The early results are highly promising and have a strong sense of organic growth, often having the appearance of grown, bone-like structures.

Patrik Schumacher, a director and senior designer at Zaha Hadid Archi-

tects and one of most high-profile advocates of this new design-by-computer-algorithm approach, believes parametricism will become the new and unified style for architecture and design in the twenty-first century. As he notes, 'A new style in architecture and design is akin to a new paradigm in science; it redefines the fundamental categories, purposes and methods of a coherent collective endeavour.' And that is exactly what parametricism is already starting to do. As computing power increases exponentially over the coming years, so will the power of parametricism to intelligently design forms that are highly complex yet also extremely rational. ∎

Feel-me-and-connect-with-me designs

IDEA № 98
HAPTICS

Divisumma 18 electronic printing calculator (1971–73) by Mario Bellini for Olivetti – this elastomer-covered device heralded a new level of functional tactility in product design.

'Haptics', or as it is sometimes referred to, 'haptic feedback', is a relatively youthful discipline in design that seeks to enhance the sensorial interaction between people and things through the sense of touch. The word originates from the Ancient Greek word *haptikós*, meaning 'able to come into contact with', and with regard to design means non-verbal communication via tactility.

Haptics can greatly help to enhance the user's experience of a product, and is increasingly a feature of designs that have a physical–digital interface. One of the simplest but also most common examples of haptics in design is when your mobile phone vibrates in your pocket to let you know that you have an incoming call or text. That inbuilt vibration feature is essentially allowing your phone to communicate with you through the sense of touch, yet it has become something that is so common in our daily lives that we just take it for granted.

At its most basic, haptics can be used to give pleasurable feedback when operating a control, such as pushing a button on an appliance. Haptic details like this provide users with better, more satisfying **connections** between themselves and a product – even on a subconscious level. But while they may seem operatively simple, haptics of this nature can in fact be quite complex to deliver.

One of the very earliest examples of haptic design was Mario Bellini's Divisumma 18 electronic printing calculator (1971–73), which incorporated an innovative tactile skin over its keyboard, made of a then state-of-the-art elastomer (synthetic rubber). This influential design, with its soft, nipple-like buttons, brought a whole new sensorial experience to the world of consumer electronics. Since then, this feature has become commonplace across many different types of product that require push-button operation, especially remote controls of different kinds. Indeed, the R&D teams at most appliance companies – most notably Apple and Dyson – go to extraordinary lengths to make sure their touch-button experiences are as pleasurable as possible. In fact, Apple seems to introduce yet another haptic **innovation** with every new product launch. For example, its latest generation Macbook and iPhone both feature haptic trackpads and screens that can detect different levels of applied pressure to enable better fingertip functionality, which ultimately enhances the interface between the user and the content being accessed.

Haptics have also long been used to enrich gaming experience, with force-feedback joysticks and steering wheels providing players with a next-level sense of tactile reality. Other areas that rely heavily on haptic feedback for more 'real' user experience are the worlds of virtual and augmented reality. Already VR- and AR-related wearables, such as fingertip 'thimbles', gloves, full bodysuits and exoskeletons with in-built haptics, are becoming a reality, and will undoubtedly become more so as each year passes.

Recently, the Bristol-based firm Ultrahaptics has developed a remarkable tactile-feedback technology using ultrasound, which allows users to 'feel' touchless buttons, get feedback from mid-air gestures, and interact with virtual objects. This type of no-need-to-physically-engage technology has numerous potential applications, not just in the gaming world, but also in the operation of vehicles, within our daily domestic environments and in medical settings, where hygienic touch-less controls could prove to be a germ-free godsend.

Today haptic design is increasingly part of larger multi-sensorial experiences that might involve sight and sound, too. It is in the realm of **robotics**, however, where haptic design will really come into its own, as the robots of the future will need an accurate sense of touch in order to make proper sense of the world around them. The haptic interface between humans and robots will also be key to their increasing acceptance into our daily lives because humans are incredibly tactile creatures who always have, and always will, respond emotionally to 'feel'. ■

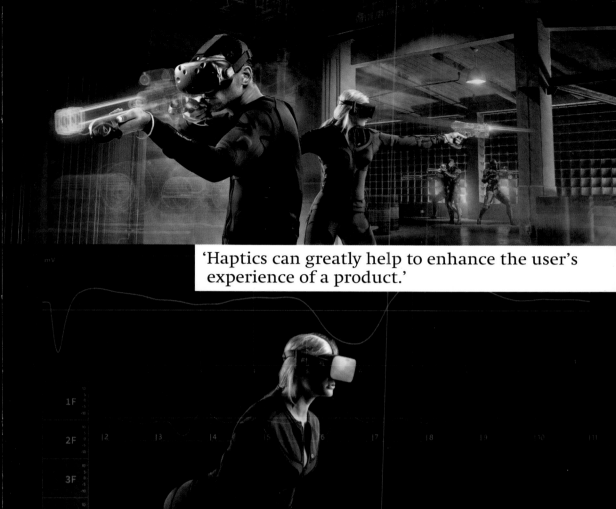

'Haptics can greatly help to enhance the user's experience of a product.'

Teslasuit (2017) – marketed as 'the world's first full-body haptic feedback, motion capture, thermo controlled suit'.

Designs that are programmed to think for themselves

IDEA № 99

SMART MACHINES (ARTIFICIAL INTELLIGENCE + MACHINE LEARNING)

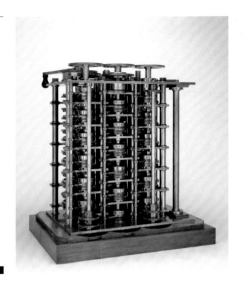

Difference Engine No.1 (1824–32) by Charles Babbage – this prototype was the first-ever successful automatic calculating machine and the world's earliest mechanical computer.

Today 'smart machines' that can truly think for themselves are no longer a matter of science fiction, but rapidly becoming design realities. Thanks to the advent of these clever 'thinking' devices, we are now on the cusp of a new design-and-manufacturing revolution that will have huge worldwide ramifications for us as individuals and for society as a whole.

The concept of smart machines not only includes various kinds of robot, but also self-driving vehicles and other designs with in-built, autonomous, decision-making cognitive capability based on computing systems. This disruptive technology will completely alter the nature of certain types of product and their capabilities, and will also transform the way we think about the fundamental design of things. Indeed, it is not inconceivable that smart machines will become the designers of tomorrow, or at the very least, helpful design assistants that will be able to process complex engineering data at incomprehensible speed and then apply it to the design of things – potentially, even to the next generation of themselves.

At the heart of smart machines lies artificial intelligence – or, as it is sometimes perhaps more helpfully termed, 'synthetic intelligence' – which can be either a simulated form of intelligence or a full-blown synthesized form of genuine intelligence, depending on the type of algorithms being used in a design's in-built computing system. In fact, artificial neural networks do not mimic the human brain, but rather work out and evolve their own cognitive capacity. Given the rapidity and complexity of this developing technology, it is not surprising that in non-techie circles there exists quite a bit of confusion as to what the exact differences are between artificial intelligence (AI) and machine learning (ML), since these two catchphrases are often mistakenly used interchangeably.

The origins of AI go back to the very first 'logical machines' devised by Charles Babbage in the early to mid-nineteenth century. His first smart machine was intended to work out complex calculations, yet over the decades, as computing shifted from the mechanical world to the electronic one, so the concept of AI evolved. Scientists and engineers working in the emerging field of computer science began seeking ways of replicating the process of human decision-making.

Eventually, in the late 1950s the American computing pioneer Arthur Samuel, while working for IBM, came up with the idea of ML, which involved machines using data analytics in order to learn for themselves. As Samuel explained, ML is a form of AI that gives machines 'the ability to learn without being explicitly programmed'.

As the power of computer processors grew exponentially over the succeeding decades, so the viability of ML (or Deep Learning as it is sometimes called) increased apace more and more data could be processed in ever-shorter times. Today increasingly complex algorithms provide machines with ever more self-generative intelligence, and that is a trajectory set to continue. The huge philosophical questions such designs with ML-based AI are throwing up, however, are only now beginning to be recognized.

Whether this development in design is going to be beneficial or detrimental to mankind's existence ultimately rests in the hands of governmental

decision-makers. At the moment, politics is on the back foot and needs to catch up fast with this rapidly advancing technology, making sure that well-thought-through global legislation is in place to ensure that the smart machines of tomorrow help us attain a brighter future rather than a dystopian one. Yet while so much is in the ethical balance concerning smart machines, one thing is for sure – their ever-onward march into our homes and workplaces will forever change the relationship between humans and machines, especially as we begin inevitably to empathize with them, and they with us. ∎

The inter-networking of connected smart designs

IDEA № 100

IOT (THE INTERNET OF THINGS)

Increasingly, everyday objects are being developed with a degree of connectivity, which means they can transmit data over the internet and 'talk' to other devices while participating together on a system. In 1999, Kevin Ashton, the founder of MIT's Auto-ID Labs, coined the phrase the 'Internet of Things' in a presentation to Proctor & Gamble to describe the future emergence of Web-connected product designs.

'Internet of Things' is also used to describe the convergence of conventionally connected devices – such as computers and mobile phones – with a new breed of smart appliances that have their own dedicated smartphone apps or can access social networks. One of the earliest and simplest connected products is the Oyster card, introduced in 2003 and widely beloved by London commuters. This contactless smartcard allows auto top-ups and gathers encrypted data with each touched-in-and-out journey. However, most connected devices have greater physicality and functionality, for example: fitness trackers that clock heart rates and step counts; smart thermostats that constantly monitor and adjust room temperature; air purifiers that can provide updates on indoor and outdoor air quality; WiFi-enabled coffee machines that can be activated by smartphones; or intelligent personal assistants capable of voice interaction.

One of the big goals behind the Internet of Things is to create homes where literally all appliances and devices, from dustbins and washing machines to lights and radiators, are inter-networked so they can 'talk' to each other via a smart hub. Early-uptake, tech-savvy IoT enthusiasts are already creating their own inter-networking domestic environments, but over the coming decades this will become a more mainstream phenomenon, with the design of everyday objects increasingly having embedded forms of connectivity. And while the IoT is still very much in its infancy, it is already leading to improvements in the automated control and monitoring of devices, while also providing more easy-to-access information to the user. In addition to making our personal lives more manageable, connected devices should also help to conserve water and energy, while making private companies and public organizations, including healthcare, educational and emergency services, more responsive and therefore efficient. Ultimately, within our increasingly connected world, collected data knowledge equals power.

Obviously, one of the primary design considerations related to connected products, other than reliable connectivity and secure data privacy, is a well-functioning user interface so that people interacting with smart devices by touchscreen or voice can do so intuitively. In this way the IoT will increasingly become an integral and highly useful part of everyday living. As for the future, the Internet of Things will continue to spread its reach and transform our world, both on a micro personal level and on a macro global level, for it is simply the result of the internet expanding into the territory of physical things – and that means into the realm of product design. ∎

'Collected data knowledge equals power.'

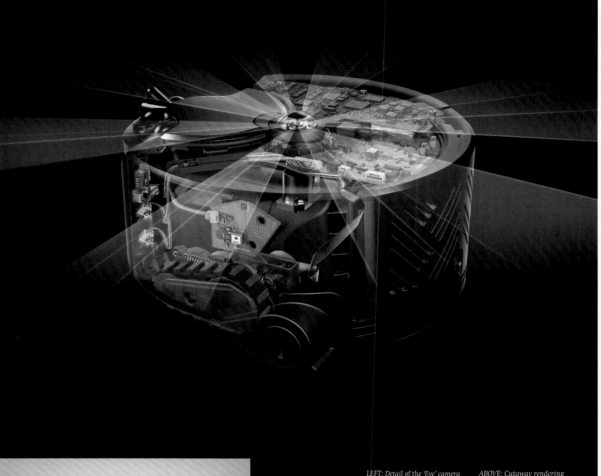

LEFT: Detail of the 'Eye' camera on Dyson's 360 Eye robotic vacuum cleaner (2015) – the product has its own linked app that tracks the course of the robot's cleaning path.

ABOVE: Cutaway rendering of the Dyson 360 Eye robot vacuum cleaner showing its vision sensor based on SLAM (Simultaneous Localization and Mapping) technology, 2015 – this smart machine features app connectivity.

Notes

1. James Dyson in conversation with Charlotte and Peter Fiell, 2016.

2. Cited in Tom Kelley and Jonathan Littman, *The Art of Innovation*, Profile Books, London, 2001, p.3.

3. Kirmo Mikkola, *Alvar Aalto vs. the Modern Movement*, Rakennuskirja, Helsinki, 1981, p.78.

4. Walter Gropius, *Scope of Total Architecture*, Collier, London & New York, 1970, pp.19–20.

5. Stephen Bayley in conversation with Charlotte and Peter Fiell, 2013.

6. Cited in Stanley Abercrombie, *George Nelson: The Design of Modern Design*, Cambridge, Mass., MIT Press, 1994, p.18.

7. Adam Smith, *The Theory of Moral Sentiments, or, An essay towards an analysis of the principles by which men naturally judge concerning the conduct and character, first of their neighbours and afterwards themselves: to which is added, A dissertation on the origin of languages*, W. Strahan, J. & F. Rivington, W. Johnston, T. Longman and T. Cadell, 1874 (first published 1759), p.263.

8. Raymond Loewy, *Never Leave Well Enough Alone*, John Hopkins University Press, Baltimore, 2002 (first published 1950), pp.210–11.

9. Herbert Read, preface to Lancelot L. Whyte (ed.), *Aspects of Form: A Symposium on Form in Nature and Art*, Lund Humphries, 1951, p.xxii.

10. Stephen Bayley, *Taste*, Faber & Faber, 1991, p.xvi.

11. Anthony Bertram, *Design*, Penguin Books, West Drayton and New York, 1943, p.14.

12. www.moma.org/documents/moma_press-release_325754.pdf

13. '"Grope" brought everything in the range of his vision' (article), *Life* magazine, 7 June 1968, p.62.

14. Parliamentary Papers, vol. 13, 1841, p.55.

15. Walter Gropius, *SoD*, quoted in Magdalena Droste, *Bauhaus, 1919–1933* (Taschen, Cologne, 1990), pp.16, 270.

16. Michael T. Saler, *The Avant-Garde in Interwar England*, Oxford University Press, Oxford, 2001, p.74.

17. William Morris, *Complete Works of William Morris*, Delphi Classics, East Sussex, 2015, p.77.

18. Christopher Dresser, *Japan: Its Architecture, Art, and Art Manufactures*, Cambridge Library Collection, Cambridge, 2015, p.319.

19. Dieter Rams, 'Omit the Unimportant', in Victor Margolin (ed.), *Design Discourse*, University of Chicago Press, Chicago, 1989, p.111.

20. *BusinessWeek*, 25 May 1998.

21. John Ruskin, *The Stones of Venice*, vol. 2, Smith Elder, London, 1850, p.208.

22. E.P. Thompson, *William Morris: Romantic to Revolutionary*, Lawrence & Wishart, London, 1955, p.248.

23. Stephen Games, *Pevsner: The Complete Broadcast Talks*, Oliver & Boyd, Edinburgh, 1836, p.33.

24. Richard Buchanan, 'Declaration by Design: Rhetoric, Argument, and Demonstration in Design Practice', in Victor Margolin (ed.), *Design Discourse – History, Theory, Criticism*, University of Chicago Press, Chicago, 1989, p.93.

25. Christopher Dresser, *Japan: Its Architecture, Art, and Art Manufactures*, Cambridge Library Collection, Cambridge, 2015, p.429.

26. Ellen Key, 'Beauty in the Home', *Modern Swedish Design: Three Founding Texts*, Museum of Modern Art, New York, pp.33–57.

27. Eric Larrabee & Massimo Vignelli, *Knoll Design*, Harry N. Abrams, New York, 1985, p.66.

28. Franz Schulze & Edward Windhorst, *Mies van der Rohe: A Critical Biography*, new and revised edition, University of Chicago Press, Chicago, 2014, p.106.

29. www.weissenhof2002.de/english/weissenhof.html

30. Karen Kurczynski, *The Art and Politics of Asger Jorn: The Avant-Garde Won't Give Up*, Routledge, London, 2017, p.110.

31. www.90yearsofdesign.philips.com/article/74

32. Robert Lacey, *Ford: The Men and the Machine*, Little, Brown and Company, New York, 1986, p.109.

33. Klaus Krippendorff, *The Semantic Turn: A New Foundation for Design*, CRC/Taylor & Francis, Boca Raton, 2006, p.1.

34. Franz Schulze & Edward Windhorst, *Mies van der Rohe: A Critical Biography*, new and revised edition, University of Chicago Press, Chicago, 2014, p.205.

35. Frank M. Gryna, J. M. Juran & Leonard A. Seder, *Quality Control Handbook*, McGraw-Hill, New York, 1962, p.1.

36. Calkins, as quoted in Carma Gorman (ed.), *The Industrial Design Reader*, Allworth Press, New York, 2003, p.131.

37. Ann Lee Morgan & Colin Naylor, *Contemporary Designers*, Macmillan, London, 1984, pp.381–82.

38. www.globalfuturist.org/2017/01/norwegian-robot-learns-to-self-evolve-and-3d-print-itself-in-the-lab

39. Silvana Anicchiarico (curator), *100 Objects of Italian Design: Permanent Collection of Italian Design, La Triennale di Milano*, Gangemi Editore, Rome, 2007, np.

40. www.ateliermendini.it

41. Victor Margolin, 'Design Discourse: History, Theory, Criticism', University of Chicago Press, Chicago, 1989, p.111, 113.

42. Andrea Branzi, *The Hot House*, MIT Press, Cambridge, Massachusetts, 1984, p.22.

43. Martino Gamper, *100 Chairs in 100 Days and its 100 Ways*, Dent-De-Leone, London, 2012, pp.82, 84.

44. Victor Papanek, *Design for the Real World*, Pantheon Books, New York, 1971, p.333.

45. Ibid, p.346.

46. http://preprints.readingroo.ms/RUR/rur.pdf

47. William McDonough & Michael Braungart, *Cradle to Cradle: Remaking the Way We Make Things*, North Point Press, New York, 2002, p.28.

48. Ivan Sutherland, *Sketchpad: A Man-Machine Graphical Communication System*, history-computer.com/Library/Sketchpad.pdf

Further reading

Åhrén, U., eds L. Creagh, H. Kåberg, B. Miller Lane and K. Frampton. *Modern Swedish Design: Three Founding Texts* (New York: Museum of Modern Art, 2008).

Bangert, A. *Italian Furniture Design: Ideas, Styles, Movements* (Munich: Bangert Publications, 1988).

Banham, J. *Theory and Design in the First Machine Age* (London & New York: Architectural Press, 1960).

Barthes, R. *Mythologies* (London: Jonathan Cape, 1972; originally published Paris: Editions du Seuil, 1957).

Baudrillard, J. *The Consumer Society: Myths & Structure* (London: Sage Publications, 1998; originally published as *La Société de consommation*, Paris: Editions Denoël, 1970).

Bayley, S. *Taste* (London: Faber & Faber, 1991).

Bayley, S. and T. Conran. *Design: Intelligence Made Visible* (London: Conran Octopus, 2007).

Benton, T. *The New Objectivity* (Milton Keynes: Open University Press, 1975).

Benton, T. and C., eds, with D. Sharp. *Form and Function: A Source Book for the History of Architecture and Design 1890–1939* (Milton Keynes: Open University Press, 1975).

Benton, T., S. Muthesius and B. Wilkins. *Europe 1900–1914: The reaction to historicism and Art Nouveau* (Milton Keynes: Open University Press, 1975).

Branzi, A. *The Hot House: Italian New Wave Design* (London: Thames & Hudson, 1984).

Collins, M., *Towards Post-Modernism: Design Since 1851* (London: British Museum Publications, 1987).

Dale, H. and R. *The Industrial Revolution* (London: British Library Publishing Division, 1992).

Dormer, P. *The Meanings of Modern Design: Towards the Twenty-First Century* (London: Thames & Hudson, 1990).

Dresser, C. *Japan: Its Architecture, Art, and Art Manufactures* (London: Longmans, Green & Co., 1882).

Droste, M. Bauhaus, 1919–1933 (Cologne: Taschen, 1990).

Fiell, C. and P. Charles Rennie Mackintosh (Cologne: Taschen, 1995).

Fiell, C. and P. Design of the 20th Century (Cologne: Taschen, 1999).

Fiell, C. and P. Industrial Design A–Z (Cologne: Taschen, 2000).

Fiell, C. and P. Masterpieces of British Design (London: Goodman Fiell, 2012).

Fiell, C. and P. Masterpieces of Italian Design (London: Goodman Fiell, 2013).

Fiell, C. and P. Modern Scandinavian Design (London: Laurence King Publishing, 2017).

Fiell, C. and P. Plastic Dreams: Synthetic Visions in Design (London: Fiell Publishing, 2009).

Fiell, C. and P. The Story of Design (London: Goodman Fiell, 2013).

Forty, A. Objects of Desire: Design and Society Since 1750 (London: Thames & Hudson, 1986).

Frampton, K. Modern Architecture: A Critical History (London: Thames & Hudson, 1980).

Friedman, M. De Stijl, 1917–1931: Visions of Utopia (Oxford: Phaidon, 1982).

Gere, C. and M. Whiteway. Nineteenth-Century Design: From Pugin to Mackintosh (London: Weidenfeld & Nicolson, 1993).

Giedion, S. Mechanization Takes Command: A Contribution to Anonymous History (Oxford: Oxford University Press, 1955).

Gorman, C., ed. The Industrial Design Reader (New York: Allworth Press, 2003).

Greenhalgh, P. Modernism in Design (London: Reaktion Books, 1990).

Greenhalgh, P. Quotations and Sources on Design and the Decorative Arts (Manchester: Manchester University Press, 1993).

Gryna, F., J. Juran and L. Seder. Quality Control Handbook (New York: McGraw-Hill, 1962).

Hamilton, R. Collected Words (London: Thames & Hudson, 1982).

Heisinger, K. and G. Marcus. Design Since 1945 (London: Thames and Hudson, 1983).

Heskett, J. Industrial Design (London: Thames & Hudson, 1980).

Hounshell, D. From the American System to Mass Production, 1800–1932: The Development of Manufacturing Technology in the United States (Baltimore: Johns Hopkins University Press, 1985).

Howard, J. Art Nouveau: International and National Styles in Europe (Manchester: Manchester University Press, 1996).

Jaffé, H.L.C. De Stijl (London: Thames & Hudson, 1970).

Kelley, T. and J. Littman. The Art of Innovation: Lessons in Creativity from IDEO, America's Leading Design Firm (London: Profile Books, 2001).

Krippendorff, K. The Semantic Turn: A New Foundation for Design (Boca Raton: CRC/Taylor & Francis, 2006).

Kurczynski, K. The Art and Politics of Asger Jorn: The Avant-Garde Won't Give Up (Abingdon: Routledge, 2017).

Lacey, R. Ford: The Men and the Machine (New York: Little Brown & Co, 1986).

Larrabee, E. and M. Vignelli. Knoll Design (New York: Harry N. Abrams, 1985).

Loewy, R. Industrial Design (London: Fourth Estate, 1979).

Loewy, R. Never Leave Well Enough Alone (New York: Simon & Schuster, 1951).

Loos, A. Ornament and Crime (1908; Riverside, CA: Ariadne Press, 1998).

Lucie-Smith, E. A History of Industrial Design (Oxford: Phaidon, 1983).

MacCarthy, F. British Design Since 1880: A Visual History (London: Lund Humphries, 1982).

Margolin, V. Design Discourse, History, Theory, Criticism (Chicago: University of Chicago Press, 1989).

Margolin, V. and R. Buchanan. Discovering Design: Explorations in Design Studies (Chicago: University of Chicago Press, 1995).

Margolin, V. and R. Buchanan. The Idea of Design (Cambridge, MA: MIT Press, 1995).

McDonough, W. and M. Braungart. Cradle to Cradle: Remaking the Way We Make Things (New York: North Point Press, 2002).

McDonough, W. and M. Braungart. The Upcycle: Beyond Sustainability – Designing for Abundance (New York: North Point Press, 2013).

Meikle, J. Twentieth Century Limited – Industrial Design in America, 1925–1939 (Philadelphia: Temple University Press, 2001).

Morgan, A.L. and C. Naylor. Contemporary Designers (London: Macmillan, 1984).

Morris, W. Complete Works of William Morris (Chichester: Delphi Classics, 2015).

Neuhart, J., M. Neuhart and R. Eames. Eames Design: The Work of the Office of Charles and Ray Eames (New York: Harry N. Abrams, 1989).

Packard, V. The Hidden Persuaders (New York: D. McKay Co, 1957).

Packard, V. The Waste Makers (New York: D. McKay Co, 1960).

Papanek, V. Design for the Real World: Human Ecology and Social Change (New York: Pantheon Books, 1971).

Papanek, V. The Green Imperative: Natural Design for the Real World (London: Thames & Hudson, 1995).

Pevsner, N. Pioneers of Modern Design: From William Morris to Walter Gropius (London: Penguin Books, new edition, 1991).

Pevsner, N. The Sources of Modern Architecture and Design (London: Thames & Hudson, 1968).

Radice, B. Memphis: Research, Experiences, Results, Failures and Successes of New Design (London: Thames & Hudson, 1985).

Read, H. Art and Industry: The Principles of Industrial Design (London: Faber & Faber, 1956).

Reilly, R. Josiah Wedgwood 1730–1795 (London: Macmillan, 1992).

Saler, M. The Avant-Garde in Interwar England (Oxford: Oxford University Press, 2001).

Schulze, F. and E. Windhorst. Mies van der Rohe: A Critical Biography (Chicago: University of Chicago Press, new and revised edition, 2014).

Schwartz, F. The Werkbund: Design Theory and Mass Culture Before the First World War (New Haven: Yale University Press, 1996).

Sudjic, D. B is for Bauhaus, Y is for YouTube: Designing the Modern World from A to Z (New York: Rizzoli, 2015).

Thompson, E.P. William Morris: Romantic to Revolutionary (London: Lawrence & Wishart, 1955).

Tisdall, C. and A. Bozzolla. Futurism (Oxford: Oxford University Press, 1978).

Triggs, T. Communicating Design: Essays in Visual Communication (London: Batsford, 1995).

Twitchell, J.B. Lead Us Into Temptation: The Triumph of American Materialism (New York: Columbia University Press, 2000).

Walker, J. Design History and the History of Design (London: Pluto Press, 1989).

Watkin, D. Morality & Architecture Revisited (Chicago: University of Chicago Press, 1977).

Whiteley, N. Design for Society (London: Reaktion Books, 1993).

Whiteley, N. Pop Design: Modernism to Mod (London: Design Council, 1987).

Whitford, F. Bauhaus (London: Thames & Hudson, 1984).

Whyte, L., ed. Aspects of Form: A Symposium on Form in Nature and Art (London: Lund Humphries, 1951).

Woodham, J. Twentieth Century Design (Oxford: Oxford University Press, 1997).

Index

Page numbers in **bold** refer to captions

Picture Credits

2 Allermuir; 8 Charlotte & Peter Fiell Design Image Archive; 9 *(both images)* Dyson Technology Ltd.; 10 © Christie's Images / Bridgeman Images; 11 *(t)* Wright, Chicago; 11 *(b)* Sony Corporation; 12 *(t)* Kartell; 12 *(b)* Vitsoe; 13 CoffeeSet, photo by Ron Steemers, Ineke Hans, © DACS 2019; 15 (t, bl) Getty Images / Science & Society Picture Library; 15 *(br)* Wikimedia Commons; 16 Getty Images – Bettmann Collection, photographer: Bettmann; 17 Fotolia / Adobe Stock; 18 The Met (Metropolitan Museum of Art, New York – Creative Commons); 19 Wright, Chicago; 20 Chanel, Paris – image courtesy of Xupes.com; 21 The Met (Metropolitan Museum of Art, New York – Creative Commons); 22 Alamy – Chris Willson / Alamy Stock Photo; 23 The Met (Metropolitan Museum of Art, New York – Creative Commons); 24 *(t)* V&A Images; 24 *(b)* RM Sotheby's; 25, 26 V&A Images; 27 Moooi; 28, 29 Seletti; 30 Dorotheum GmbH & Co AG (Dorotheum, Vienna, auction catalogue 20 June 2017); 31 Bukowskis, Stockholm; 32 *(t)* Fiell / Laurence King, photo: Andy Stammers; 32 *(b)* Fiell Archive – Courtesy of Carlton Publishing; 33 *(t)* Fiell / Laurence King, photo: Andy Stammers; 34 Dualit; 35 The Dunsfold Collection Archive; 36 Alamy – Florilegius / Alamy Stock Photo; 37 *(t, b)* Getty Images – Anadolu Agency; 38 *(t)* Alamy – Andrew Jackson / Alamy Stock Photo; 38 *(b)* Alamy – World History Archive / Alamy Stock Photo; 38 *(b)* Getty Images – Hulton Archive, photographer: Fox Photos; 40 Mondaine – design copyright SBB AG; 41 IKEA; 42 Alamy – Granger Historical Picture Archive / Alamy Stock Photo; 43 *(l)* Alamy – Stan Tess / Alamy Stock Photo; 43 *(r)* Alamy – Maurice Savage / Alamy Stock Photo; 44 Getty Images – AFP, photographer: Joel Nito; 45 National Archives (USA); 46 Kartell; 47 Moooi; 48 Fiell / Laurence King, photo: Andy Stammers; 49 The Met (Metropolitan Museum of Art, New York – Creative Commons); 50 *(t)* Alamy – Zoonar GmbH / Alamy Stock Photo; 50 *(b)* Mary Evans Picture Library – © Illustrated London News / Mary Evans; 51 Bauhaus Archiv, Berlin, © DACS 2019; 52 Charlotte & Peter Fiell Design Image Archive; 53 Museum der Dinge: Werkbundarchiv, Berlin; 54 Alamy – Ian Dagnall / Alamy Stock Photo; 55 Ducati; 56 Fiskars; 57 Plank; 58 Vitra, © The Isamu Noguchi Foundation and Garden Museum/ARS, New York and DACS, London 2019; 59 Fiell / Laurence King, photo: Andy Stammers; 60 Quittenbaum Kunstauktionen GmbH, Münich; 61 Getty Images / Science & Society Picture Library; 62 The Old Flying Machine Company Ltd.: photo John Dibbs; 63 Alamy – age footstock / Alamy Stock Photo (Friends of the American Wing Fund, 1966 / MET Museum NYC); 64 V&A Images; 65 Yves Béhar / Fuseproject; 66 Getty Images / Science & Society Picture Library; 67 Great Caricatures (www.greatcaricatures.com); 68 Covo, Italy; 69 *(t)* Iittala; 69 *(b)* Fiell Archive – Courtesy of Carlton Publishing; 70 Fiell / Laurence King, photo: Andy Stammers; 71 Magis; 72 *(l)* Fiell Archive – Courtesy of Carlton Publishing; 72 *(r)* Habitat; 73 IKEA; 74, 75 Getty Images – The LIFE Picture Collection, photographer: Bernard Hoffman; 76, 77 *(t)*, 77 *(b)* Geffrye Museum, London; 78 Philip Lighting

Holding B.V.; 79 Tesla; 80 *(t)*, 80 *(b)* Black Diamond; 81 *(t)* Wright, Chicago; 81 *(b)* Getty Images – Science Faction, photographer: U.S. Air Force; 82 Wikimedia Commons; 83 *(t)*, 83 *(b)* Howe; 84 Creative Commons; 85 Quittenbaum Kunstauktionen GmbH, Münich; 86 Alamy – Gregory Wrona / Alamy Stock Photo; 87 Charlotte & Peter Fiell Design Image Archive; 88 Wikimedia Commons; 89 Fiell Archive – Courtesy of Carlton Publishing; 90, 91 *(t)* Alamy – Arcaid Images / Alamy Stock Photo; 91 *(b)* Alamy – D.G. Farquhar / Alamy Stock Photo; 92 Wikimedia Commons; 93 *(t)* Dreamstime – © Kaprik / Dreamstime.com; 93 *(b)* Alessi; 94 *(t)* Mass Modern Design (www.massmoderndesign.com); 94 *(b)* Wright, Chicago; 95 Herman Miller (© Vitra); 96 Wikimedia Commons; 97 *(t)* Konstantin Grcic; 97 *(b)* Wikimedia Commons; 99 *(t)* Getty Images – The LIFE Picture Collections, photographer: Gjon Mili; 99 *(bl)* Getty Images – Archive Photos, photographer: American Stock Archive; 99 *(br)* The Henry Ford, Dearborn (MI); 100 Alamy – Archive Pics / Alamy Stock Photo; 101 *(t)*, 101 *(b)* The Henry Ford, Dearborn (MI); 102 Quittenbaum Kunstauktionen GmbH, Münich; 103 Fiell Archive – Courtesy of Carlton Publishing; 104 *(t)* Brooklyn Museum – Creative Commons, © DACS 2019; 104 *(b)* Wikimedia Commons; 105 Getty Images – Hulton Archive, photo: Courtesy of Apple Inc.; 106 Iittala; 107 *(t)* Bukowskis, Stockholm; 107 *(b)* Scala Archives – The Museum of Modern Art, New York/Scala, Florence, © DACS 2019; 108 V&A Images, © DACS 2019; 109 *(t)* Quittenbaum Kunstauktionen GmbH, Münich; 109 *(b)* Rex by Shutterstock; 110 Shutterstock; 111 Wright, Chicago; 112 Cassina; 113 Hybrid Air Vehicles/Philippa Murrey Photographer; 114 DLR-Archiv Göttingen; 115 Alexander Schleicher GmbH & Co. – photographer: Manfred Münch; 115 *(t)* Wright, Chicago; 116 Getty Images – Getty Images Publicity, photographer: Ken Ishii; 117 Wikimedia Commons; 118 Ecolean; 119 *(l)* Wikimedia Commons; 119 *(r)* © Nordiska Museet, photographer: Birgit Brånvall; 120 The Henry Ford, Dearborn (MI); 121 Rex by Shutterstock; 122 US Patent Office; 123 *(t)* Bic, France; 123 *(b)* Alamy – Steve Trewhella / Alamy Stock Photo; 124 Scala Archives – The Museum of Modern Art, New York/Scala, Florence; 125 Charlotte & Peter Fiell Design Image Archive; 126 PriestmanGoode; 127 Wright, Chicago; 128 Fiell Archive – Courtesy of Carlton Publishing; 129 *(t)* Wright, Chicago; 129 *(b)* Venetia Stadium; 130 Charlotte & Peter Fiell Design Image Archive; 131 Alamy – picturesbyrob / Alamy Stock Photo; 132 Magis; 133 *(l)* Ross Lovegrove Studio (sketch for Ty Nant bottle – sketch by Ross Lovegrove / www.rosslovegrove.com); 133 *(r)* Ross Lovegrove Studio (Ty Nant bottle – John Ross / www.johnross.co.uk); 134 Fiell / Laurence King, photo: Andy Stammers; 135 Alamy – Glasshouse Images / Alamy Stock Photo; 136 Design: Peter Opsvik, Photo: Tollefsen; 137 *(t)* Veryday / Ergonomi; 137 *(b)* Fiell Archive – Courtesy of Carlton Publishing; 138 Braun; 139 Just5; 140 *(t)* Herman Miller; 140 *(b)* © 2018 Eames Office, LLC (eamesoffice.com); 141 Wright, Chicago; 143 *(t)* Alamy – Stop Images GmbH /

Alamy Stock Photo; 143 *(b)* VICIS; 144 Flos; 145 *(both images)* Zanotta; 146 XO, France; 147 Alessi; 148 Sony Corporation; 149 Smart; 150 *(t)* Alamy – Urbanbuzz / Alamy Stock Photo; 150 *(b)* Alamy – ImageBroker / Alamy Stock Photo; 151 Alamy – Bailey-Cooper Photography 3 / Alamy Stock Photo; 152 Wikimedia Commons; 153 *(l)* Jonathan Schwinge; 153 *(r)* Ignazia Favata / Studio Joe Colombo; 154 Andreas Fuhrimann; 155 Quittenbaum Kunstauktionen GmbH, Münich; 156 Scala Archives – The Museum of Modern Art, New York/Scala, Florence; 157 *(t)* Modernity, Stockholm; 157 *(b)* Herman Miller; 158 RePack, Finland; 159 *(t)* Yves Béhar / Fuseproject; 159 *(b)* Getty Images – Bettmann Collection, photographer: Bettmann; 160 Fiell Archive – Courtesy of Carlton Publishing; 161 © Atelier Mendini; 162 Fiell Archive – Courtesy of Carlton Publishing; 163 B&B Italia – photographer: Klaus Zaugg; 164 *(t)* Wright, Chicago, © ADAGP, Paris and DACS, London 2019; 164 *(b)* Wright, Chicago; 165 © WWRD United Kingdom, Ltd.; 166 Die Neue Sammlung – The Design Museum – photo: Die Neue Sammlung (A. Laurenzo); 167 *(t)* Martino Gamper – photo: Angus Mills and ÅBÄKE; 167 *(b)* Tom Dixon; 168 Charlotte & Peter Fiell Design Image Archive; 169 *(both images)* Yves Béhar / Fuseproject; 170 Smart Design / OXO; 171 PriestmanGoode; 172 *(t)* Alamy – Richard Baker / Alamy Stock Photo; 172 *(b)* Anglepoise; 173 Louis Poulsen, Copenhagen; 175 *(t)* Getty Images – AFP Collection, photographer: Yoshikazu Tsuno; 175 *(bl)* NYPL Collection; 175 *(br)* Getty Images – Nur-Photo Collection, photographer: NurPhoto; 176 *(t)* Sharklet Technologies Inc.; 176 *(b)* Alamy – Stephen Frink Collection / Alamy Stock Photo; 177 Festo, Esslingen am Neckar; 178 Alamy – ZUMA Press, Inc. / Alamy Stock Photo; 179 © Courtesy of Apple Inc. – images designed by Susan Kare of kareprints.com; 180 Herman Miller; 181 Ross Lovegrove Studio (Solar Tree); 182 *(all images)* Allermuir; 184 Fiell Archive – Courtesy of Carlton Publishing; 185 *(t)* Jasper Morrison – Office for Design, London; 185 *(b)* Moroso; 186 Gufram; 187 Ben Brown Fine Arts, London, © ADAGP, Paris and DACS, London 2019; 188 *(t)* Kartell; 188 *(b)* Scala Archives – The Museum of Modern Art, New York/Scala, Florence; 189 Ross Lovegrove Studio (Basic flask); 190 Mathias Bengtsson; 191 Siemens; 192 history-computer.com; 193 Ross Lovegrove Studio (CAD drawing of Supernatural armchair); 194 Victorinox; 195 *(t)* Bukowskis, Stockholm; 195 *(b)* Courtesy of Apple Inc.; 196 Ross Lovegrove Studio (Foliates rings); 197 *(t)* DUS Architects – Ossip van Duivenbode, Sophia van den Hoek, DUS Architects; 197 *(b)* Joris Laarman Lab; 198 Pieter Stoutjesdijk; 199 Defence Distributed; 200 *(t)* Ross Lovegrove Studio (Diatom chair); 200 *(b)* Oleg Soroko; 201 Zaha Hadid Architects / photographer: Iwan Baan; 202 Fiell Archive – Courtesy of Carlton Publishing; 203 *(both images)* Teslasuit; 204 Science & Society Picture Library; 205 Herman Miller; 206 Amazon; 207 *(both images)* Dyson Technology Ltd.

Acknowledgements

To bring a book like this into being requires a big team effort. We
are enormously grateful, therefore, to everyone at Laurence King
Publishing who worked with us on this project. Special thanks
must go to: Jo Lightfoot and Sophie Drysdale for commissioning
us to write the book in the first place; Andrew Roff for his
good-natured editorial project management; Angela Koo for her
skilful copyediting; Patricia Burgess for her thoughtful
proofreading; Angus Hyland for his skilful creative direction;
Jon Allan for his stunning graphic design work; Anna Pauletti for
overseeing the book's exacting production and, last but not least,
Laurence King himself for his enthusiasm for the project right
from the beginning.

We would also like to thank all the many designers, design studios,
manufacturers, museums, auction houses and picture libraries
that have allowed us to use their images in this book.

With particular thanks to:

Alamy
Alexander Schleicher GmbH & Co
Allermuir
Anglepoise
Apple
Aprés Furniture
Atelier Mendini
Alessi
B&B Italian
Bauhaus Archiv
Stephen Bayley
Yves Béhar / Fuseproject
Ben Brown Fine Arts
Mathias Bengtsson
Bic
Black Diamond
Braun
Brooklyn Museum
Bukowski's
Cassina
Chanel
Christie's
Covo
DLR-Archiv Göttingen
Die Neue Sammlung
Tom Dixon
Dorotheum
Dualit
Ducati
DUS Architects
Dyson
EcoLean
Festo
Andreas Fuhrimann
Martino Gamper
Geffrye Museum
Getty Images

Konstantin Grcic
Great Caricatures
Gufram
Habitat
Henry Ford Museum Archive
Herman Miller
Hydrid Air Vehicles
Iittala
IKEA
Ineke Hans
Jaguar Land Rover
Jasper Morrison
Jonathan Schwinge
Joris Laarman Lab
Just5
Susan Kare
Kartell
Kunstbibliothek der Staatlichen
    Museen (Berlin)
Louis Poulsen
Ross Lovegrove
Magis
Mary Evans Picture Library
Mass Modern Design
Metropolitan Museum of Art, NY
Modernity (Stockholm)
Mondaine
Moooi
Museum der Dinge (Berlin)
National Archives (USA)
New York Public Library (NYPL) Collection
Nordiska Museet
OXO
Peter Opsvik
Philips
Plank
Priestman Goode

Quittenbaum
RePack
RM Sothebys
Scala Archives
Science & Society Picture Library
Seletti
Sharklet Technologies Inc.
Shutterstock
Siemens
Smart
Sony
Oleg Soroko
Pieter Stoutjesdijk
Tesla
Teslasuit
TetraPak
The Old Flying Machine Company Ltd.
Tom Dixon
V&A Images
Venetia Studium
Veryday (Ergonomi)
VICIS – Artefact Group
Victorinox
Vitra
Vitsoe
Wedgwood
Wright (Chicago) – Richard Wright
    and Todd Simeone
XO
Zanotta

LAURENCE KING

Published in 2019 by
Laurence King Publishing Ltd
361–373 City Road
London EC1V 1LR

e-mail: enquiries@laurenceking.com
www.laurenceking.com

A catalogue record for this book is available from the
British Library.

ISBN: 978 1 78627 343 7

Design: Two Sheds Design
Senior editor: Andrew Roff
Printed in China

Cover image: *Model 1227 task light (1934–38) by George
Carwardine for Herbert Terry & Sons (later Anglepoise) –
image courtesy of Anglepoise (see p.172).*

Frontispiece: *Axyl stacking chair (2017) by Benjamin Hubert
for Allermuir (see p.182).*

Charlotte and **Peter Fiell** are leading authorities on
the history, theory and criticism of design and have
written and edited over 50 books on the subject,
including *Industrial Design A–Z*, *The Story of Design*, *Modern
Scandinavian Design* and the bestselling *1000 Chairs*.